Women at the Wheel

WOMEN AT THE WHEEL

A Century of Buying, Driving, and Fixing Cars

KATHERINE J. PARKIN

PENN

University of Pennsylvania Press
Philadelphia

Published by
University of Pennsylvania Press
Philadelphia, Pennsylvania 19104-4112
www.upenn.edu/pennpress

Printed in the United States of America
on acid-free paper

2 4 6 8 10 9 7 5 3 1

Library of Congress Cataloging-in-Publication Data
Names: Parkin, Katherine J., author.
Title: Women at the wheel : a century of buying, driving, and fixing cars / Katherine J. Parkin.
Description: 1st ed. | Philadelphia : University of Pennsylvania Press, [2017] | Includes bibliographical references and index.
Identifiers: LCCN 2017009400 | ISBN 978-0-8122-4953-8 (hardcover)
Subjects: LCSH: Women automobile drivers—United States—History. | Sex role—United States—History—20th century. | Automobiles—United States—History. | Automobile driving—United States—History. | Automobiles—United States—History.
Classification: LCC HE5620.W54 P37 2017 | DDC 629.28/3082—dc23
LC record available at https://lccn.loc.gov/2017009400

To Quinn and Vivian,
my daughters, my loves

CONTENTS

PREFACE

Driving in Circles

LIVING IN THE SUBURBS in the late 1950s, author Betty Friedan preserved her writing time by having a taxi transport her children to school. Friedan realized that driving did not free her from the yoke of domesticity she so famously exposed in her classic, *The Feminine Mystique.* Instead, she recognized that for most women the car was principally a tool in service of the type of never-ending domestic work expected of them. Not only did women not find liberation on the road, but they also found themselves targeted by spurious stereotypes of "women drivers." These myths, including a belief that women were excessively cautious, spatially inept, and fundamentally incompetent drivers, persisted with little change over the course of automobile history.[1]

Yet at the same time, in spite of these negative associations, women needed cars. The country's shift to the suburbs, facilitated by the emergence and eventual dominance of the automobile, meant that women had to go out and get products and services once delivered to the home. While one historian contended that driving "represented liberation from the household," home economist Christine Frederick noted that moving to the countryside meant that in addition to all of the farm production she was responsible for, she also had to serve as a *chauffeuse.* Most women discovered that to facilitate everything from daily milk delivery to doctor's care, they needed to drive. Their work also included taking their husbands to the train or their jobs and their children to school and activities. Across the century, even those women with the means to drive did so almost entirely in service of their domestic responsibilities and identities.[2]

Most twentieth-century white, middle-class, American women found their lives defined by domesticity, and the use of their car principally affirmed their gender identity. Friedan's decision to pay someone to drive her children to school reflects the insights she brought to bear on a nascent feminist movement. Few have questioned, as Friedan did, the value of having women spending hours behind the wheel chauffeuring their husbands to work and their children to school, practices, and lessons. Yet women discovered that driving mirrored their other domestic responsibilities, as it was structured around others' needs, it was rote, and it was never-ending. For millions of women, their experience with the car fundamentally differed from that of men. The car was for most men an assertion of masculine identity, predicated on power, control, and freedom. Even when men drove in more mundane circumstances, ferrying their families or driving to work, their ownership and default position behind the wheel of the car left them with more authority than women could generally assert.[3]

Most women found their legitimacy as drivers compromised by a cultural expectation that placed men in the driver's seat and relegated women to the passenger side of the car whenever both were present. The cultural representations of men's control of cars served to dissuade women from assuming an identity as a driver. Women's historical association with the car, therefore, was primarily as a passenger or as a driver in service of their work as wives and mothers. The number of women who found independence when they slid behind the wheel was relatively small.

In part because of their customary role as passenger, some women also found themselves vulnerable to men who had control of an automobile and whisked them away from the watchful eyes of their families and communities. Moving beyond the front porch or the neighborhood created both opportunity and vulnerability for women. From their earliest experiences with cars, young women were taught to be wary of men, especially those offering rides or assistance. Cautioned about the risks of predators and the "devil wagon," most women, into the twenty-first century, had a much more circumscribed automotive experience than men.[4]

One need only look at the language used to describe drivers. In the nineteenth century, a professional woman who challenged gender expectations and entered a male field received a gendered title, such as "doctress" or "lawyeress." As women took the wheel when automobiles emerged in the late 1890s, however, no new word emerged to describe them. With the introduction of mass production and the growing embrace of cars in the early 1900s, both men and women became known as "drivers." A gender-neutral identity was possible, but instead the language that emerged identified women with a gendered qualifier. They were "woman drivers," "lady drivers," or "female drivers," with a host of pernicious assumptions surrounding them. Conversely, we see no deployment of terms such as "man drivers," "gentleman drivers," or "male drivers." Even in countless newspaper and magazine accounts of men causing automobile accidents, the gender qualifier did not appear. While the novelty of women driving dissipated over time, the desire to delineate who was driving and demean women with these monikers persisted into the twenty-first century.[5]

Contemporaries of the first women to drive cars generally did not consider their actions significant, or even positive. More than a dozen men laid claim to being the inventor of the American automobile, dating to 1893, and countless more sought acknowledgment as the first to break driving records for speed and distance. Before the emergence of the women's movement in the 1960s and 1970s, however, few women celebrated their vehicular accomplishments as the first American woman to drive a car, be licensed, or drive long distances. While some have imagined the role of cars as transformative, in truth cars only offered women "a wider range of possibility in their everyday lives."[6]

Indeed, it was a man who made one of the earliest claims of a woman behind the wheel. Automobile inventor and manufacturer Elwood Haynes proclaimed that his secretary, Mary Landon, had been the first woman ever to drive, in 1899. Businessmen like Haynes needed to grow the number of drivers nationally; into the 1920s, only a small percentage of women drove. His story line was clear: Driving is so easy and safe that even women have historically done it, and he either resurrected or created a story about Landon's adventure. Highlighting Landon in 1928, though,

AUTOMOBILES
59
Miss Maud Leroy of Weber & Fields Co. in her Haynes-Apperson Runabout.
The HAYNES=APPERSON
is the only powerful automobile simple enough for a lady to run *easily*, and reliable enough for her to take far from home and count on getting back without trouble.
The Haynes-Apperson Cars have been started under conditions officially imposed by others, not once or twice, but 1, 2, 3, 4, 5, 6, 7, 8, 9, 10, 11, 12, 13, 14, 15, 16, 17 separate times, winning first honors EVERY time with stock cars. That means reliability of the kind no one else has PROVED.
Our catalogue gives full information. Inquirers are urged to visit our factory, where every detail of HAYNES-APPERSON superiority can be seen and fully understood. Call and see our exhibits at New York and Chicago Shows.
HAYNES=APPERSON CO., Kokomo, Ind., U. S. A.
The Oldest Makers of Motor Cars in America.
Members of the Association of Licensed Automobile Manufacturers. Branch Store: 1420 Michigan Ave., Chicago. **Eastern Representatives:** BROOKLYN AUTOMOBILE CO., 1239-41-43 Fulton Street, Brooklyn, N. Y., and 66 West 43d Street, New York; NATIONAL AUTOMOBILE & MFG. Co., Pacific Coast Agents, San Francisco.

Figure 1. Manufacturers sought out women drivers in the early twentieth century by assuring them that their cars were easy to drive and reliable. This 1904 Haynes ad drew on the popularity of a vaudeville performer to explain why a woman would need a vehicle to take her "far from home and count on getting back without trouble."

also revealed how short-lived her automotive independence was, as she no longer drove and had not even owned a car for twenty years.[7]

Driver's licenses also helped establish the identities of early women drivers. *Life* magazine ran an article in 1952 on the woman they claimed had been the first to be licensed in Washington, D.C., Anne Rainsford French. The author praised French's independence motoring a steam car in 1900 but noted that she stopped driving in 1903 when she married. After living without a car for ten years, when the couple did finally acquire one, French's husband proclaimed to her and their children, "Driving is a man's business. Women shouldn't get soiled by machinery." The article, ostensibly written to demonstrate that French was a woman of accomplishment, concluded that in response to her husband's contention that cars were only for men, the capitol's first licensed female driver replied meekly, "Yes, Walter." Even in a popular national magazine's article on the significance of early women drivers, the underlying message to readers was that women should not identify with the car as a source of pride or freedom.[8]

This type of backhanded acclaim pervaded the attention accorded to early women drivers. As Kokomo, Indiana, residents celebrated their centennial in 1965, they revived the claim that Mary Landon was the first woman driver. A newspaper article celebrating her history and participation in the festivities, however, still concluded that the explanation for her revolutionary turn behind the wheel stemmed from the fact that she was "tricked into it" by Haynes. Even as the local media granted Landon recognition and thought her story newsworthy, they simultaneously characterized her as "duped into driving."[9]

As with Landon, it was only on the fifty-year anniversary of Alice Ramsey's pioneering 1909 cross-country adventure that people began to credit her, as well. The trip from New York to San Francisco had also been a promotional affair for the Maxwell-Briscoe car company. Traveling with three female companions, a young friend and her husband's two sisters, Ramsey drove nearly 4,000 miles, heralding the ease with which even a woman could handle the car and its reliability over thousands of miles and difficult terrain. The 1909 journey of "Mrs. John R. Ramsey," a married, wealthy woman, generated only a handful of small notices appearing in local papers en route and a few longer pieces celebrating the launch and Ramsey's triumphant arrival on the West Coast. Ramsey's more extensive media coverage began in the late twentieth century when the visually driven media relished the wonderful pictures of Ramsey in her duster, accompanied by brief stories that heralded a pioneer whose husband did not like to drive and acknowledged that she had left behind her year-old son to undertake the trip. Accounts of the trip still maintained a fiction about her single-handed ability to manage repairs and navigation, relying principally on her own 1961 account of her trip, written more than fifty years after the fact.[10]

Newspaper and magazine articles, and even obituaries in the 1960s and 1970s, touted the accomplishments of early female drivers, perhaps inspired by the feminist movement that was asking of history, "What was *her* story?" In addition to highlighting national figures, local papers began to feature the first women to drive, maybe not in the country or across the country, but certainly in their town or city. The 1961 obituary of Frances Senteney Carey, for example, proclaimed that she "was the first woman to drive an automobile in Hutchinson, Kansas." These later twentieth-century accounts uncovered women's early embrace of the automobile and positioned them as progressive and accomplished. Second-wave celebrants touted women's heroism in asserting their equality in this new arena.[11]

Most women, however, did not find dignity and independence in driving. Any attempts to develop their automotive acumen and disrupt the prejudice against them challenged cultural definitions of women's gender and sexual identity. The evidence suggests that the only kind of woman believed to be good at driving or repairing a car would be one without a man. The phenomenon of women taking the wheel could have been empowering, as many proved their mettle as drivers and mechanics, but in spite of occasional celebratory reflections, the broadest, most frequent response to women driving has been mockery and dismissal. For most women, characterized as terrible drivers, harping passengers, and naïve mechanics, the car represented not freedom and power but only the likelihood of ridicule. The emergence of the car, therefore, led to an expectation across the century that women would buy cars, drive them, and fix them, but not be good at any of it. Even as the car became an increasingly important part of American life, women found themselves isolated on the fringes of this national obsession.[12]

Automobiles became a defining aspect of American culture and identity, and the many stereotypes that existed adapted to drivers and passengers. Just as the public and the police made reflexive conclusions about cars and drivers based on race, so too has the nation made parallel assumptions based on gender. A quick glance informed attitudes about the motivations and aptitudes of those at the wheel.[13]

Women have often been behind the wheel, but when it comes to directing the cultural conversation, men have done the driving. This story of American automotive history reveals a long-standing pattern of according men respect and women disdain. When it came to automobiles, people continuously evaluated cars and drivers on the basis of their gender. One of the earliest assumptions came with the early contest for supremacy waged among inventors of steam, electric, and gasoline cars.

The conceit that women only drove electric cars persisted even though historians have only a loose grasp on how many people of either sex drove, and even less on what kind of car, in the first decades of the twentieth century. Historian Clay McShane found in his analysis of early 1900s car registrations that "women owners preferred more powerful, heavier cars." While historian Virginia Scharff contended that advertisements in the first two decades of the century targeted electric cars to women, it is not evident that women predominated in driving electric cars or that women forsook steam or gasoline cars. The suggestion that men only drove gas cars and women only drove electric cars inaugurated a mythical belief in gendered automotive preferences.[14]

While various automobile models vied for dominance in the early years, including the long-forgotten steam cars, Henry Ford's introduction of the gas-powered Model T in 1908 led to a staggering rate of adoption in the United States. In 1900, there were about 8,000 registered automobiles. Historian James D. Norris discovered that, by as early as 1910, the automobile had moved beyond a "passing fad or an expensive plaything for the rich." By 1923, more than half of the nearly 23.5 million American families owned an automobile, far more than paid federal income tax or owned a telephone. According to historian Margaret Walsh, "Those who

Figure 2. History has principally told the story of gas- and electric-powered cars, but women and men also drove steam-powered cars in the early twentieth century, as in this 1901 Toledo ad.

owned these vehicles were likely to be white and middle-class. Only small percentages of minority families owned cars." In the middle of the Depression, in 1935–36, 15 percent of African American families had a car, as compared to 59 percent of white families.[15]

Still, understanding that the American driver was most likely to be white and have reached the middle class does not reveal women's relationship to the number of cars produced, automobile registrations, number of licensed drivers, or what analysts call VMT, Vehicle Miles Traveled. Walsh points to women's embrace of the car, noting their pleasure in it and asserting its importance to them. In a 1920 interview, one woman explained her family's decision to buy a car before installing indoor plumbing: "Why, you can't go to town in a bathtub." While we know, too, that African Americans drove, including women like cosmetics entrepreneur Madam C. J. Walker, who used the car to both acquire and showcase their wealth, their relatively small numbers left a historical record with little trace of their role in shaping the automobile experience.[16]

While it is nearly impossible to know how many women were car owners and drivers, the historical record suggests miniscule numbers that grew slowly across the first half of the twentieth century. Breaking down the larger population into likely owners is revealing. According to a 1921 report in the *Automotive Manufacturer*, only 5 percent of native-born, white men of voting age owned a car in 1912. Even by 1920, only 42 percent of those Americans imagined to have had a car, wealthy, white adult men, apparently did so. Analyzing these numbers, informed by women's relatively smaller population, compounded by their reduced social and financial power, it becomes clear that driving a car persisted as being an exceptional activity for women. A 1920 article in the *Literary Digest* found 15,000 women licensed to drive in New Jersey. With a total population greater than three million, this made women drivers a mere half a percent of all drivers in New Jersey in 1920. While the author extrapolated to imagine about 300,000 female drivers nationwide, the social map of the United States—with many western states such as Wyoming and Nevada boasting populations with 10, 15, and 20 percent more men than women, and with much more rural, unpaved terrain—does not support this conclusion. Still, increasing suburbanization, greater affordability and accessibility of the car, and women's growing public responsibilities all led to increasing numbers of women drivers, and by 1963, the ratio of male-to-female licensed drivers stood at 60:40. The numbers then accelerated rapidly, with the number of women drivers growing 39 percent between 1980 and 2000. By 2012, there were more women than men licensed as drivers in the United States for the first time.[17]

Across the automotive age, images and stories of women and cars filled internal industry newsletters, automotive periodicals, and popular media. What may have seemed a universal experience is revealed to have been a distinctive one for women. From their earliest efforts to learn to drive to their attempts to secure driver's licenses, women generally found taking control of cars to be fraught with aspersions of their competency and appearance. Automobile companies used magazines and advertisements to shape the discourse. In the process, they played two opposing roles, seeking both to legitimate women as car enthusiasts and to reify men as "natural" drivers.[18]

The next step for women, after learning to drive and securing their licenses, was to acquire a car to drive. Most automotive companies expressed continual surprise when they discovered evidence of women's economic power, and they consistently approached women as a narrowly defined, monolithic market they could ignore. This reveals an inherent contradiction: Although automobile companies did occasionally seek out female consumers, their fundamental inclination was to ignore them. This pattern is perhaps easiest to understand at the point of purchase. Women buying an automobile did so in a decidedly male space and, into the twenty-first century, faced a consistently uninterested reaction from the salesmen. While other industries that sought female customers invested money in women's media, car companies were reluctant to do so. Only designating paltry advertising budgets of 3 percent or less and creating intimidating, sexist showrooms hampered the already limited number of marketing approaches the automotive industry believed key to winning women's business.

Many auto enthusiasts and companies then and now condescended to women by crediting them with making cars more comfortable and practical, but, in truth, throughout the car's evolution people always sought to improve the car. From the complex, wide-ranging efforts to create the car itself, to the continuing endeavor to make the best car possible, there has been a constant quest for improvement. Windshield wipers, heaters, turn signals, and seat belts emerged, not because women demanded it but because competition for consumers of both sexes inspired it. As exceptions became the rule, more innovative features developed to further improve the automotive experience. Often initially attributed to women, once unique, significant technological developments quickly became de rigueur for a modern automobile.[19]

Driving a car was perhaps the most visible way that someone was identified as a "woman driver." Women faced the reality that although driving a car could offer freedom, real and perceived vulnerability also shaped their driving experience. From the day-to-day concerns of seeking out gasoline stations with "Rest Rooms" to the prospect of facing sexual violence in cars, women's experiences behind the wheel shaped their national experience as drivers. Beyond their individual driving experiences, women also faced the perennial question, asked from the earliest days of automobility: Who were the better drivers, women or men? This question permeated the debate and helped perpetuate the myth of men's superiority. Unlike other racial and ethnic assertions of inferiority that became gauche and self-evidently false, it remained acceptable, for more than one hundred years, to persist in asking the gendered question of who was better. Moreover, the question principally served to continually assert that men were superior drivers, in spite of evidence to the contrary.[20]

While we might imagine maintaining a car historically to have been men's work, women in the first decades of the twentieth century quickly found themselves responsible for their family's car care. Solicitous companies assured women that taking care of a car was just like taking care of a child, with the presumption that this type of knowledge was "natural." In general, though, the small number of women who mastered their own cars' mechanical makeup discovered that they risked their femininity. For most women, tasked with selecting a garage to perform the work and knowing what services and costs were appropriate, they discovered that they were rarely afforded respect even in their quest to find others to care for the car.

Although the culture featured a number of stereotypes regarding women and cars, one of the most enduring associations concerned identity. Americans considered the car to be female, regularly referring to the automobile as a "her" and "she," adorning the car with feminine markers, and sometimes naming it. The car's female identity, then, gave rise to a number of unexpected outcomes, including the love and even lust that men, in particular, felt for their cars. With both women and cars having bodies, car talk often blurred the lines between the two.

In spite of the many changes in women's lives, the historical evidence reveals a significant continuity of cultural and behavioral impulses regarding American women's experience with cars. Patriarchal attitudes and assumptions of male superiority continue to dominate our understanding of the car and inform our study of history. By focusing their analyses on changing trends, historians have underappreciated the permanencies of ideological power in American culture. Automobiles offer an opportunity to analyze the ways this power has been wielded to great effect. Principally looking for change over time in such attitudes obscures their longevity. Asking different questions about women's experiences offers insights into what it was like for women at the wheel.[21]

1

Learning to Drive

FROM THE VERY INTRODUCTION of the car into American lives, instructions for how to drive evolved in a gendered manner. The physical demands of early cars, combined with an early, entrenched belief that only men should drive, set the stage. Although secondary schools, organizations, and corporations sought to educate teenagers on driving, they remained convinced that young men were the *real* drivers. This expectation undoubtedly contributed to the relatively smaller percentage of younger women who drove and the later need to target women for instruction as older adults. The tensions over who should teach women to drive and how to teach them revealed a consistent expectation that men had natural driving ability and women did not.

Driver's licensing, while a more uniform process, also created different outcomes for women and men, as issues of marital status and the significance of appearance weighed differently on them. Instead of acquiring a key to freedom, women found their weight, age, and appearance documented and exposed for all to judge. Indeed, their very identity, their name, remained something to be contested with each application and renewal, and potentially varied with each change to their marital status.

Many critics used humor to disparage the driving skills of novice female drivers. As early as the 1930s, a strong cultural response suggested that women who could not drive were shrews who chose instead to critique men's driving. The stereotype of women as "backseat" drivers empowered men to mute women's guidance and feedback.

"I'm a Typical Teenage Girl"

The question of whether women should learn to drive began simultaneously with the introduction of motor vehicles. An early publication, *The Horseless Age*, sought to answer the question in 1898, assuring readers of the ease in driving the new "motor carriage." The author recounted a story of a young woman who had seen but never ridden in a car. After about an hour of riding, she took her place behind the wheel and quickly learned to drive. Challenging a belief that drivers needed "skill and long experience" to operate this new machinery, the author hoped readers would recognize women as able drivers and the automobile as readily accessible to all who tried it.[1]

According to an article in the *Woman's Home Companion* in 1900, "Several manufacturers have opened academies where instruction is given in the operation of the motor carriages." While society remained conflicted about the notion of women drivers, manufacturers had a stake in encouraging women to learn to drive. Acknowledging that only a few motorists existed in America's large cities, the article nonetheless promoted the automobile's qualities and established women's aptitude for it.[2]

Women, though, continued to make up only a small percentage of drivers, and the number of driving instructors remained miniscule. A 1914 *New York Times* article featured one female instructor who claimed that the number of women remained small because driving challenged their gender identity. She noted that initially women were thought to be "too frail to drive a 'devil wagon,'" and that those who did "were looked upon as being mannish" as they cranked a car to start it, manipulated the steering apparatus, and shifted gears.[3] She believed that the key to increasing the number of women behind the wheel would come in women's growing confidence as they drove and cared for a car.

Rural farm women used the car as an important tool to aid their housewifery, bringing goods to market. They also used the car to seek out social opportunities to sew and cook with other women, including family and friends. Women also sought urban fashion and used cars to acquire new styles. One 1930 study of Midwestern farm families, for example, discovered that women made about "two-thirds of all clothing purchases out of their country environs." That did not mean, however, that girls and women necessarily had licenses to drive. Historian Mary Neth found that girls were the "least likely to know how to drive" and discovered one study that revealed "that while 81 percent of country boys in Missouri drove cars, only 46 percent of the rural girls did."[4]

Instilling that confidence increasingly fell to organizations and schools offering driving instruction. Although most targeted both sexes, they occasionally singled women out. Motivated by the exigencies of war, many private organizations offered driving lessons in the buildup to America's entry into World War I and during the war. Thereafter, the urgency fell off and did not pick up again for about a decade. The American Automobile Association (AAA), for example, recorded praise for its first "women drivers" course offered in Washington, D.C., in 1929. The local assistant superintendent of police thought the AAA course would improve public safety but also wondered, "Why confine this instruction course to women drivers only as I am sure we have some male drivers who would find that an instruction course of this nature would materially help their driving." While occasionally someone made such an observation, frequently assumptions about women's inabilities coexisted with blind faith in men's ability to drive.[5]

In the 1930s, Americans embraced driver's education for young adults in the nation's secondary schools. There continued to be stand-alone programs for adults, like the St. Louis Women's Safe Drivers' School, but for the most part instructional efforts centered on teenagers. Enrolling students as young as fourteen, these elective school programs maintained that instruction was a critical part of the country's growing automotive safety imperative. Even before they could drive, girls and boys were taught about the car and the driving laws. The schools joined forces with the automobile and insurance industries to teach young people with replica automobiles that featured driving simulators.[6]

Before they could teach young people how to drive, however, schools needed trained instructors. This initially proved problematic, with only a

Overland
TRADE MARK REG.
$1075
F.O.B. TOLEDO
FIVE PASSENGER TOURING CAR
Every Woman Can Drive an Overland
Tens of thousands of American women drive their Overland every day—daughters, sisters and mothers.
It is the simplest car in the world to drive.
In the first place, practically everything is done by electricity—just as it is on the most expensive cars.
On the steering column, where your hand naturally rests, are the electric control buttons. These buttons start the car, light the head, side, tail and dash lights, and sound the electric signal.
The clutch, operated by foot, takes no more strength than you exert in walking.
The levers are within natural reach of your right hand.
So all you need is a few lessons, and before you realize it you are unconsciously driving with as much skill and confidence as those who have driven cars for years.
As far as care goes, the Overland requires about as much attention as your sewing machine.
Prices: Overland Model 80 T, $1075 Overland Model 81 T, 850 Overland Model 80 R, $1050 Overland Model 81 R, 795 Overland Model 80 Coupé, $1600 Overland Six—Model 82, 1475
All Prices F. O. B. Toledo

Figure 3. This 1915 Overland ad featured a woman at the wheel, with men in both the passenger seat and the backseat. The text assured women that its care required "about as much attention as your sewing machine."

few colleges and institutes offering training. Moreover, safety fears pervaded accounts of the instruction, with one of the pioneers of driver's education, Amos Neyhart, remarking in 1937 that past instruction had only enabled people to "drive after a fashion." By joining forces with AAA, he sought to exceed the minimal state expectations and truly empower drivers to "manage and control today's fast-moving automobiles" to lower the number of fatalities on the road. Even with the growing feminization of the teaching profession, few women appeared in the front of driver's education classrooms.[7]

In addition to saving lives, individuals, organizations, and corporations also saw the potential for sales in instruction manuals and advertising their products. Although occasionally they were even targeted to young children, most efforts centered on teens. General Motors, for example, issued its first printing of *We Drivers* in 1936, and updated it through the 1960s. Companies undoubtedly hoped high school or college driver's education classes would adopt their guidebooks and build brand loyalty for their cars and services. The AAA's *Sportsmanlike Driving*, for example, was first printed in 1936 and continually updated through the late 1980s. It centered on the social and emotional issues drivers must consider, including "The Psychology of the Driver" and "Courtesy." While most twenty-first-century Americans likely consider "road rage" a modern problem, concern with "overgrown babies" at the wheel appeared in early guidebooks as well. The books generally did not offer written gendered guidance, although the driver imagery was decidedly male. A 1955 *Sportsmanlike Driving* text made references to men as "the unpopular show-off" and "baby blow-horn."[8]

Although ubiquitous in American culture and required in about half its states, driver's education has never been nationally mandatory and many studies revealed its ineffectiveness in decreasing the number of automobile accidents for young people. As one 2008 government report concluded, "Teens do not get into crashes because they are uninformed about the basic rules of the road or safe driving practices; rather, studies show they are involved in crashes as a result of inexperience and risk-taking." Indeed, some studies even found that those who took the classes had a higher rate of accidents than those who did not. Most states recognized that the primary reason for those accidents stemmed from putting young people on the road and embraced graduated license programs that limited when and how teens could drive at ages sixteen and seventeen. Still, in spite of its limitations, driver's education remained a part of the process of learning to drive a car. Insurance and automotive companies, therefore, continued to seek opportunities to put their products in the hands of the millions of new drivers, especially teenagers without established brand loyalties.[9]

Popular driver's education portrayals generally spared girls and women no criticism in their depictions of poor drivers. In a 1969 television commercial, American Motors touted that professional driving schools used more of their cars than any other manufacturers' cars and, to demonstrate their durability, the ad showcased six bad drivers. While the featured men drove jerkily, panicked, and hit a fire hydrant, the portrayals of the three women were much worse. The first ground the gears, trying to find first, and then could not stay on the road; another was told to turn left and claimed she could not with the instructor watching, and then turned too soon over the traffic island; and the last one, when told to look out for the truck and bus replied in a high-pitched voice, "What truck? What bus?" as she wove dangerously through oncoming traffic. The company portrayed the men as novices and the women as incompetents.[10]

This condemnation of women's driving continued into the twenty-first century, with a 2010 Allstate Insurance commercial that featured a spokesman acting as though he were a teenage girl. It opened with him in a pink, oversized sport utility vehicle (SUV) in a parking lot. His pink sunglasses and the script conveyed his "girl" identity. In the thirty-second spot, he drove carelessly, holding his cell phone, and telling the viewer, "I'm a teenage girl. My BFF Becky texts and says she's kissed Johnny. Well that's a problem cause, I like Johnny. Now, I'm emotionally compromised." He then threw the cell phone into the back and slammed the SUV into another car's front fender. He then concluded of his "Mayhem," "Whoopsies. I'm all 'OMG, Becky's not even hot.'" After suggesting that teenage girls are reckless, bad drivers, he warned motorists that they unknowingly share the road with these terrible drivers and had best get Allstate insurance. The fifteen-second spot was even less subtle. It opened with him announcing, "I'm a typical teenage girl," getting a text message on the phone, slamming the SUV into a car's fender, and driving off. According to Allstate, it was typical of teenage girls to text and drive, as well as to crash into other cars because they were emotionally unstable. Other ads included poor behavior by teenage boys and men. Female behavior, however, was singled out as "typical teenage girl" behavior, while that of males was more individualized. Advertisements and the broader culture consistently portrayed women, and girls in particular, as poor drivers.[11]

"Drive with Both Hands if You Expect to Live and Marry Her"

Female passengers admonished individual young men not to endanger young women with their driving. An early cartoon chastised men, "Drive with both hands if you expect to live and marry her." Companies commonly premised ads promoting driving safely on women's preference for safety and young men's recklessness. Placed only in periodicals targeting boys, such as *Boys' Life* and *Hot Rod*, with no comparable ads appearing in *Seventeen*, the ads used shame, humor, and adult mentors to send the message to boys that driving dangerously could leave you without a date, a license, or your life or someone else's. Headlined "That's the Last Time I Ride with That Show-off," one 1939 ad for Ford had a girl resolving never to go out with a "cut-up" whom she deemed an "infant," who "doesn't know enough about driving to put out his hand at a turn." A 1960 General Motors ad maintained, "The cars are safer . . . the roads are safer . . . the rest is up to YOU!" and targeted boys in their role as both driver and protector. Beneath the photograph of a girl and boy headed off in the car to go ice-skating, the text recounted their conversation, " 'Don't worry, Mom, we'll be careful.' She says that as you're walking her out to the car. And what a responsibility this means for *you*, the driver! Her folks, your folks, the parents of everyone riding with you depend on your safe driving ability and mature judgment."[12]

The rhetoric about bad male drivers centered principally on individual men and their immature behaviors. Men's deadly actions did not indict the male sex, but they supposedly reflected a limited number of exceptions to the sacrosanct expectation that men were the better drivers.[13]

Starting in the 1950s, driver's education classes relied on films to communicate their safety messages and tried to scare young people straight. The stories centered on traditional gender roles with a reckless male driver and a victimized female passenger. These movies grew increasingly terrifying, and eventually used actual graphic footage shot by police officers arriving on the scene of accidents to emphasize that young men, particularly in cars with souped-up engines, needed to drive more carefully and considerately. The narration of the movies underscored the carnage. The male narrator of *Mechanized Death* warned, "These are the sounds of excruciating agony. . . . This is not a dream, not a nightmare. This is real." The opening of *The Last Prom* asked, "Was it a pretty face that made this gaping jagged hole in the windshield?" The films used girls' facial scars to drive home that a poor decision by male drivers would end a girl's life, if not literally, figuratively. *Last Date* had the girl who survived a boy's deadly crash narrate the movie with her back to the camera because the accident left her face so disfigured that she would not show it. The movies suggested that a girl who lost her beauty in a car crash suffered a social death, so women had a vested interest in controlling male behavior behind the wheel.[14]

According to New York University's director of the Center for Safety Education in 1960, "The major accomplishment in the field of driver education may be described as moral. The willingness of the schools to include this instruction implies a feeling of moral responsibility for the preservation of lives from death and injury." Trying to reach young people's impressionable minds and emphasize ethical concerns about taking the wheel, instructors wanted to temper young people's egos by reminding them of the obligations of citizenship. They did so primarily by assuming that the driver was always male and the passenger and potential victim was female.[15]

In 1971, the AAA magazine *American Motorist* highlighted the success of Cissie Gieda in becoming the president of the American Driver and Traffic Safety Education Association. While recounting some of her successful teaching strategies, Gieda revealed that she believed that "the bad reputation credited to women drivers is probably deserved. She says women drivers, in general, are less polite and not as safe as most men drivers in general. And she lets her students know it. Her humorous lamentation of the poor quality of women drivers is a source of challenge to her girl students and a source of delight to boys in her class."[16]

Gieda denigrated women to gain credibility with her students, themselves immersed in a cultural expectation of women as poor drivers. Even in a setting where everyone was there to learn how to drive, the expectation that male drivers came in with authority pervaded the curriculum and informed the instructors. Female drivers, consistently relegated to seeing themselves as victimized passengers, had no models for how to proceed and their instructors, including the rare female ones, taught their coed classes that women deserved their reputation as bad drivers.

"DON'T Let Your Husband Teach You!"

While teenagers remained the primary focus of driver's education schools, large numbers of adult women remained without a license. A gendered understanding of driving, fueled by the relatively small number of women drivers, fed a belief that women needed special instruction to acquire licenses. Women flocked to driver training programs, particularly in the second half of the century. Of AAA's 12,236 pupils in 1956, "*75 per cent* of the students who took those lessons *were women*!" Ads for their driving schools usually featured women, as with one 1969 ad that had a forlorn-looking woman transformed into a joyous one: "It's sad to hear a housewife say, I'm marooned at home the livelong day! Her life's now changed—she's always gay! She's Learned to Drive the AAA Way!" The number of women seeking instruction remained high because even as late as the 1970s only about half of American women had a driver's license. In spite of the natural decline in population of elderly women who never drove, the numbers seem to have remained high for two reasons: (1) many immigrant women arrived not having learned to drive in their home country (American rates of women drivers remain among the highest in the world) and (2) many urban women never learned to drive.[17]

Many adult women who had never learned to drive sought out lessons. In a 1959 account, for example, a woman acknowledged that her family and friends had tired of her "carefree-state" and subsequent dependence on them, so at age thirty she enrolled in driving school. In addition to learning to drive, she also discovered that some driving instructors seduced women with supportive encouragement and a calm, patient ear. Her forty-five-year-old male instructor told her, "You not only meet a lot of beautiful women, you meet a lot of rich ones. There are all kinds of ladies who have got nothing better to do. Sometimes they will take driving lessons for four hours at a stretch." Some women, then, seduced their instructors, paying for attention under the guise of learning to drive. Whether they gained mobility, confidence, or companionship from driving instructors, the experience of learning to drive later in life was more distinctly a female one.[18]

Driving instructors, such as the head of the AAA's driving school in 1965, commented on the importance that they believed women placed on driving, contrasting it as greater than men's. Some women, recounting their experience learning to drive, reflected on the importance of controlling an automobile to their life experience. Feminist writer Katha Pollitt saw it "as a metaphor for taking control and breaking through and doing things that are difficult for you. And not depending so much on men." Undoubtedly, the fact that many of these women apparently made the decision to take lessons after losing their male driver to disability, divorce, or death heightened the significance of the car to their independence. Regardless, some women attested to the value of being able to drive as part of a modern, adult repertoire.[19]

Occasional reflections, especially popular for the urban readers of the *New York Times*, explored the many roads to not driving for women, which, beyond those who never learned, included those who, even with a permit, never pursued a license; those who let their licenses lapse; or those who, even with a license, chose not to drive. In 1987, one woman who grew up driving in California found herself letting her husband do all the driving. She explained, "What I don't like . . . is getting on the highway or getting off and doing either one fast. I don't like to switch lanes, and I don't like night driving, snow, or parallel parking." Many women also professed a need to take lessons to learn to drive "for real," even if they had a license or experience driving, reflecting the tendency for both women and the culture to undervalue women's skills.[20]

Fueling the emphasis on professional instruction was a long-standing conceit that husbands were ill suited to teach their wives. An eighty-year-old, retired schoolteacher drove home the importance of driving schools to teach women. She pronounced, "Don't ever let anyone who loves you or cares for you teach you how to drive. . . . My husband taught me how to drive in the beginning, and it was a terrific strain for both of us. You need a stranger to teach you." Women across the century reiterated the importance of driving schools to marital harmony. An anonymous columnist not only beseeched women on behalf of safety experts who did not think husbands should teach their wives, but also warned, "HOME INSTRUCTION CAN BE MURDER!" Cataloging the reasons for this, the article noted that men were not necessarily modeling good, safe behavior, and would bring both a lack of objectivity regarding their wives' performance and a hypersensitivity to their car's well-being. Women concluded, "This sort of do-it-yourself project can result in a wrecked car or a wrecked marriage." One woman interviewed about the subject implored, "If you want to learn to drive, don't let your husband teach you! . . . Go to driving school! You'll learn more, and you WILL eventually get your license. When you're taught by someone you know, you're a nervous wreck."[21]

While some women argued that husbands made poor driving instructors, one popular columnist, in a column titled "Teaching Wife to Drive Called False Economy," blamed women for their inability to drive. Citing a study by a Dr. Luther Limpenberger, "Maids, Motor Cars, and Madness," the columnist claimed that women responded to their husbands' "gentle and loving tone" teaching them to drive by yelling, bawling, and threatening to jump out of the car. He concluded that women "generally had tantrums." The syndicated columnist, Henry McLemore, completely fabricated the cited author and the study to advance his own prejudiced thinking to readers across the nation. As he divulged on the television program *You Bet Your Life* in 1956, in response to a question from host Groucho Marx, "There are times when a columnist just has to dream up things." There were no studies that showed women could not learn to drive and nothing to substantiate his assertion that, in women's efforts to learn, "the fault is wholly attributable to the wife." Publishing a column that claimed to be based on "studies on four continents," which found that women went into hysterics if their husbands taught them to drive, but that they could learn easily from "deaf pygmies" and "defrocked railroad firemen," McLemore perpetuated his larger message that women could not drive. A popular, public figure, McLemore maintained that women, not the men teaching them, were the problem, running counter to the experience women professed.[22]

Empowered by McLemore and a cultural dismissal of women's driving aptitude, other men also wrote to columnists to complain about their wives. Their response to female drivers also reveals disdain for their wives' aptitude for driving. One man's 1965 letter to syndicated columnist Dr. Joyce Brothers suggested that teaching his wife to drive was the most trying experience of his life. He claimed that he needed help to save his marriage because his wife proclaimed "Don't tell me what to do!" every time he instructed her on how to drive.[23]

Unlike McLemore, who professed the fault was all women's, Dr. Brothers acknowledged the stress inherent in the process and supported women's efforts by citing the statistical record, which revealed women to be safe and good drivers. She also built on a concept introduced by theorist Michael Kaufman that men were seeking to create differential participation in driving with their attitudes and behavior. As Kaufman found with social and political participation, one of the powers wielded by a process that principally empowered men as instructors and evaluators was the ability to render women's driving experiences invisible and invalid.[24]

Not content to refute a man's assertion that his wife's alleged poor driving skills meant an end to his marriage, Dr. Brothers also built on his complaints to counter them as well. She wondered if perhaps husbands thought their wives too old to learn but cited evidence that women's prime driving age was in their forties and early fifties. As all studies found, she also indicated that what drivers should fear most were young men, ages 20–24, who had the most dangerous accidents. While the discourse abounded with criticisms of women learning to drive, female columnists consistently responded with reasoned evidence to counter male hysteria.[25]

One woman's letter sent to popular advice columnist Ann Landers in 1968 revealed what was at stake for male power in enabling women to drive. After an accident necessitating that her husband leave work to come home and drive their child to the hospital, the woman told Landers that she was determined to learn to drive and enlisted her husband to help her. He did so, "But he made me so nervous (called me dumb and a fraidy cat) that I gave up trying to learn from him." After that failed effort, she announced that she was "enrolling in driving school." Just as women's efforts to go back to school or work for wages outside the home created tensions, women learning to drive elicited anger from some men. In this case, "He screamed, 'No man is going to teach MY wife anything. It would be a reflection on me.' " In first failing to teach his wife to drive and then denying her the opportunity to learn to drive from others, he attempted to keep absolute control over his wife's movement. Kaufman notes the significance of violence in contributing to women's self-doubts and limiting their participation in the broader community. In this instance, though, the woman knew full well her husband was wrong and sought public affirmation in a letter to someone she believed not only would offer wise counsel but also would make public the emotional abuse she and other women were experiencing.[26]

As columnists commonly acknowledged, learning to drive can be a stressful experience and the car can serve as a site of intense, focused emotion as people confront each other in a small space. Filmmakers have used the car to explore tensions between races, ethnicities, and the sexes, evident in films as far reaching as the award-winning *Driving Miss Daisy* and the renowned filmmaker Mike Leigh's *Happy-Go-Lucky*, which explored a woman's fraught interactions with an unstable driving instructor. Women more often than men found themselves vulnerable in this proximate space, as they faced continual criticism for their driving, risked their identity as morally upright, and endured physical violence, including sexual assaults.[27]

Although vehicles provided the opportunity for romance and consensual rendezvous, they also empowered men to jeopardize a woman's status as morally "good" with behavior ranging from keeping her out past her curfew to committing sexual assault. If riding with a familiar man was dangerous, doing so with a total stranger seemed even more terrifying. Society held up hitchhiking as inherently dangerous for women, yet riding with a driving instructor, someone paid to teach her how to drive, generally did not raise red flags. Most women learning to operate a car acquiesced to the authority of male instructors and the risk of sexual harassment and violence they carried.[28]

Some male instructors used the isolation and privacy of the car to harass and assault their students. Exploiting their authority as instructors and their advanced age, men harassed and assaulted women. To address the concern, some companies confronted it forthrightly in their contracts. The Behind the Wheel Driving School, for example, based in Manhattan Beach, California, included their resolve to disallow any harassing behavior of their students. While less explicit, the emergence of woman-owned and operated schools from coast to coast sought to assure female students of a safe driving environment.[29]

Assaults by driving instructors were frequently bemoaned in England where news reports abounded with accounts of "pervert" instructors assaulting students, yet it was a 1992 rape case in Italy that made headlines for the next decade in the United States as the case wrangled its way through the courts. An eighteen-year-old girl accused her forty-five-year-old male driving instructor of taking her to a remote location and raping her. He did not deny that they had sex, but he maintained it was consensual. The courts sided with him; they claimed he could not have removed her jeans without her willing assistance because the jeans were too tight. Taken up as a cause célèbre in states like New Jersey that heralded "Denim Day" to decry judging women for their appearance when deciding a rape case, coverage of the case also reminded women of their vulnerability in riding in the car with men.[30]

In the early 1990s, gender analyst Virginia Rinaldo Seitz found that the economic vulnerability of Appalachian women's lives translated into an inability to afford a car and severely limited their work opportunities. Their socioeconomic status also likely dissuaded many women from learning to drive or from getting a license. As Kaufman noted about women's participation, patriarchal power often meant that men contributed to dissuading or disallowing women from seeking the independence the car could have provided. Indeed, Seitz noted that women found themselves not just dependent on others (usually a man) for rides but also dependent on receiving permission from their husbands and male relatives to ride with another man, further complicating their dependence on others for transportation.[31]

Battered women's accounts dramatically illuminated the freedom having a license represented for women generally. Legal scholar Margot Mendelson, for example, discovered in her interviews with battered women in the late twentieth century that they consistently referred to their driver's licenses as central to their lives. For many, their inability to drive (or to drive legally) "contributed to a general sense of unease, disorientation, and dependence." These women contrasted these feelings to the empowerment they felt in relation to their husbands once they could drive, which "altered the gender and power dynamics to which they had become accustomed." One woman characterized getting a license as the defining experience in her emergence from the hard times that marked her early years in the United States. For some women, this freedom and their skills remained bounded by the limits of socioeconomics, ethnicity, and geography, but most women embraced their licenses and the independence they proffered.[32]

However, even for those who could drive, fear tempered their freedom. Some women professed a fear of highway driving, preferring to take the longer route by navigating the side streets. Columnist Richard Shepard contended that his wife and others like her were competent drivers, but they feared bridges, tunnels, highways, and city driving. In some instances, these limits stemmed from individual comfort levels, while in others, women squarely placed the blame on men. They asserted that men had belittled their competence and made them too nervous to take the wheel. Men made comments and decisions that left women doubting their own driving abilities and limited their overall agency. Sometimes it was a husband's doubts about their daughter's driving (compared to a son's driving) that sent the message to his wife that he doubted her, too.[33]

Women occasionally reported that their fears stemmed from the poor care their husbands afforded their cars. It was not so much that they were afraid to drive, but that they were afraid to break down. One woman, for example, reported in 1982 that her husband would not buy her car new tires, even when three of the four had worn smooth, while another complained that her husband would not leave his incompetent mechanic, placing her life in jeopardy when the repair work was faulty. Although freedom seemed within their grasp, some women continued to find themselves limited by their own doubts and men who undermined their abilities.[34]

Certainly some observers suggested that women struggled more than men in their quest to learn to drive. One such critic was England's chief driving examiner, Richard Cummins, who in 2005 pointed to women's lower pass rates in that country as evidence of their poor driving skills. While not disputing Cummins's claim that British women passed at a rate of 40 percent as compared to men's pass rate of 46 percent, American authorities weighed in to refute the notion that pass rates equated to being good drivers. They argued that while men may pass the driving test more quickly, women's cautious performance behind the wheel made them safer and, therefore, better drivers. To support their claims, they cited statistics showing that women and men drove similarly, except in certain categories, such as men ages seventeen to twenty-five, who have more crashes.[35]

When Registering They Must Tell Their Age

The automobile emerged in advance of laws and guidebooks, so millions of Americans drove before there were any rules and without taking any formal lessons. Millions more eventually got licenses without necessarily passing formal written or road tests. Many early licenses merely let states account for who was on the road and enabled the states to charge, fine, or ticket drivers, none of which encouraged people to get licenses. Reflecting the cultural disrespect accorded women drivers, some people did not think the rules applied to women as they were not "real" drivers. For several decades, individuals could easily acquire licenses by mail in many states, including not just renewals but also the initial application. States often required only a name and an address. As more states began to require licenses and increased their testing requirements, they also determined with which states they would have reciprocal relationships, as well as what content would be essential to their license.[36]

The history of driver's licenses reveals a patchwork quilt, with each state, territory, and the District of Columbia making independent decisions. These decisions, including the fundamental one to license at all, were often contentious. In 1919, for example, the introduction of a new law in New York brought heated responses from advocates who thought questions about a driver's "past imprisonment in jail or insane asylums, if any; bodily infirmities, addiction to drugs or drink, and other physical and moral conditions" were relevant to licensing, as well as protests from those who saw testing as irrelevant. Whether to license women remained a point of contention. Even in a time of war, a critic of the New York law tersely noted, "I know a great many women drivers who could answer every question satisfactorily and yet, within ten minutes, if I took them out on the road, they would make fools of themselves." Furthermore, exemptions such as applying by mail undermined examination requirements and efforts to teach rules and safety.[37]

Historically, the most common identifying categories on a license included a number and an individual's first and last names and address. Over time, in different places, licenses also included information such as the driver's race, sex, height, weight, date of birth, social security number (created in 1936), occupation, whether corrective lenses were required to be worn while driving, the driver's photograph (starting in 1966), and organ-donor status (starting in the mid-1970s).[38]

Most states used paper licenses, in spite of their fragility. Other states used metal badges stamped with the state, year, and license number but no other identifying information about the driver. These pinned badges seem to have been a particularly popular style for regulating early professional drivers, such as chauffeurs and taxi drivers, although some states, including South Carolina and Arizona, appear to have used them for individual drivers as well, with Kentucky doing so into the 1950s.[39]

In a 1947 exposé in the popular magazine *Saturday Evening Post*, David Wittels sought to demonstrate that "the states in which it is hardest

FIGURE 4. These metal pinned licenses for Pennsylvania (1919) and Kentucky (1954) offered only an identifying number, while the more common paper ones revealed age, weight, and an often unflattering photograph, which made seeking a license an unpleasant undertaking.

to get licenses have the best safety records." He discovered that South Dakota did not even have a driver's license, and that Wyoming and Louisiana had just recently introduced them. Alarmed by the large number of accidents nationally, Wittels wanted to expose the lax attitudes states took in licensing drivers. He recounted a blind man in Montana who acquired a license, as well as young people of fourteen and fifteen who drove without restriction in some states, and the fourteen separate state driver's licenses he was able to secure by mail, using a false name and a completely concocted address.[40]

State and federal concern with fraudulent behavior came fairly late, with states only slowly requiring that signatures be in pen; using lamination to shield the cards from tampering; and later instituting holograms, magnetic strips, and other efforts to thwart forgeries. The terrorist attacks on September 11, 2001, prompted a number of uniform changes in driver's licenses, reflecting their growing importance as de facto national identification cards. While Americans consistently resisted the introduction of an actual national ID card, they largely accepted their state's Department of Motor Vehicles monitoring them. Although militia adherents often rejected driver's licenses and libertarians contested their encroaching reach, most citizens acquiesced. With increased security measures, people needed identification to fly even within the country, and the Department of Motor Vehicles issued identification cards for nondrivers. The most significant changes in the twenty-first century included disentangling the social security number from the license and every state ensuring IDs had a photo, with New Jersey the final straggler in 2008.[41]

Women have had a number of distinctive experiences with licenses. A long-standing etiquette allowed women to hide their age from public knowledge. Customarily, it was also improper to ask a woman's weight. Yet the driver's license often laid bare this information for all to see. Early applicants, particularly women, attempted to leave this revealing information off their applications or applied by mail so that they did not have to confront the clerk processing their information. One 1903 *Boston Daily Globe* article, for example, reported, "Much amusement is derived from guessing at age before glancing at the birthday entry for verification. Women autoists from out of town avoid exposing their blushes over the age requirement by doing business by mail." Nor did this desire to shield themselves abate easily. In 1934, a Minnesota newspaper relished the discomfort Minnesota's new licensing law elicited. It recounted an incident in which a "young lady was asked her weight she replied, 'Do I have to tell that!—Well, I-I weigh close to two hundred—Yes, I know it's entirely too much!'" A 1955 account reported that Connecticut returned more than 5,000 applications for driver's licenses because women failed to state their age. Early licenses did not have photographs, but this later development meant that drivers found themselves having to share three elements of themselves: an often-unflattering photo, their age, and their weight. For women, such exposures left them vulnerable to social critiques on these fronts.[42]

For most women, changing their driver's license when they changed their name upon marriage or divorce has been a long-standing headache and cost, with each state stipulating its own process. Most women changed their surname upon marriage and sometimes licenses even identified women by their husband's full name, as with a 1951 Connecticut license for Mrs. Truman W. Gilbert and a 1954 Pennsylvania license for Mrs. Harvey Shelly. Those who kept their maiden names ran up against laws that held that a woman had to change her name to her husband's in order to apply for a driver's license. She could then change it back, but upon marriage the state required her to apply for a driver's license using her husband's surname. Licenses reflected this tension over names, as with a 1968 Kentucky license issued to Ann Hudson Wild that she signed as Mrs. David W. Wild. Although Wild preferred the formal, traditional manner of address, some women wanted to maintain their maiden names legally.[43]

The importance of women's maiden names appeared in the courts early in the twentieth century as women challenged archaic laws predicated on coverture. This legal concept asserted that men legally covered women, either as fathers or husbands, and that married women could not "own or inherit property, sign a contract, or pursue their business interests in court." In the nineteenth century, laws of coverture began to face challenges from women's rights activists such as Elizabeth Cady Stanton. By the 1920s, state courts heard challenges from divorced women who still found their names linked to a man's and from professional women who sought to maintain separate, distinct identities from their husbands as early as the 1930s.[44]

A few women in the late 1960s and 1970s emerged as part of the feminist movement to challenge these antiquated laws. A federal court defended the first challenge, by Wendy Forbush in Alabama in 1971, by citing the "considerable investment" in the state's licensing system and pronounced "'the inconvenience and cost of a change to the State of

Alabama far outweighs the harm caused' to women." She took the case all the way to the U.S. Supreme Court, but the court affirmed the constitutionality of the law requiring her to apply in her husband's name for a driver's license without comment. Then, in 1976 and 1977, Sylvia Scott Whitlow fought to get a driver's license in her name, challenging Kentucky's law that she must do so with her husband's name as Mrs. Van Tubergen. The Supreme Court refused to hear her case, claiming the 1971 Alabama case settled the question when it concluded that the "existing law in Alabama which requires a woman to assume her husband's surname upon marriage has a rational basis." Most court briefs concerned with these issues in the 1970s continually returned to the custom of women assuming men's names upon marriage. They tended to assert that the process was automatic and inevitable; that disrupting the custom would create chaos for the woman's identity (how many names could she have?); and that forcing a woman to change her name upon marriage was not a violation of her rights because she had a right to apply for a change of name subsequently.[45]

Women, though, did keep asserting their right to apply for licenses in their names at the local level. In the midst of Whitlow's case in 1976, Barbara Roos applied for a license in her own name in Florida. The deputy director of the driver's license division reported that they had several dozen requests a year to issue such licenses and denied them all. Roos took her case to court and the hearing, she recounted, began with the judge looking

> down at his notes, then he glanced up at me with a twinkle in his eye! Then he slammed his hand down on the table and told the license bureau rep that he had a lot of nerve wasting the Court's time with this case!!! The judge listed a couple of other serious cases he had before him that day and repeated that he had too much to do to be bothered with what was obviously my perfectly legal status! The license plate guy blushed. Case was dismissed. Then the judge came up to me in the hall afterwards and in the friendliest possible way with a really sweet smile he told me that he'd graduated from the University of Michigan Law School in

> Ann Arbor: he knew this was the same school where I [had] gotten my degrees. The U of M was an early supporter of the rights of women students in the 19th century.[46]

Not surprisingly, given its recalcitrance, the division of driver's licenses appealed. The First District Court of Appeals of Florida upheld the ruling and found that the driver's license division had to issue Roos a license in her own name. It did so, acknowledging the precedent set in the 1971 Forbush case but with the assertion that

> Alabama has adopted the common law rule that upon marriage the wife by *operation of law* takes the husband's surname. Such may well be the common law as construed by the Alabama courts, however, after reviewing the extensive authorities on the subject, we conclude that the common law of England on July 4, 1776, did not by operation of law engraft the husband's surname upon the wife. In Florida there is no statute or judicial decision requiring a woman to take her husband's surname upon marriage. Although it is the general custom for a woman to change her name upon marriage to that of the husband, the law does not compel her to do so. [Emphasis added][47]

Eventually, enough women kept their maiden names in the later 1970s and 1980s that, although far from universal, they constituted a challenge to the status quo. Even when the numbers of women keeping their name declined in the twenty-first century, the legal and bureaucratic tradition had been broken. Women could now apply in their own names, even if they were married. The onus was now on women to change their license if they changed their name.

Those women who did change their names often faced an additional quandary about what to do with their middle names and their maiden names, and for many it involved a lengthy, costly bureaucratic undertaking. Across the nation, women had to contend with varying rulings, like those in Texas where they had to provide three names and other constricting provisions that limited their ability to reflect their identity. In the twenty-first century, perhaps encouraged by growing numbers of gay and lesbian couples who sought name changes, states began to ease the way. In 2007, California passed its Name Equality Act, which allowed "one or both applicants for a California marriage license to elect to change the middle and/or last names by which each party wishes to be known after solemnization of the marriage." In 2013, the New York state legislature passed a law allowing women who sought to take their husband's last name to change their middle name to their maiden name with a marriage certificate. However, the Department of Motor Vehicles in New Jersey, Ohio, Pennsylvania, and Washington State, as well as rogue clerks in states such as Florida, Indiana, and New Hampshire persisted in making women petition the court or deterred them from making this change.[48]

The growing adoption and eventual requirement of driver's license photos proved to be the subject of great humor and heartache, particularly for women. All women confronted gendered expectations of beauty in the driver's license photo, while men generally did not share this concern. The importance of women's appearance contributed to the license being one more opportunity for angst. The early license photos, taken on basic cameras that only allowed for one exposure often left people with an embarrassing form of identification. Humorist Erma Bombeck played her driver's license photo for laughs in a 1973 column, angry with the checkout girl who surveyed Bombeck's license photo and then her and said, "That's you all right." Bombeck claimed her picture looked "like a 50-year-old woman who has just been told by her obstetrician that the rabbit died" (i.e., that she was pregnant). She continued, "Not that I expect the department of motor vehicles to have you moisten your lips and say 'sex,' but after you numbly fill out 36 questions, identify 18 road signals, are told you have to drive with your glasses on and relieved of $2, they direct you to stand in front of a machine and while you are picking a piece of bacon out of your teeth with your tongue, you are photographed." Twenty years later, comedian Ellen DeGeneres made her repeated, failed attempts to secure an attractive driver's license photo the basis for the pilot of her first television sitcom, laughing with women who spent considerable time, money, and effort on appearance, and frequently still suffered a disappointing result.[49]

In the late twentieth and early twenty-first centuries, religious photo exemptions evaporated. Mennonites still sought to avoid violating their faith's stipulation to not "make any images of themselves," while some Muslim women claimed the right to cover their hair and face with a veil by doing so in their license photos. Women's religious desire not to seek vanity or expose their bodies to male scrutiny fell away under the pressures of national security. The seemingly minor matter that some states began to forbid individuals from smiling in their license photos so that the technology could detect fraudulent duplicates affected women more acutely than it did men. American culture expects women to smile most of the time, while allowing men to look dignified and handsome with a straight face, thus forcing women to violate their gendered role as warm, welcoming smilers and further contributing to the photo being a source of gender tension for women.[50]

"She Drives Like Crazy"

Throughout the twentieth century, comedians, cartoonists, and artists have created indelible pictures of women as poor drivers, as well as women harping from the backseat. Comedians and cartoonists in particular loved the premise of women drivers as pathetic, and they played to a public that generally laughed along. A 1916 poem by Edgar A. Guest, "Ma and the Auto," offered such a popular depiction of women as insufferable backseat drivers that it went on to inspire a recording of Guest reading it in 1921, a musical score in 1928, an illustrated broadside in 1931, and even a film version in the 1930s. A 1945 cartoon appearing in the Ford Corporation's in-house publication, *Ford Times*, featured a woman in a full-body cast, telling her husband by phone, "Guess what, George? I learned to drive today!" The highbrow *New Yorker* featured several cartoons with women struggling in their driving lessons, including one that had a woman at the wheel of a driving-school car that was being towed. She remarked, "It's like everything else, I guess—you only learn by doing."

Another had a female student at the wheel, asking her instructor, "What's the signal to show I've changed my mind?" In spite of the social success evident in being able to afford driving lessons and in being married, these women served as stand-ins to ridicule all women's efforts to learn to drive.[51]

Renowned comedian Bob Newhart centered one of his most famous comedy bits on the premise that he was a driving instructor for a fictional Mrs. Webb. The audience knew where the story was going as soon as he set the stage with a woman learning to drive and quickly filled in the details: She backed out of the driveway going seventy-five miles an hour as the last instructor dove out of the car. She drove too fast, turned recklessly, found herself on a traffic island and a newly seeded lawn, and finally struck someone. His audience brought to the skit an expectation that women drivers were a joke. Newhart acknowledged in his 2006 autobiography that some women found it to be a "sexist routine." He mockingly suggested that he would seek absolution by changing it to a Chinese driver before continuing on with his routine. To Newhart and many late twentieth-century Americans, a belief that women were terrible drivers existed along with a parallel expectation that Asians could not drive either, making an Asian woman the alleged epitome of a bad driver. Newhart helped contribute to an expectation that women were clueless drivers and did so despite the fact that he did not learn how to drive until he was thirty-two years old.[52]

Comic singer "Weird Al" Yankovic also got in on the joke when he set his 1989 song "She Drives Like Crazy" to the Fine Young Cannibals' song "She Drives Me Crazy." In one stanza he parodied,

> Where'd you learn how to steer?
> You do 80 in second gear
> When you drive, I can't relax
> Got your license from Cracker Jacks
> You just hit another tree
> These fender benders are killin' me.[53]

While some women may have laughed along initially, by the end of the century, a *Chicago Tribune* survey of women found that the number of women annoyed by the jokes about women drivers grew from nearly a third in 1970 to more than half in 1990. Still, instead of objecting to these slights, women often continued to join in with the jokesters, decried women who could not drive, and asserted themselves as the exception to the rule. As with so much other humor at the expense of women, objecting reinforced the idea that "thou doth protest too much" or that women were humorless.[54]

Given the expectation that women did not know how to drive, one of the prime sites of humor, then, was women's driver's education and status as new drivers. Early television programs began to use women and driving as a gag in their shows. Lucille Ball used the conceit twice, first in her 1955 *I Love Lucy* show that had Lucy's husband teach her to drive. After only one lesson, she attempted to teach her friend Ethel, with disastrous results. In *The Lucy Show* (1969), she used her teenage son getting his license to contrast his exceptional male abilities in the driver's seat with her female ineptitude in the backseat. After listening to her carping from the backseat, the driving examiner told him, "If you can drive under these conditions," you can drive under any circumstances.[55]

Comedian Dick Van Dyke used the fear of women drivers in his namesake show's 1964 episode, "Scratch My Car and Die." His paranoia about his new car had him scolding his wife, complaining that if she drove she would run into something. Ultimately, she took the car and someone did scratch it while she was parked at the supermarket. Later in the episode, he became so enraged that he drove into cement posts and rosebushes, and then ran out of gas. Under the subtext of criticizing bad women drivers, Van Dyke poked fun at men for their hypersensitivity about their cars, misplaced suspicions about women, and their own poor driving behavior.[56]

The Brady Bunch also wrestled with the issue of women drivers in its 1972 "Fender Benders" episode, with Mrs. Brady accused of bad driving by a disdainful, chauvinistic man but staunchly defended by her eldest daughter, Marcia. The script used the man's nonfamilial, deceitful status to dismiss his rantings. It concluded with the court finding in Mrs. Brady's favor and restored all women's honor as good, innocent drivers.[57]

While denigrating humor seemed to haunt women drivers throughout the twentieth century, their designation as "backseat drivers" evolved from the gender and power relationships within the car. Boorish women who heckled their husbands' driving also served as a staple type, ripe for ridicule. One common joke was the jokester license, awarded to backseat drivers. American popular culture eventually equated backseat drivers with women, although into the 1920s the culture embraced both men and women as backseat drivers. A 1924 poem included the stanza,

> So, when your wife is driving, please
> Don't tell her what to do;
> To see that other auto she's
> As competent as you.
> If you will leave her quite alone
> You likely will arrive;
> She doesn't need a megaphone
> To tell her how to drive.[58]

There was a fleeting moment when the culture imagined defending women from male "backseat drivers," but the possibility quickly faded.

Several factors conspired to solidify the backseat-driver identity for women. Initially the most significant variable was that the vast majority of women chose not to learn to drive. For example, a 1934 article reported that women made up less than 25 percent of drivers, and it categorized the women as "members of the 'backseat club.'" A Minnesota man, contending with new licensing rules, wondered if he would have to apply for a driver's license for his wife, "since she drives from the back seat?" However, throughout the twentieth century, even with growing numbers of women driving, in households in which both women and men were available to drive, Americans persisted in making driving a man's job. Women avoided listening to men's criticisms of their driving by largely having men assume the driving responsibility when they both rode in the car.[59]

Many articles and cartoons critiqued women's behavior by asserting that they did not have the authority to criticize men. In many families with sons, women gave up the passenger seat to the boy when he became a teenager and moved to the backseat. This helped contribute to a male sense of entitlement and authority, along with a commensurate belief that women took a backseat to men in the car. An October 1927 story in *Popular Science Monthly* had the mechanics fixing a wrecked car and taking the woman's backseat driving to task for the accident. One said to her, "You do all your driving from the backseat. No man can drive a car and do a good job of it with somebody pouring advice into his ear all the time. You probably kept telling your husband how to drive until he got so flustered he didn't know what he was doing . . . you admit you don't know how to drive so your advice wouldn't be worth much anyway!"[60]

To illustrate their disapproval of her ugly behavior, artists usually made the backseat driver unattractive. Frequently they contrasted a woman's oversize body—open, yelling mouth and large hat—to the man's meeker, smaller stature. This enabled them to suggest that women's criticism physically diminished men and cautioned that men should not let their wives' talk belittle them. A 1939 cartoon had a male driver explaining to the gas-station attendant, "I got another muffler and it stopped all that knocking." His oversized wife sat in the backseat, yelling angrily through the scarf (muffler) that covered her mouth. In a 1947 *New Yorker* cartoon, the backseat held an adult woman, while a young boy who could barely see over the dash sat in the passenger seat next to his father; the woman received a ticket from a police officer for her crime of being a backseat driver. The discourse supported men in maintaining their prerogative to silence any criticisms from women.[61]

When it served to validate the claims they wanted to make, occasionally articles, cartoons, or advertisements conceded that women critiquing men had merit. For example, in a 1938 radio broadcast, the chief executive of the Traffic Audit Bureau asserted that some men might conclude from their "consistently obnoxious back-seat companions . . . that they have married a shrew." However, he also considered that men might realize that it was more likely that "their driving is not so perfect as it might be." He teased men about their objections to women's critiques and questioned whether women were truly jeopardizing men's driving. Does the male driver, he wondered, have "such a sensitive, nervous constitution that he ought, under any circumstances, to resign his position"? The Better Vision Institute ran a series of ads in the 1960s concerning the dangers of people renewing their licenses by mail and foregoing eye exams. In one, beneath a photograph of a car with a crumpled back fender, they suggested to their imagined male audience, "When a certain backseat driver suggests you may be too close to the car ahead, it might be wise for once to heed her."[62]

At the end of the twentieth century, technological developments introduced a game changer into the tensions between drivers and passengers. The Global Positioning System (GPS) had the potential to revolutionize how people got from point A to point B. A 1998 reflection on the "Backseat Driver That Sits in Front" maintained that the age-old tensions couples have over who was at fault in getting lost evaporated with the dashboard device guiding them. While an undoubtedly significant change, it did not address controversies over speeding, tailgating, road rage, and a myriad of other driving choices that continued to divide passengers and drivers.[63]

Although the subject of much ridicule and condescension, with their driver's education under their belts and their license in their wallets, the next step for women drivers was to buy a car. The next chapter will explore how manufacturers and advertisers approached women as consumers. Although their research had long revealed the significance of female consumers, most car manufacturers—into the twenty-first century—disbelieved the power of the purse.

2

Buying a Car

THROUGHOUT ITS HISTORY, the automotive industry remained perplexed by women's interest in cars and uncertain as to how to approach women as buyers. Companies created gendered sales approaches primarily directed at men, contributing to a sense that men and women had unique, separate relationships with the automobile. While the culture embraced the idea of young men getting a car so that they could pursue women, there was no commensurate expectation of agency or action for young women. Middle-aged men continued to need cars to showcase their freedom and power, from the open Jeep, to the convertible, to the expensive sports car. Middle-aged women were supposed to expect their vehicle to serve as a protector. These contrasting messages of men as independent and women as dependable pervaded car buying. Businesses persisted in shaping women's experience buying cars in distinctly gendered ways in spite of emerging evidence in the late twentieth century that both women and men responded positively to gender-neutral approaches. Advertisers held an unshakable belief that whatever motivated women's car buying was fundamentally different from whatever compelled men's buying behavior.[1]

Despite sporadic, targeted efforts, the most surprising decision automotive businesses made across the century was to largely ignore women as consumers. Confronted with irrefutable evidence that "women already have the full suffrage—in the selection and operation of motor cars," most companies persisted in neglecting women as consumers most of the time. A survey of car dealers in 1916 reported that they believed women influenced between 50 and 90 percent of automobile sales. Women's role expanded to include not just shaping their family's choice of car but also purchasing their own automobiles. For one hundred years, those in the auto industry never ceased to be astonished by women's social and economic power. They treated each revelation as new and insurmountably complex. Instead of finding greater clarity over time, automotive companies faced continual confusion over whether women even constituted a market.[2]

It is helpful, therefore, to examine women's experience considering and buying cars, as well as the market studies and advertising that companies used to shape women's behavior. As scholar Deborah Clarke maintains, it is likely that ads "have the widest and strongest impact in shaping our awareness of cars and car culture," and so this analysis is centered on the ads, as well as what the automotive industry knew and what it did, or did not do, with its analysis of female consumers. While Clarke contends the automotive industry was "reluctant to offend women," the consistent evidence suggests that few companies cared what women thought, either while perusing ads or when entering a showroom.[3]

When businesses did decide to include women in their marketing campaigns, they did so based on an assumption of absolute differences between men and women. We see this belief in the dichotomy in the industry language and in the categorization of women, into the twenty-first century, in minority marketing campaigns in which companies paired women with Asians and African Americans.[4] And we see this belief in three key principles that evolved over time but remained the thread weaving together corporate thinking across the century. The first principle was that women did not know anything about cars and were not serious consumers. The second was that women cared only about domesticity and safety. And the third, was that women's car buying was unique and gendered. Belief in a distinctive experience led corporations to key into women as a "special group." They tried to persuade Americans that women needed a car of their own to achieve a circumscribed, domestic freedom and they formulated seemingly countless ways to gender car ownership.

Chapter 2

"What Happy Intuition for Quality Which a Woman Carries"

Across the century, automotive companies contended that women had no technological expertise and were not "real" consumers. They granted women authority to weigh in on the quality and value of a car by suggesting that women's only knowledge came "naturally." Advertisers who embraced this validating approach gave women the upper hand in *knowing*; women knew just by intuition. Their authority extended only to having a feeling that a car was of a good quality and therefore a wise investment. In a 1912 brochure, *The Woman and the Ford*, the company affirmed, "Trust women to find the bargains." Cadillac maintained that women were "equipped with a sort of sixth sense." A 1923 Marmon ad used Helen Keller, who they described as "blind, deaf, and dumb," as the epitome of women's intuition. The image of Keller delicately touching the window of the car was accompanied by her recommendation, "To my touch the workmanship seems perfect." Women did not have rational or scientific evidence; their expertise allegedly came through their innate understanding of the car.[5]

Of course automobile companies' use of intuition in ads did not mean they believed women truly understood the car's inner workings. The Rollin car company flatly stated about women in a 1924 dealer brochure, "Don't bother with mechanical data, of course. . . . Point out the finish of the interior. *They* know quality of fabrics." A 1925 Chrysler ad drew the parallel between women's fashion acuity and their understanding of cars, noting that women needed a car to suit their style. The ad claimed, "And unless her car can be worn with the same ease, the same careless grace, it is as irritating as a disappointing hat." Advertisers asserted that women would "wear" the car, while men intellectually understood it.[6]

Women's intuition was useful in selling cars, but—the ad men believed—it was in no way equal to the masculine claim on factual knowledge. Occasionally, therefore, advertisers credited women's contributions in designing the car and their discerning taste in selecting it, but they drew on husbands and sons to assert technical information to the reader. In a 1964 Buick Riviera television commercial, a man and woman playfully raced through the countryside in their Buicks. The narrator concluded, with the man depicted having smugly won the race, "Riviera by Buick, a

First it warms your heart...
(That Thunderbird Styling!)
It's amazing how just looking at the '55 Ford gives so many people that wonderful feeling. Why not? There's "Thunderbird" written in almost every line . . . from the hooded headlights to the flat rear deck. Inside, you'll see new exciting color harmonies in durable fabrics. All in all, there isn't a more pleasing car in sight.

Behind the wheel of the new Ford, you become a new man. For under your foot lies response so eager and alive, you almost believe it's clairvoyant! This is Ford's Trigger-Torque power . . . and it replies to your driving demands with split-second agility. There's safety in power like this . . . to whizz you out of traffic snarls . . . and to pass you ahead when passing is called for. Three new stout-hearted engines to choose from. And at least a score of other new engineering features. Reading about it is nowhere near the fun of driving the new Ford. So why not visit your dealer today?
Then it reads your mind...
(That Trigger-Torque Power!)
Treat yourself to a Trigger-Torque Test Drive in a new
'55 Ford

Figure 5. "There's safety in power like this," promised this 1955 Ford ad that contrasted women's love of styling with men's intellectual insights into "Trigger-Torque" power.

great and rare machine that a woman can enjoy and admire to the fullest, but only a man can really understand." The idea that, unlike men, women could only begin to grasp the full greatness of cars continued throughout the century. The belief that women only cared about a car's aesthetics, while men exclusively valued the mechanical, set up a persistent divide. Occasional efforts were made by automobile companies to counter the claim, such as a 1986 Chevrolet brochure written for Chevrolet's salespeople that pleaded, "Forget Women's Intuition. Give Women Information." However, across the century, most companies remained skeptical about women's technical interest and knowledge and they tried to assure women they would just *know*.[7]

Another way that advertisers used women's purported intuition was in thrift, and they frequently touted women's *natural* understanding of a car's value. Advertisers flattered women with being "purchasing agents" and asserted that they excelled at comparison shopping. In 1928, the president of Auburn Automobiles pronounced women "shrewd buyers" who "will not tolerate mediocrity in motor cars." A 1968 ad proclaimed, "Women who check contents, read labels, know quality and compare prices steer their shopping carts to '68 Chevrolet Wagons."[8] While advertisers generally credited women with appreciating value, extending from the grocery store to the showroom floor, they believed women's knowledge stemmed from an intuition that they came by naturally, rather than rational knowledge, which advertisers believed men continued to command. The stereotyped conception of women only intuiting knowledge about cars dominated the industry's approach to women across the century and reflected a long-standing "essentialism" in marketing to women.

One of the most visible examples of the tendency both to neglect female consumers and to dismiss women's automotive acumen was found in automotive showrooms, with an almost exclusively male sales force. The people and place were both structured around male consumers. Salespeople believed women who walked through the doors to be naïve, misguided, or looking for love.

There were exceptions, though. The Maxwell-Briscoe Company, which had sponsored Alice Ramsey's cross-country trip in 1909, "explicitly aligned its marketing goals with women's political and professional emancipation." In 1914, the company announced "a plan to hire automobile saleswomen on an equal basis with men." They even "held a reception at a Manhattan dealership . . . featuring not only speeches by prominent suffragists such as Crystal Eastman but a woman dressed in a leather apron and blue jeans assembling and disassembling an engine in the showroom window."[9]

This extraordinary exception notwithstanding, most women across the century bought cars in what observers described as a negative, male space, with one marketer describing it in 2010 as having a "locker room" mentality. Most women believed it was more difficult for women to purchase a car than it was for men, and they cited problems securing credit and the patronizing attitudes of the salesmen as their biggest complaints. Women confronted a sales force that was unsure how to sell to them.[10]

More than uncertainty reigned, however; salespeople across the century did not respect women as consumers. As early as 1927, car companies recognized that poor behavior in the showroom could hurt their sales. A Dodge brochure guiding salespeople on "The Woman Buyer" cautioned, "Be careful about making a remark or giving a shrug or a sneer behind the back of the woman buyer. There are often windows and other highly polished parts of the car in which she can see reflections of your actions." Surveys of women consistently found them disappointed in dealers. One 1958 study discovered that "28 per cent of the women reported 'the dealer has no interest in me or my car.'" An observer recounted that in the 1970s, salesmen interpreted women's presence in the showroom as an opportunity for sexual pursuits and "would offer 'a discount for a date.'" Showrooms persisted as a male domain. Salesmen belittled women with "honey," "babe," and "sexually pushy" behavior, rather than treating them respectfully as prospective buyers of an expensive item.[11]

To try to effect change, companies relied on brochures, training tapes, and study guides to reform their sales forces. Ford instructed their dealers in 1980 "to stop patronizing women, suggesting instead that they 'talk to women as you would to any young-thinking, intelligent people.'" Pontiac pleaded in a 1986 memo, "Selling to women assumes greater importance with each passing day and each sales opportunity. For your own success, it is important to show that you respect women as being fully competent

Figure 6. The automotive industry made only sporadic efforts to train salespeople on treating women as valued consumers; this 1958 Chevy brochure is one such example. Women continued to complain about their poor treatment into the twenty-first century.

buyers." Chevrolet cautioned its sellers that same year, "Women shouldn't be 'dear' to you or 'honey' or 'sweetie,'" and used a quiz titled "Are you Ms. Informed?" to educate them about women's car-buying acumen. The need for these training materials reflects an intractable misogyny, with salesmen so certain that women were not legitimate buyers that they could persist in their boorish behavior without consequence.[12]

Makers of upscale models like Cadillac and Lincoln recognized in the 1980s that their salespeople were hurting their business and led the way in conducting seminars promoting selling to women. They tried to disrupt the "macho approach" of the "good ol' boys and chauvinists." Cadillac made a concerted effort to circumvent this minefield by appealing directly to women. Targeting women in fifty upscale malls across the country and bringing the cars to them there, they paired with *Vogue* to offer a sweepstakes that included a shopping spree in Paris. Their director of merchandising conceded, "An automotive showroom is not always the most pleasant thing in a woman's life. We're trying to reach out to women in a relaxed, positive environment." They hoped that by forgoing the traditional showroom for the mall they could disrupt the dealers and link their brand to a place women already trusted to shop. Even when the industry tried to focus on women as consumers, they could only understand women as completely different from men and had to completely jettison salesmen and showrooms to do so.[13]

Ten years later, Cadillac still insisted publicly that it was prioritizing female customers. With coverage in both the *New York Times* and industry magazines, company executives echoed that they needed to change but had little sense of how to do so. In 1994, Cadillac instituted "a national dealer training program to help old-fashioned salesmen understand [that] women have the money to buy their cars." This nearly one-hundred-year-old sales problem had one Philadelphia dealer musing, "We have to treat everyone the same here, even if they are a pig farmer with mud on their boots." Salesmen remained fundamentally confused, rarely believing that even the well-attired woman in front of them had money or would be the critical decision maker. Challenged to question their prejudice, they equated female consumers with the unlikely country bumpkin walking into their dealership. For such an established brand with a unique history of embracing female consumers to be so confused about the prospects who presented themselves in showrooms suggests an entrenched industry problem in respecting women as knowledgeable consumers. While it was surprising that Cadillac made the effort to include women on the front end of their efforts and then failed to close the deal, Cadillac's inability to contend with women as legitimate consumers was not unusual. A belief that women had no automotive knowledge paired with car sales being gendered as male shaped dealers' thinking so much that dealers had a hard time imagining a woman buying a car. Indeed, most automobile companies struggled into the twenty-first century to take women seriously as consumers.[14]

By and large, in one of the most exclusively male occupations, salespeople across the century continued to disregard and mistreat women, dismissing their buying power, knowledge, and value as a consumer. Salesmen quoted in one 1989 *Washington Post* article demeaned female customers that came in "well-armed for price negotiations" as "Bitches." They said of these women, who they expected to know nothing, "They already know the manufacturer's suggested retail price, and usually know what's realistic in terms of dealer and options costs. They ask specific questions and get upset when specific answers aren't forthcoming. They can make a salesperson invest an enormous amount of time in a sale—and then walk away, leaving the salesperson empty-handed."[15] Preferring to treat female consumers as naïve rubes they could ignore or patronize, salespeople loathed the women who comparison shopped or tried to bargain. Companies made sporadic efforts to remedy the intimidating setting and transform the showroom to make it inviting to women. Efforts to physically make over the showrooms reveal that typically the space and the audience was indeed entirely male. In 1986, a Lakewood, Colorado, Chevrolet dealership went so far as to create an automotive showroom designed for women, replete with "deep rose carpeting . . . soft lighting, and plants." The dealership may have been responding to the corporate distribution of a 1986 brochure called "Pretty Soon Every Other Guy Who Walks into Your Showroom Will Be a Woman" that cautioned their salespeople, "Women influence over 87% of all car purchases. Women. You can't live without them." More than one critic pointed to the difference between established dealerships and the newer ones for imports, noting that the salespeople for imports tended to be "more sensitive to the way women want to be treated." In spite of occasional changes and superficial efforts, a 2004 study continued to find that "the number one complaint women have with dealerships is how they're treated as customers."[16]

In the twenty-first century, General Motors won over a lot of consumers with its "no-haggle" brand, Saturn; women in particular reported a better consumer experience. Hyundai garnered attention for its "Power of the Purse" program, which focused on helping women learn "how to deal with car salesmen." Hyundai also marketed its cars in a largely gender-neutral manner. The Hyundai corporate office helped empower women to be better consumers and made sure its dealers understood the importance of women, who comprised upward of 50 percent of Hyundai sales. Internet companies, too, like CarMax, emerged to offer information and clear pricing, and women responded positively to this gender-neutral sales pitch.[17]

A 2014 *Wall Street Journal* article that assessed how companies pitched their cars to women noted that more women than men were driving in the United States, and "Ever since, researchers have been wondering why the car-shopping and buying experience is still such a man's game." Even though automakers had known about the significance of women to their sales for a hundred years, they continually expressed surprise that women had considerable influence. Motor vehicle companies and dealers struggled to offer customers a welcoming, forthright, and open buying experience and particularly failed to treat female consumers respectfully. Automotive companies began and ended the century believing that women did not know anything about cars.[18]

"Women Care About Car Interiors"

Advertisers who did overcome the prejudice that women did not know anything about cars still believed that women's only interests were in domesticity and safety. Women increasingly found the car central to their household responsibilities. Transporting children and provisioning for her family took center stage as a woman's job. Belonging to modern America and performing such gendered work, the advertisers suggested, demanded that women have a car. The widespread embrace of the closed car by the 1930s inspired a long-standing assertion that the car could provide the same comforts as a living room. Automobile advertisers intentionally blurred the lines between the home and the car, and called on women to consider it an extension of their domestic lives. Cars were expected to provide the same level of comfort in this intimate space, as well as to entertain family and friends, so ads promised the comfort of sofa-like seating, "Picture Window," "closet space," "climate control," and, eventually, radio, television, and computer systems.[19]

Ads integrated home imagery with the car to encourage the comparison. A 1931 ad for the Hudson Essex showcased an elegant woman reclining on a settee in her living room, and suggested to women, "You might as well ride comfortably . . . it really does not cost you any more." In 1955 another ad contended that car designs were inspired by the fact that "many people spend almost as much time in their cars as in their living rooms." Buick even laid down carpeting in the back of their 1966 Opel wagon.[20]

Promises of comfort and safety also assured consumers that the car's interior would be easy—for women—to clean. A 1967 *Ford Times* magazine described a woman who ensured that the family car was "as clean as her living room. She's the hostess, see, on her day with the car." This responsibility for cleanliness persisted throughout the century and companies shared an expectation that women were "as concerned about the appearance of the family car as about the neatness of her home." As American cars acquired even more amenities and got larger, it was even easier to describe them as simulated living rooms. Automotive companies like Ford and Chevrolet also sought to capitalize on an accessory market that brought home conveniences on the road.[21]

Vans in particular lent themselves to campaigns that suggested expanding a family's entertainment space. As technology advanced, some minivans and SUVs even laid claim to trumping the home. One 2000 Oldsmobile ad for its minivan contended, "Tree forts. Family rooms. Even remodeled basements can't compete," as the ad touted dual climate controls, seats with leather trim, and the built-in video entertainment system. It assured women, "all you need to add is the popcorn," as the mom brought snacks to the family nestled in the van watching a movie, parked in the driveway. Car manufacturers even sought to make sure the family pet was included. In 2012, Ford offered a dog-"Sealed & approved!" model of its Escape, which let animals "jump in and out of the vehicle more easily," as well as providing places to clip leashes and floor compartments to store pet food.[22]

The promise of safety undergirded domestic comforts. Advertisers presumed women to be slow, careful drivers, concerned for their family's well-being.[23] Therefore, companies created ads predicated on an expectation that women would be predisposed to buy products to ensure greater safety, as opposed to greater speed, which the firms understood to only be valued by men. At first, ads struggled to assure consumers that it was safe for women to drive and often framed their inventions as justification for women entering the ranks of drivers. Safety was believed not just to be a primary consideration for women but also to fundamentally undergird the identity of women as drivers.[24]

Ads with infants and small children targeted parents and sought to threaten them to ensure that they protected their "precious cargo." The American Chain Company was the first to take this tack and drew attention for its 1921 ad that suggested "the not yet born child asks and has the right to ask for protection when the prospective mother is motoring, through the use of chains to prevent skidding." Little cherubic children reached out to a woman serenely riding in an automobile, her portrait encircled by the chained tire. Other ads intoned, as one did in 1936, "It costs so little to protect lives worth so much," and often included images of a mother and young daughter smiling safely in the backseat.[25]

Early ads called on vague endorsements from doctors who testified that the product offered "The safest way" to transport children, as well as claims by advertisers, columnists, and the Children's Bureau of the United States Department of Labor. Early automotive writer C. H. Claudy termed the electric car itself "the modern baby carriage." Ford began to promote the invention of the "Comfy-Safe" child seat in 1939. Automotive advertisers consistently marketed children's safety in the car to women. They acted on a sentiment embraced by the industry and verbalized in the twenty-first century by marketing strategist Clotaire Rapaille, that "women care about car interiors because they're 'programmed to create life' inside their wombs." Scholar Deborah Clarke argues that the automotive industry is ruled by a belief in "automotive maternity" and contends that women and the cars they drive are both understood to be shepherding children to safety.[26]

One popular trope of advertisers was women *nearly* hitting children as the "fear appeal" to sell their products. A 1958 Buick ad had a woman backing out of her garage as a young girl on a tricycle approached the car; "We designed this car with mothers in mind." Even into the twenty-first century, these depictions continued. Mr. Goodwrench television commercials promoted their services, including free brake inspections and recommending new tires, as the savior for women who otherwise would have hit something . . . or someone.[27]

Tire manufacturers in particular distinguished themselves by preying on fears of catastrophe. Ads regularly referred to flat tires and blowouts, and the Goodyear Company even named one of its tires Life Guard. No

We designed this car
with mothers in mind
SUPER
1958
When better automobiles are built Buick will build them

WE KNEW you wanted a car of true modernity—and this 1958 Buick fairly sings with it.

From its graceful grille to its gleaming tail towers to its luxurious décor inside—this is the freshest fashion in town.

But we also knew you wanted other things—like fenders you can see over *clearly* when you're backing out of the drive. And wait till you see how easy it is *here*.

We knew you wanted a car with roominess and comfort, a luxurious ride and beautiful performance. And this gorgeous Buick has all that and more.

Above all, we knew you wanted a car that's quick handling—light on its feet. And this one's a joy. It seems to respond to your very thoughts.

It handles with the airiness of a ballerina—so you can slip into tight parking spots—swing around curves or into narrow drives with the greatest of ease.

When you try this 1958 Buick you'll see how completely we designed it with you in mind.

Your Buick dealer will gladly arrange matters. Call him soon.

BUICK *Division of* GENERAL MOTORS

See TALES OF WELLS FARGO, Monday Nights, NBC-TV and THE PATRICE MUNSEL SHOW, Friday Nights, ABC-TV

First big car that's light on its feet

the AIR BORN B-58 BUICK

FIGURE 7. Ads showed women nearly hitting people and vehicles to sell their cars' safety and maneuverability. This 1958 ad promised that the Buick "handles with the airiness of a ballerina—so you can slip into tight parking spots—swing around curves or into narrow drives with the greatest of ease."

other automobile component advertised so directly to the dangers inherent in traveling by car. These fearful ads most often featured girls and women who pulled at the heart. Sometimes the warnings were only suggestive, as with images of children in the rain or a couple leaving the hospital with a newborn. Others featured just-shattered vehicles, leaving the reader's imagination to wonder at the consequences to human life.[28]

Goodyear relied particularly on the vulnerability of babies, starting in the 1960s, and began to intensify their baby appeals in the 1980s. Michelin deployed a similar, long-running campaign in the late twentieth century, starring a baby and the tagline "Because so much is riding on your tires." Pairing babies and the threat of loss left no question that parents should prioritize purchasing these tires if they wanted to protect their children.[29]

Advertisers also presumed women would insist on seat belts, shocks, and safety alarms to care for their children and protect themselves. In particular, advertisers believed women would be the force behind the purchase of seat belts when they appeared in the second half of the century. While some safety appeals were understated, one of the most dramatic ads selling fear and safety featured a young child with a gun pointed at her head. The 1971 headline read, "A car with worn-out shocks can be as dangerous as a child with a loaded gun." OnStar, the remote assistance service introduced in the 1990s, was fairly general in its advertising and did not explicitly suggest the device only for women, but Cadillac issued this press release in 1996: "OnStar Provides Peace of Mind to Cadillac Women Drivers." Buyers were told in many ways, both subtle and melodramatic, that safety was of paramount importance to women buying car parts.[30]

One car brand, however, managed to create an explicit association between its cars and safety. Volvo, based in Sweden, consistently promoted its cars' safety features in its advertisements. Volvo's confidence in the design of its cars led the company to engage consumers with the very real dangers of driving, even using an emergency room doctor to vouch for the importance of driving a Volvo. A belief that women valued safety above all else led Volvo to make safety the foundation of its sales pitch. As the brand floundered in the United States in the late twentieth and early twenty-first centuries, the company invested in a technological simulation of a pregnant crash test dummy, so the company could continue to

FIGURE 8. Believing women's preeminent concern with automobiles was safety, in 1971 the Columbus company advertised in *Life* magazine that having worn-out shocks was equivalent to the danger of letting a child play with a gun.

assert its safety claims. Volvo claimed it led the automotive industry with innovative research to help ensure the safety of pregnant women. Advertisers consistently appealed to women to buy their vehicles by demanding that they prioritize the comfort and safety of their family and strive to create a home on wheels, to protect them from the outside world.[31]

A "Special Group"

Industry leaders persisted throughout the century in being convinced that what motivated women's car buying was fundamentally different than what drove men to make a purchase. Automotive analysts tended to disparage women as either insignificant or misguided in their choices, and this contributed to the industry-wide practice of devoting very little effort and very little money to courting women.

This disregard is apparent even when it was encouraging action. A late 1940s report emphasized women's role in selecting the family car and argued that Ford ought to consider women a "special group." The company believed that its ads "ignored the basic psychological differences between men and women," as well as "a woman's love for gadgets and detail." Generally critical of the job to date, the analysts suggested that the company use "stunts," such as press releases, to "contrive to build up an impression that we actually are doing a great deal of research to find out what women want." Ford contented itself with creating "filler" material and stunts to make it look like the company was interested, rather than ascertaining what media women were consuming and placing noninsulting ads there.[32]

Despite its awareness of women's significance as consumers, Ford's superficial analysis and poor behavior remained intractable. A 1952 Ford press release confidently stated: "Indications are that women are basically slower to make up their minds than men. So, Ford engineers designed quicker-acting brakes." A 1954 article about male car designers credited them with listening to women and using a lot of chrome, because "Women love glitter." After fifty years, car makers were still discovering that women were shorter, on average, than men and finally factoring that knowledge into their calculations about the location of the seats, foot pedals, and steering wheel. Even though appeals "to dominant, aggressive, and sex expressions" fell flat for women and even though Chevrolet was outselling Ford with a more tempered strategy, Ford persisted in appealing to male consumers in 1958 with aggression and sex. An allegiance to narrow, fixed-gender stereotypes left most automakers flat footed in their efforts to respond to the growing potential to attract female consumers.[33]

Entering the second half of the century, in particular, it was readily apparent that more women worked for wages and had begun agitating in earnest for equality and rights. Increasingly, advertisers recognized that for women the car made possible the "triple parlay of wife/mother/worker." Researchers began to understand that there was an incredible diversity of women, segmented in a variety of ways, including age, marital status, and, most important, whether they worked outside the home and if they did so part time, full time, or in a career capacity. Some companies affirmed that not only could their cars work for business, but they could also work a second shift, like the women themselves.[34]

Companies initially proved reluctant to advertise sport utility vehicles (SUVs) and pickup trucks to women. Market researcher Jill Avery drew on the anthropological term "gender contamination" to capture the fears expressed by automotive companies that advertising "men's vehicles" to women risked "poisoning the well" for sales to men. Others, however, believed companies could claim to empower women by putting them in larger, higher vehicles to "be in the dominant position on the road." Campaigns like those for the Chevy Blazer sought to persuade women that SUVs were perfect for them, suggesting that SUVs, in the words of their creative director, were an " 'urban safety vehicle,' dodging potholes and surviving harsh winter conditions while emphasizing a secure feeling of sitting up high." A Chevrolet dealer reported to the company, "I'm having women in heels and short skirts buying pickup trucks." In the 1980s and 1990s, advertisers even began to place truck ads in women's magazines; Chevy did so in a series of 1990s ads that included a suited professional and a pregnant woman. As women made SUV and truck purchases as equals, a few ads encouraged and reflected the practice.[35]

In the 1990s, the *Marketing to Women* newsletter reported that women were spending $65 billion annually on cars and trucks, but bemoaned the fact that "auto manufacturers are still ignoring the needs of women." Among the litany of complaints women had: air bags that "can kill smaller women drivers and small passengers in the front seat," "seats that don't get them close enough to floor pedals and dashboards," and "seat belts that cut across their chests in the wrong place." Instead of explicitly responding to consumer feedback and improving its vehicles and marketing, Ford relied on research that suggested women viewed the Expedition as a "5,000-pound security blanket." Ford's vapid, allegedly female-inspired innovations were limited to optional illuminated running boards, in the unlikely event that someone "was hiding under the vehicle, you'd be able to see them and get help," and "a hook on the back of the center console from which to hang a purse." Ford also continued its effort to key into fashion by "marketing a line of nail polish in Mustang paint colors." Ford believed that women accounted for about half of all sales for the 2005 Mustang model, but instead of making substantive changes to address women's needs, the industry continued to dress up their vehicles with stylistic camouflage.[36]

Advertisers spent only miniscule percentages of their advertising budgets on women's media and the women's market generally. As late as 1981, for example, General Motors spent only 3 percent of its advertising budget to reach women's magazines. The company also suggested that its dealers "host tea parties for its female consumers," which only reached a sliver of female consumers. The totality of its efforts is questionable. Studies continually revealed that, with no guidance from ads in women's magazines, women relied on word of mouth and consumer research reports to make automotive purchases. Companies typically devoted large portions of their budgets to sports marketing for men, generally ignoring women's media and only slowly realizing that broader media buys could reach both women and men.[37]

In those instances when they did advertise to women, women did not tend to favor the ads. Advertisers reading their trade journal *Printers' Ink* in 1961, for example, discovered that "Homemakers want fact, less fluff, in ads." Car advertisers read that women generally "disliked 'half-dressed women' trying to sell a product." Still, this clear, direct criticism did not reach its target. A creative director for the Ford account in 1977 asserted that "Detroit is still the national stronghold of selling with sex. Why? The male is still the decision maker in car buying ('Our research tells us it is so'); and the auto is still an extension of the American male libido." Of their Lincoln-Mercury commercial featuring Catherine Deneuve, "who slips inside [the car] to fondle the plush interior," he noted, "she is the 'garnish on the salad.'" Corporate efforts to appeal to women tended to be lackadaisical, with most epitomized more by hyped, fragmented press releases and exceptional efforts.[38]

With decades of research amassed, advertisers knew that both men and women prioritized detailed information regarding technical features and that there were "*no major differences between women and men in reasons for purchase*" (emphasis added). Yet most automotive companies continually refused to place car ads in women's magazines. Research abounded, with Condé Nast discovering in 1986 that "almost 50% of the women interviewed felt they weren't being reached adequately by advertising in dual-audience media." Women they surveyed also claimed that "they would respond more readily to advertising in women's magazines." Still, spending remained miniscule and a J. D. Power study reported in 1990 that, "65% of the women surveyed were not aware of any automotive-related material included in women's magazines." Advocating for a thoughtful, concerted campaign, feminist Gloria Steinem, who had long sought advertising for *Ms.* magazine, noted in 1991, "Detroit never quite learned the secret of creating intelligent ads that exclude no one, and then placing them in women's magazines." Even when the women's market was worth billions of dollars, the automotive industry persisted in treating women like a "special group" they could ignore.[39]

Facing a number of hurdles, unclear of what to say, how to say it, and where to say it to female consumers, car advertisers generally did not make much of an effort. While seeking to reach women online in 2007, Chrysler still considered it "a challenge to attract women to a culture centered on an engine." Its website Dodge.com created a "'mom hostess' with tips on how to learn more about" the Grand Caravan. Women's role in car buying continued to be staggering; twenty-first-century analyses continually reflected on the importance of the female market but also recognized automakers' slow learning curve in tapping into it.[40]

"Prisoners in Their Homes"

In 1928, General Motors announced hopefully in a newspaper ad, "America is now a two-car country." This early, explicit push for two cars reflected the industry's hunger for new markets. Manufacturers had continually moved the cost of the automobile down, through greater efficiency and corporate organization, and there was a used-car market as well. What automakers believed they needed was not only to expand their base by reaching new families but also to persuade those who already owned a car to purchase another.[41]

Targeting heterosexual couples made excellent sense, particularly as middle-class women who sought more active roles outside the home likely would need their own cars. Social changes, starting in the early twentieth century, made these appeals particularly germane to women's lives. Women's growing public presence, including those who graduated from high school, college, and graduate school, and women who found paid work and even professional identities, as well as an expectation that marriage should be a fulfilling partnership, centered on domestic life, meant that an emphasis on women's circumscribed independence increasingly resonated with consumers.

Chevrolet ran an advertising campaign in the late 1920s and early 1930s, proclaiming "A car for her too!" One ad insisted that the time had come when two cars was "a necessity." Asking men, "Is Your Wife Marooned During the Day?" another ad encouraged readers to consider the car's usefulness in "shopping, calling, taking the children to school in bad weather, etc." Advertisers assured women that part of being modern, stylish, and successful rested on having two cars. Another had a maid helping to remove a woman's coat as she arrived for a bridge game, her car visible through the expansive window, just below the contrasting image of a bird in a cage.[42]

Car ads largely disappeared during World War II, as plants shifted production to war materiel, but the emphasis on two cars returned with gusto in the 1950s, with the postwar economic boom. In 1956, a series of cheeky advertisements encouraged women to take the lead in getting their husbands to check out Chevrolet's new cars. Asserting that women needed a car to do their homemaking job effectively, one ad eavesdropped on a

THE SATURDAY EVENING POST 39

The Car for the Girl in Business

The modern business woman needs her own personal transportation medium. It saves time and increases her efficiency and earning power. Yet, because she is a woman, she also insists that her car shall measure up to a high standard of quality.

The Chevrolet Utility Coupé with Fisher Body, refined gray cloth upholstery, plate glass windows, Ternstedt window regulators, and other artistic fittings, stream lines and riding comfort, fully meets her quality requirements. Its mechanical efficiency and ease of handling make strong appeal, and finally its surprisingly low price and lowest per mile cost decide her choice.

Chevrolet Motor Company

Division of General Motors Corporation

Detroit, Michigan

for Economical Transportation

CHEVROLET

Utility Coupé

$680

F. O. B. Flint, Mich.

Prices F. O. B. Flint, Mich.

SUPERIOR Two Pass. Roadster	$510
SUPERIOR Five Pass. Touring	525
SUPERIOR Two Pass. Utility Coupé	680
SUPERIOR Four Pass. Sedanette	850
SUPERIOR Five Pass. Sedan	860
SUPERIOR Light Delivery	510

There are now more than 10,000 Chevrolet Dealers and Service Stations Throughout the World.

Applications will be considered from high grade dealers in territory not adequately covered.

FIGURE 9. This 1923 ad for the Chevy Utility Coupé appealed to the growing number of women in the 1920s pursuing advanced education and careers; the ad was unique in promising them increased "efficiency and earning power."

couple's conversation: "Now, darling, let's be reasonable. Can I go bargain hunting over the telephone? Not really. But if I had my own pickup and delivery service—a new Chevrolet—I'd track those bargains down like a treasury agent in action." Another distinctive ad had a woman proclaiming, "You want me to come home from work and fix a six-course dinner? Fine! Then I want a Chevrolet of my own." Ads that acknowledged women's paid labor were unusual and the suggestion that women merited assistance to complete their two jobs made it truly unique.[43]

Much more common in postwar era automotive advertising was the notion that women were "virtually prisoners in their homes because they do not have a car of their own." Advertisers continued to emphasize that women needed a second car to do their jobs as wives and homemakers, frequently showing the car loaded with groceries and children. The industry's success in making two-car status a common middle-class aspiration proved to be as remarkable as the initial mass-consumption stage. In 1950, "only 7 percent of families owned more than one car." By 1960, that figure had grown to 19 percent, and it reached 34 percent by 1980. Advertisers encouraged families to buy cars tailored to the family's needs, which increasingly meant cars for women.[44]

By the late 1960s, reflecting women's dissatisfaction borne out by the electric response to Betty Friedan's *The Feminine Mystique*, Chevrolet's ads began to shift. In a startling exploitation of what Friedan termed "the problem with no name," one 1967 Chevy headline suggested, "If your wife keeps rearranging the furniture, maybe you ought to think about getting a second car." The text of the ad, alongside a picture of an unhappy woman in a bathrobe, pronounced, "She's bored silly. She knows there's a lot she could be doing during the week if she had a car of her own. You know, the stuff you wind up doing on Saturday." Chevrolet framed a second car as not just women's liberation but also as liberation for men because women would be able to independently do more household chores. As they had historically, car companies continued to frame independence for women as the ability to fulfill domestic duties. Ads like this one encouraged men to see the benefits of a second car so that women would continue to undertake unpaid labor for men's benefit.[45]

The F-Series

Although most car ads reflected a conviction that men and women had oppositional priorities in choosing a car, they also confronted the reality that not all buyers could afford a "his and her" pair as they selected a car. Ads used words like "rugged," "solid," "quick," "power," and "speed" to attract men's interest; they hoped "beauty, luxury, and comfort" would lure in women.[46]

To bridge the imagined divide, advertisers sometimes promised that a single car would respond differently to women and men. One 1926 Marmon ad featured both illustrations and descriptions that contrasted a woman and a man driving. She asserted, more mildly, "It's a Great Automobile! [A Woman's Intuition]," while below the man's image he proclaimed, in bold-faced type, "It's a *Great* Automobile! [A Man's Decision]." The text of the ad promised, "Obediently yielding to the silken touch of feminine hands, or in quick response to the hurried stress of masculine needs, *it's all the same to a Marmon*." This double talk persisted and even grew in intensity across the last third of the century.[47]

A 1966 Jeep Wagoneer ad appealed to couples, promising dual effects from their vehicle. First, addressing its performance for women, the ad claimed to men, "Your wife will be twice as safe this winter with a 'Jeep' 4-wheel drive . . . she's got *twice* the traction of ordinary station wagons. . . . And she's twice as safe on slippery streets." Without skipping a beat, the ad revealed the Jeep's male identity. "That same extra grip will take *you* off the road . . . up onto the ski slopes, hunting, or just plain exploring." Domesticated and safe for women; wild and daring for men, Jeep made safety a gendered trait.[48]

Locked into the baseless assumption of difference, advertisers sought credit for reconciling this supposed gap with cars that could meet supposedly wildly divergent requirements. Motivational researcher Ernest Dichter encouraged this gendered understanding of car buying, with men seeking powerful, aggressive vehicles (Charger, Fury) and women seeking cars to provide "womb-like security." He wrote that women believe "the inside of the car is like a home where her family can be cuddled and feel safe."[49]

Your wife will be twice as safe this winter with 'Jeep' 4-wheel drive.
In a 'Jeep' Wagoneer with 4-wheel drive, she's got twice the traction of ordinary station wagons...twice the "bite" in deep snow. And she's twice as safe on slippery streets. That same extra grip will take you off the road...up onto the ski slopes, hunting, or just plain exploring. Choice of engines: 'Vigilante' V-8, or new Hi-Torque 6. Turbo Hydra-Matic* automatic transmission, other power options. Your family will be safer on the highway...on city streets...or off the road...have more fun this winter, in a 'Jeep' Wagoneer with 4-wheel drive.
NOW! THESE 10 SAFETY FEATURES ARE STANDARD:
☐ Seat belts front and rear
☐ Padded sun visors
☐ Padded dashboard
☐ High-impact windshield
☐ Outside rear-view mirror
☐ Dual brake system
☐ Self adjusting brakes
☐ 4-way warning flashers
☐ Back-up lights
☐ Windshield washer and dual-speed wipers
KAISER Jeep CORPORATION
TOLEDO 1, OHIO
'Jeep' Wagoneer
You've got to drive it to believe it. See your 'Jeep' dealer.

Figure 10. Jeep made safety a gendered trait in this 1966 ad, with a presumption that only women valued safety and that it was all that women valued.

One difference advertisers presumed existed between men and women drivers was their respective preference for manual or automatic transmission. The widespread improvements to shifting gears and the eventual introduction of automatic transmission in the 1930s and 1940s led advertisers to frequently focus on women, although they did not do so exclusively. One Buick ad claimed, "Ladies . . . we built this car for you." Another had a baby at the wheel and proclaimed, "It almost drives itself." According to Chrysler, the Fluid Drive transformed women into "confident drivers." A 1958 ad assured women about driving the Plymouth: "It's as simple to master as your familiar washing machine. Push a button and you're in gear. No shifting, no nerve-racking shudder. Stop quickly without bounce. . . . Go with the light, no honking behind you; the new Plymouth goes from a full stop into smooth, immediate action. Even parking is easier because the wheel never fights back."[50] Automatic transmission meant that women avoided challenging men's role as "real" drivers because they used invisible technology to operate the car, as opposed to demonstrating mechanical know how.

Yet for all their gendered language and imagery, advertisers did not always position automatics as something only women wanted. Ads also had men at the wheel, depicted men's shoes at the pedals, and otherwise had men delighting in the modern ease of "No Clutch! No Shift!" Particularly with the war effort in the 1940s and the embrace of aerodynamics in the 1950s, advertisers promoted the smoothness of driving their "supermatic," "hydra-matic," "automatic" cars with both men and women.[51]

By the 1960s and 1970s, however, a cultural expectation emerged that held that only women (and not men) preferred to drive an automatic-transmission car. A few ads presented women as fickle, changing their driving preference along with their hairstyle, while most suggested that women preferred to drive an automatic transmission. In doing so, advertisers commonly challenged women's competence; a 1973 Volkswagen ad had a woman kissing an automatic wagon, touting it as "Mommy's big helper." Companies crafted these ads in spite of research that found that many women "appear to prefer manual transmission to automatics." One analyst suggested that "myopia" might have prevented the male leadership of the auto industry from heeding the data. Women reported that they

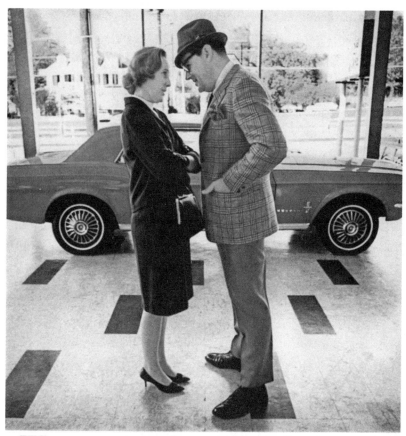

Why see a marriage counselor?
Get a Select Shift.

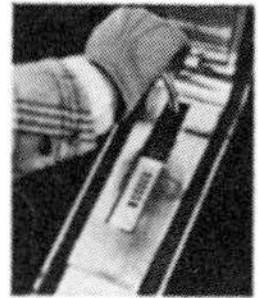

You want a stick shift. *She* wants an automatic. And your budget says: "one car!" No problem anymore. Get *one* car. And get it with a Ford Motor Company Select Shift. The Select Shift is standard equipment with every automatic transmission. Comes on the steering column or on the floor. Works like this: Shift the Select Shift into first or second gear; it works like a *manual shift*. Real control in snow or mud. Assists braking on hills – helps handle heavy trailer loads. Shift the Select Shift into automatic. It's *automatic*. The Select Shift. *You* get your way. *She* gets hers. Ford has a better idea . . . Shift for yourself!

Ford

...has a better idea

Figure 11. In this 1967 ad, Ford suggested that its Select Shift could satisfy the tension between women who preferred an automatic and men who wanted to drive a stick shift, and it did so despite the evidence that many women liked to drive a manual and many men preferred to drive an automatic.

thought manual transmission gave them fuel savings and "greater control over their car." Despite the evidence, Ford disparaged women's abilities and preferences. They developed a "Select Shift" that would let drivers choose whether to operate their car's transmission manually or automatically. A 1968 Mustang ad, however, asked women to make a pledge: she should vow to "keep the 'helpless-female' look by shifting manually only when I'm driving alone. All other times I will let the Select Shift work automatically." Ford asked its female consumers to publicly deny their ability and preference for manual, to help maintain the façade that women were "helpless" and incapable. Companies that advertised automatic transmissions as something women would prefer had the consequence of alienating women who preferred manual, as well as men who preferred automatic. They also contributed to a discourse that would not even entertain the idea of women preferring to drive stick shift because, they asserted, it was a threat to women's femininity and men's masculinity.[52]

Another way advertisers suggested women and men approached cars (and trucks) differently was in their portrayal of men with one type of vehicle and women with another, often encouraging a comparison side by side. Sometimes they tied the difference to the style of car, featuring men with a car appropriate to business or leisure, while encouraging women to buy practical cars that could transport children and groceries. Another favorite contrast focused on size, as with a 1986 Ford ad that had a man posed next to the Bronco and a woman next to the smaller Bronco II, suggesting that gender helped determine the best vehicular fit.[53]

This fundamental belief in difference was at the root of the decision for companies to create separate cars for women and men. Drawing on European panache, Chrysler created "his-and-hers concept vehicles" in 1954, Le Comte for men and La Comtesse for women. In this case, the cars were identical Imperial sedans, outfitted in bronze and black paint for men, with cream and pink styling for women. Between 1954 and 1962, Nash put out the Metropolitan, hoping, in particular, to attract women. They hired Miss America Evelyn Ay as their spokesperson, developed Nash jewelry to enhance their connection with women, and targeted their audience in magazines like *Women's Wear Daily*.[54]

FIGURE 12. Ford's 1967 ad wanted women to pledge to use the automatic setting on their Select Shift to achieve a "'helpless-female' look" when men were around, and also had women promise to stick to their diets, to highlight that the wheel could be tilted away from the driver.

Most famously, Dodge thought it had found the key to women's hearts when it designed and brought to market the pink La Femme in 1955. Its brochures proclaimed "By appointment to her majesty . . . the American Woman" and explained that "the interior was all pink, from the steering wheel to the Jacquard upholstery to the small leather handbag that came with the car. At auto shows, [Lucille] Pieti described the car and its accessories: 'A raincoat, rainhat, rain shoes and a collapsible umbrella, all of which match the interior upholstery, come with the car and fit into this special storage compartment on the back of the driver's seat.'"[55] An *Auto Week* writer suspected that in spite of the many consumer studies that existed and an ostensible interest in female consumers, "Chrysler marketing guys never bothered to actually *ask* women what they wanted in a car." Produced in 1955 and 1956, the car did not sell well and stood as a reminder of the pitfalls of "Ms.-Marketing" and narrowly gendered design in general.[56]

Still, the failure of La Femme did not slow the fascination with feminine-inspired display models. Oldsmobile put forward two such cars, the Chanteuse and the Mona Lisa, in 1957. With colors stylized by designer Peggy Sauer, "without influence by the men," "the Chanteuse came with a "matching violet full-length umbrella," "map pockets in both doors," and "a small vanity case bound in matching leather" designed for the glove compartment. The Mona Lisa model was outfitted in "brilliant tangerine" and cream leather.[57]

Of course, marketing cars as designed for women was not a new strategy and dated most conspicuously to the electric car. From the electric starter to automatic transmission, the assurance that women needed car driving to be "effortless, the lady-like way" remained a message from automobile manufacturers. These would not be the last cars marketed in this way. DeSoto, in 1957, claimed that its newest model was "perfect for a woman," and highlighted five ways that the car was designed to be "easy" for women: to park, to drive, to stop, to enter, and to own. Automakers continued to gravitate toward oppositional, gendered thinking in designing and promoting cars just for women.[58]

Although advertisements consistently targeted women for "female" car styles throughout the century, most automakers did not bring to market cars designed only for women. That, however, did not stop them from thinking about it; never far from their minds were "feminine" colors or women's domestic life. In 2000, Ford revealed its Windstar "Solutions" minivan, replete with Maytag domestic appliances; the car featured, among other things, a microwave, washing machine, and refrigerator. Honda then brought forward its 2012 minivan, with a ShopVac vacuum. In the corporate telling of the story, headlined by one hard-hitting reporter as "Honda Odyssey's New Onboard Vacuum Surprisingly Easy to Use," the company claimed it was a six-year-old American girl who suggested to her Honda engineer father that their minivan needed a vacuum.[59]

More revealing than their stylized accessories and onboard appliances was that so many companies proudly asserted that their designers used paper clips or glued-on fake nails to test their new models. In 1996, Cadillac described their male engineers donning paper-clip nails as "part of a dedicated effort to better reach women customers." In 2002, the line director for full-sized trucks had a hundred male General Motors employees "wear skirts made from plastic garbage bags and high-heeled shoes, sport long fake fingernails, and carry a purse and a baby doll" in an exercise called "Mr. Mom." Along with pregnancy suits and short skirts, male engineers continually claimed in press releases to approximate the female experience but mainly revealed how few women worked on car design and how superficial all of the carmakers' efforts to appeal to women tended to be. The press releases, following decades of counsel to promote any consideration of women, continued apace. At the end of the twentieth century, Cadillac proudly asserted that their new Catera model was designed for women; it boasted an "air-conditioned glove box, to preserve items like lipstick and film, and the use of yellow markings to highlight important under-the-hood fluid fills." The industry's understanding of women's concerns and its expectations of what the companies should do to address those concerns remained weak and limited.[60]

Emphasizing cars designed with an eye toward women buyers also risked alienating women and men buyers. A 1980 ad headlined "Some Companies Talk About the Women's Market, Ford Motor Company Has Been Doing Something About It" asserted that Ford had "involved" women and introduced an illuminated, keyless entry system. A number of women surveyed, though, "responded negatively to the approach." Irritated that the "new" feature was not, in fact, new and benefited both men and women, they called it a con. They also took issue with the ad highlighting "stereotyped weaknesses," when "men too lose their keys and have difficulty getting in an automobile when it's dark." The popular animated television series *The Simpsons* parodied this in a 1999 episode that had Homer Simpson rejecting the F-series SUV he bought because he believed it was branded *F* for *females*. The only difference in the models was that the F-series came with a lipstick holder instead of a horn and a cigarette lighter, but Homer refused to drive it because it threatened his masculine, heterosexual identity. Subverting the identity of the minivan as a vehicle for "soccer moms," one company tried to alter the identity of its "new" minivan in 2011 by asking, "Are You Tough Enough for Chrysler's 'Man Van'?" As was evident in general marketing campaigns, the effort to segment the market in explicit ways often fell short with both men and women.[61]

Despite the pitfalls to the strategy, companies continued to market to what they claimed were women's needs and preferences. The Girl Scouts, in a 2006 booklet called *On the Road: The Savvy Girl's Guide to Cars*, called for more attention to women's power in the marketplace; asked for a suggestion to improve cars for women, the girl scouts they surveyed suggested that companies place "vanity mirrors in the back seat." Volvo, facing falling market share in the early twenty-first century, went all out promoting their efforts to cater to women. Just as Harley Earl had done at General Motors more than forty years earlier, Volvo put together an all-female design team. They tasked the team with developing an ideal car for women. Able to proclaim themselves committed to learning about women ("All decisions made by women"), without actually bringing a car to market, they mercifully avoided creating a pink car. They claimed women's priorities included "Smart storage solutions," "A car you can personalize," and "A car that is easy to park." After one hundred years of automotive design, automakers' expectations for women's "unique" desires continued to be decidedly banal, universally appealing, or insulting. Volvo's all-woman team created headrests that could accommodate ponytails and removable, washable upholstery "that can be swapped in

THE SATURDAY EVENING POST 129

Somewhere West of Laramie

SOMEWHERE west of Laramie there's a broncho-busting, steer-roping girl who knows what I'm talking about.

She can tell what a sassy pony, that's a cross between greased lightning and the place where it hits, can do with eleven hundred pounds of steel and action when he's going high, wide and handsome.

The truth is—the Playboy was built for her.

Built for the lass whose face is brown with the sun when the day is done of revel and romp and race.

She loves the cross of the wild and the tame.

There's a savor of links about that car—of laughter and lilt and light—a hint of old loves—and saddle and quirt. It's a brawny thing—yet a graceful thing for the sweep o' the Avenue.

Step into the Playboy when the hour grows dull with things gone dead and stale.

Then start for the land of real living with the spirit of the lass who rides, lean and rangy, into the red horizon of a Wyoming twilight.

FIGURE 13. Unlike the language and imagery of this exceptional 1923 Jordan Motor Car Company ad, depictions of women's automotive lives tended to be much more circumscribed by their domestic life.

two minutes" "to fit the season—or your mood. . . . 'It's a bit like a living room.'" They introduced electronic sensors to help with parallel parking, along with "dent resistant rubberized bumpers." The company hoped that by publicizing their purported effort to listen to women and employ female designers, women would buy their cars.[62]

Conclusion

While the automobile has been synonymous with freedom in our collective memory, for the most part automobile companies did not include women in this vision. Historians showered attention on a beautiful, distinctive 1923 car ad "Somewhere West of Laramie" that stood as a stark exception. Created by Edward S. "Ned" Jordan for the Playboy brand automobile, scholars and enthusiasts claimed that the ad was "one of the most famous of the 1920s," "one of the most celebrated in advertising history," and "changed automobile advertising from that point." Yet the ad, aggressively courting female consumers, reveals what was more mundane in all other car advertising. Jordan addressed the ad to "a bronco-busting, steer-roping girl," while other ads only valued women in their roles as daughters, wives, and mothers. His romantic pitch granted women knowledge, power, and the freedom to escape "when the hour grows dull with things gone dead and stale." Most car companies did not promise women freedom or power; they only assured consumers that their vehicles would help women succeed in the everyday workings of their home, work, and community. Finally, the famous ad offered the unusual image of a woman racing a car (against a horse), while other ads targeted to women fixated on their imagined predilection for automotive safety. Like the Playboy automobile brand itself, the message of independence faded quickly, leaving the automotive giants to create a monolithic, constricted vision for women and their cars.[63]

Buying a car continued to be a distinctly gendered experience into the twenty-first century. The expectation that women would be best served by marketing that treated them as unusual, indeed, rare and exceptional, rather than typical consumers shaped the experience from start to finish. Perhaps the only thing even more fundamentally gendered would be women's experience driving a car.

3

Driving a Car

HISTORICALLY, WOMEN FOUND THEMSELVES motivated to drive by the same allures that captivated men. If gender did not provide the impetus, class did. The wealthy enjoyed cars as playthings, while the middle and working classes used their cars for both job opportunities and social excursions. Early automobiles demanded physical strength and automotive know-how, which served to lower the expectation that women would be in the driver's seat. However, as cars became easier to maneuver, the perceived accessibility of driving increased dramatically. As cars became more affordable and assistance more readily available to all, women increasingly embraced the prospects the car afforded.

Three major opportunities for women to drive came in the first decades of the century. Early on, women who participated in automobile races and who undertook cross-country expeditions served to establish that cars were reliable machines. These events also assured the public that women and this new contraption, both popularly believed to be weak and vulnerable, were in fact strong and dependable. The cumulative effect of these company-sponsored advertising efforts was to establish the relative safety and pleasure of automobile driving generally. In the midst of these campaigns came the outbreak of the First World War. Volunteer organizations serving Europe called for women to bring their cars and a driver's license to serve as ambulance drivers. For those who remained on the homefront, the absence of men created demand for women to drive, shuttling people and goods around the country. Finally, suffragists used the automobile to establish women's competence and promote the importance of women's rights. Used to create publicity in everything from local parades to cross-country jaunts, automobiles gave the cause visibility and strengthened women's efforts waging state and national battles.[1]

Entrepreneurial women also used cars to create markets for their products. Traveling salesmen, etched in national lore as archetypal figures, such as Willy Loman, blot out the experiences of saleswomen who also traveled the countryside. Whether representing their local chamber of commerce businesses with Welcome Wagon–type organizations or selling kitchenware and beauty supplies, ambitious women such as entrepreneur Madam C. J. Walker understood a car to be an investment in their business.[2]

Across the century, however, in spite of the obvious societal benefits and the overtures businesses occasionally made, Americans believed women who drove faced a number of vulnerabilities. The most fundamental risk, according to the discourse, was that women were not good drivers. This baseless stereotype plagued women consistently into the twenty-first century, frequently advanced through a disingenuous consideration of whether women or men were better drivers. Many maintained that it was a given that women could not park because of their genetic makeup. A close second, in asserting women's driving as a risk, was the belief that women were in constant jeopardy from strange men, especially if they had to stop for gas or if they got lost.

Businesses regularly exploited the dangers of driving to persuade women to read their periodicals or buy their services. Companies did so, however, in a context of a real potential for danger. As increasing numbers of women secured their driver's licenses and drove independently, their vulnerability grew. It did not require a long-distance trip to put them in harm's way; crimes occurred in their own towns, at their local mall, and in lovers' lanes. Even those entrusted to protect women proved to be potentially dangerous offenders, as police officers also assaulted female drivers. Some businesses sought to profit by tapping into the legitimate fears of women behind the wheel.

As women hit the road, gas stations welcomed this growing population of travelers who, companies believed, played a critical role in selecting where and when families would stop. They also shared an expectation that women would be responsible for caring for their passengers and hoped to entice women with appealing services and facilities. Gas companies even employed uniformed, trained women to staff their stations, offering sanitation inspections and nursing expertise.

"If She Can Dance, Then She Can Drive"

Early newspaper and magazine articles about the phenomenon of women drivers tended to comment on their growing numbers or offer guidance to help steer women toward successful command of a car. While most of these forays did not center on comparisons with men drivers, some did question who was better behind the wheel. One 1912 newspaper article, for example, headlined "Women Drivers Increase," was subtitled "Men Often Inferior in Handling a Motor Car." After several paragraphs detailing the importance of the car to women, especially to farm women's physical and mental health, it concluded of women, "As a rule they are better drivers than men. They are not speed fiends, and operate a car with more care and wisdom than do the majority of men." A 1913 *American Homes and Gardens* article devoted to giving women detailed guidance on how to drive and care for a car, premised its argument that women could become "successful and expert" drivers by maintaining that there were already many such women who were as skillful and successful as male drivers, and that the number grew considerably each year.[3]

Newspapers featured articles and debates about women's mental fitness as drivers. An op-ed in the *New York Times* in 1915 challenged a judge who maintained, "In my opinion, no woman should be allowed to operate an automobile. In the first place, she hasn't the strength, and, in the second place, she is very apt to lose her head." The op-ed and subsequent letters in response debated women's propensity for reckless driving. A male medical doctor in Bergen County, New Jersey, wrote in to take issue with the characterization of women as poor drivers. He stated that in three years of treating victims of automobile accidents, "in no case was

SUNDAY MAGAZINE

Of the Buffalo Courier

BUFFALO, N. Y.
DECEMBER 18, 1910

PART 3
20 PAGES

Beginning PHILIP VERRILL MIGHELS' THURLEY RUXTON

Figure 14. For more than a hundred years, American society has asked the question of whether women or men were better drivers, principally to assert that men are superior, despite the evidence that there has been no significant difference between them. This 1910 magazine cover captures a woman confidently in command of the car, sitting tall, while the man next to her simmers and shrinks in his seat. This is also an early example of the uncertainty of where American cars would ultimately place the steering wheel.

a woman the driver of either car where two automobiles were involved," and he challenged readers to consider whether this meant, then, that only men were too weak or lost their head while driving. These debates also filled legislative hearings and fueled the research agendas of professors like Charles Sherwood Ricker, a philosopher at Harvard, who argued that "a great many persons, both men and women, are physically and temperamentally unfit to operate motor vehicles, except at the lowest possible rate of speed on wide highways."[4]

The presumptions about women's driving were plentiful and often contradictory. A young woman, fined for reckless driving, was told by the judge during her sentencing, "Women drivers are incompetent and unfit to operate automobiles. . . . Since universal suffrage came into existence you have shown the men no consideration. In traffic you ride roughshod over everybody and expect to get away with it because you are the gentler sex." The assertion that women were simultaneously gentle and careless brutes appeared in the courts and the court of public opinion and helped to shape the different ways women were understood to be engaged with the car.[5]

Another analytic approach also found its way into the discourse about women drivers. Edna Purdy Walsh, writing in *Motor Life* in 1924, maintained that through physiognomy it was possible to discern which women were capable drivers. She asserted that a woman could look in the mirror and ascertain from her eyebrow ridge, lips, and ears if she had motoring ability. In addition, Walsh also believed that a woman's body also told the story. "If she can dance, then she can drive. . . . It is the woman's muscular temperament and sense of balance that qualify her to guide her car." Evaluating the size of her hands and feet, the color of her hair, and even whether "she likes a variety of clothes in her closet, in many colors," all informed whether a woman would be a good driver. Other people also asserted their observations as fact; for example, a driving instructor in Texas who maintained that women with red hair were the fastest to pick up driving and that "stout women make 'crackerjack' drivers, while schoolteachers are about the hardest women to teach how to manipulate a machine." This suggestion that women's driving capability was discernible on sight fed the notion that some women should not be driving, which contributed to their differential participation. There were no suggestions made that any man could be immediately categorized as a good or bad driver based on his looks, because men were understood to be, as a group, the "good drivers," while all sorts of strategies emerged from those who sought to categorize women as "bad drivers."[6]

While some people relied on "natural" markers to identify good drivers, most authors interviewed psychologists, police officers, neurologists, and driving instructors, and, of course, they relied on studies and statistics to ground their arguments. One influential article, written in 1925 by the head of the psychology department at George Washington University, asked, "Are You a Better Driver Than Your Wife?" The author used scientific tests to determine the relative skills of women and men and analyzed the arguments made to support the contention that women were poor drivers. In addition to evaluating the IQ tests that revealed the sexes to be equal, he also challenged the cultural expectation that women expressing their emotions undermined their ability to cope with a crisis while driving. Crying or screaming, he maintained, did not necessarily affect women's ability to respond well to an emergency.[7]

Esquire magazine apologized to its male readers for a 1936 article titled, "Women Are Good Drivers." Although 76 percent of the men questioned by an insurance company gave a resounding "NO" to the question, "Can women drive as well as men?," the article systematically debunked the myth of male supremacy. It concluded that if men admit that they tend to be more likely to speed, and if speeding is the "most prolific cause of accidents today," then their arguments against women turn into a confession about men behind the wheel. This prejudice in the face of rational arguments persisted. A headline in the *Pittsburgh Press* proclaimed, "Public Would Rather Ride in Auto Driven by Man," with the subhead "But Women Motorists Have Fewer Accidents and Drive Cars Slower."[8]

For almost one hundred years, the assertion that women were to blame for making driving dangerous and unpleasant fueled both serious criticism and ridicule of women drivers. Newspaper articles reported topics like "Buffalo Men Blame [Women] for Traffic Jams" in 1925, and millions watched youtube.com compilations of women's parking and driving disasters in the twenty-first century. More than just a reflection of the broader gender inequality that existed throughout society, humor about women drivers helped assert the differences that defined gender expectations. The humor worked, as critic Joanne Gilbert contends, as "an important rhetorical tool . . . limiting options as it amuses." While E. B. White wrote his "Notes and Comment" in the *New Yorker* for humor, he was not joking when he proclaimed in 1931, "Men, in general, drive better than women." "Women, in general," he concluded, "are incurious about anything mechanical—incurious and intolerant . . . women are too self-absorbed to drive well." Tempering his charges with "in general" allowed for exceptions while maintaining his shallow assessments. Even more significant, these kinds of characterizations were not limited to local newspapers and women's magazines. White's casual dismissal of women drivers played to an audience of highbrow readers and joined countless other columns and articles marketing male superiority.[9]

Following women's illustrious contributions to World War II, one community protested the 1946 comments of Gerald Barker, a local safety official in Akron, Ohio, who proclaimed, "After careful deliberation, I've decided they are not fit to sit behind the wheel of a car. . . . Take them from the highways, and you will see a big decrease in Akron's accident record." Taking to the phones and the newspaper, women responded with outrage. One of the "thousand telephone calls" was for the man's wife, wondering "who could live with" him. His wife responded publicly, "He's not such a hot driver, himself. Sometimes on trips, I feel like using a crank handle on him because he's so confident he's the best driver in the world. He misses that by a big, big margin." To answer the broader question of whether women or men were the better drivers in Akron, the Goodyear Tire & Rubber Co. and the Akron and Summit County Federation of Women's Clubs sponsored the Battle of the Sexes. After scoring women and men across ten days, the women emerged victorious. That did not stop Barker, who would only concede that their situation in Akron was different from the national picture.[10]

The casual dismissal of women as poor drivers also served to justify men's driving malfeasance. Courtrooms heard accounts of women's exploits behind the wheel, especially regarding signaling not matching their intentionality. The expectation that women's turn signals did not truly indicate their intended action left women not only charged as fickle but also accountable for the ensuing accidents—even when men were to blame. In 1952, fifty women had had enough and argued in court that their "'civil rights' had been encroached upon in the dismissal of charges against a man who had refused to believe a woman driver's signal and had crashed into her automobile." The man admitted to the judge that he had seen the left turn light on, "But I didn't believe she actually was going to turn. . . . She was the first woman driver I ever saw who turned the same direction she signaled."[11]

Occasionally companies asserted that women's driving abilities surpassed those of men. A 1930 ad headlined "Women Drivers Are Safe Drivers" and the accompanying asterisk noted "24% of the licensed drivers in the USA are women, yet they are involved in only 6% of all automobile accidents." The subject of this ad in the *Ladies' Home Journal* was a woman confronting her husband about his misdeeds as a driver, "A summons for speeding? A dent in the radiator? Another fender? Now really John . . ." Texaco sought to appeal to women decision makers, who were well aware of men's fallibility at the wheel.[12]

More often, though, companies premised their ads on an expectation that women were bad drivers. The trope was so popular even non-car companies used the idea of bad women drivers to sell their products. A 1969 American Tourister suitcase ad featured a woman, door open, leaning out to look back and assess the damage. The text read, "I backed our car over the suitcase. Inside was my husband's portable radio. . . . I got so rattled, I put the car in drive and ran over it again." The woman's husband assured men, "My heart was in my mouth, but the radio wasn't even scratched." Claiming that American Tourister suitcases were so durable they could be run over again and again was outlandish; claiming that women were such poor drivers that they would do so multiple times was beyond the pale.[13]

Newspapers and magazines also traded in these claims as well. One AP story, carried by the *New York Times*, maintained that the man recounting "swears this story is true—but even if it isn't true it has to be told." The short account alleged that a woman who was supposed to nudge the car with a dead battery by bringing her speed up to thirty to thirty-five mph, instead rammed into the stalled car at that speed. Under the guise of reputable reporting, even esteemed newspapers indulged in jokes about women drivers.[14]

Volkswagen was even less subtle. As part of the irreverent campaign created by the Doyle Dane Bernbach ad agency, a 1964 ad appeared in newspapers and *Life* magazine proclaiming, "Sooner or later, your wife will drive home one of the best reasons for owning a Volkswagen." With false flattery they agreed, "Women are soft and gentle," and then they added "but they hit things" to the litany, making being poor drivers a "natural" part of women's identity. The ad promised that "VW parts are easy to replace. And cheap. . . . It may make you furious, but it won't make you poor." Companies continued to assert that men dealt with the presence of women drivers with tolerant exasperation and that they feared the large and growing number of women drivers in the United States.[15]

Researchers for organizations and professors at universities historically considered female drivers distinct from male drivers. They frequently plucked out findings to make arguments both for and against women driving automobiles. Efforts to parse the numbers often contended with the relative numbers of drivers (with arguments for weighting their relative proportion), the type of driving (commuting, errands, highway), and miles driven per violation or accident. They sought evidence of differences in qualities like reaction times and vision, as well as more unusual measures, such as the "strength of grip."[16]

Throughout the twentieth century and into the twenty-first, the assumption that women were worse drivers than men persisted, appearing as the lead for a story or the premise of an advertisement. Interestingly, the contention that women were bad drivers frequently served as a myth to disprove, rather than affirm. The general acceptance and expectation of women as poor drivers withstood all of the scientific evidence amassed over the decades of study that demonstrated otherwise. A 1937 *Time* article comparing male and female drivers concluded with a man stating, "The ladies may not find it tactful to cite that men have higher blood pressure, because the men might say it's caused by women drivers." Even in the debate over who was a better driver, men asserted that women were the cause of their problems. Of course, some women blamed men, as well. One psychiatrist maintained that "women have heard their driving disparaged so often that they get a bit tense about it, and then don't do as well as they might."[17]

Women penned a growing number of the articles that challenged the defamation of female motorists. While male authors had predominated, starting in the post–World War II era, newspapers and magazines began to feature more articles about women drivers by women. These writers rejected the fallacy of the poor woman driver and believed that their arguments and evidence would serve as the "nail in the coffin," ending the inane debate. As one declared, "So to the graveyard goes one more myth of woman's inferiority, to rest comfortably with others of the kind—the defunct legends of women's incapacity to become doctors, architects, or machinists." The newspaper editors, however, consistently undermined women's arguments by placing detrimental photographs and cartoons alongside their stories. One 1951 article, titled "So You Think Women Can't Drive!" promoted women's abilities, but the editors captioned the accompanying photo, "As this young woman demonstrates, a girl can back up into a parking place without bumping anything—provided she looks behind her and follows the directions some man will be glad to give her." Even more damning, the cartoon that the editors placed in an adjoining column had a wide-eyed husband taking in the sight of his disheveled wife as she announced, "They've made a one-way street out of Thirty-sixth." The author concluded that winning the debate about superiority was more complicated than one might imagine. She asked, "But will men admit it? You know they won't. Being the vain, stubborn creatures that they are, they will go right on preening their feathers as they always have. They'll laugh and sneer at us, print their cute cartoons—ignoring all truths save those that support the laughable theory of male superiority." Instead of outrage at this injustice, however, the author suggested that women use the myth to their advantage, getting "the sucker to park our cars, change our tires, drive us through frustrations of city traffic. . . . Eve taught us long ago that it pays to let the chump think he is superior."[18]

Generally, the evidence either declared the battle between the sexes to be a draw or gave a slight edge to women as the better drivers. In spite of the evidence, one hundred years after the cars' introduction and embrace by women, many still contend that women are not good drivers.

A male Fox News reporter in 2013 declared that women "clearly are" worse drivers, assuring viewers, "if you could just see the women I know . . . they can't maneuver as well. But, what's the bigger measure, which is how many people do they kill . . . we men are much worse. We're much more likely to run stop signs, speed, and kill other people." When Golden Globes host Ricky Gervais skewered Caitlyn Jenner in 2016, he did so by feigning respect for all she had done "in breaking down barriers and destroying stereotypes," but his takedown followed: "She didn't do a lot for women drivers, but . . ." According to the premise of Gervais's "joke," when men were men they were good drivers, but a biological man who transitioned to become a woman immediately became vulnerable to her true identity: bad driver.[19]

It was not just a one-time "bad joke." The assertion of women being bad drivers persisted into the twenty-first century. Two wide-release movies in 2016 trotted out this well-trod joke. The trailer for the Tina Fey film *Whiskey Tango Foxtrot* used the first licensed female driver in Kabul, Afghanistan, to ridicule women drivers everywhere. As she reported on the event of a new driver taking the wheel in a country that had denied women opportunities both for education and for employment, Fey's character pronounced, as the driver backed into some debris instead of driving away, "Oh, that sucks. That sucks for women." One mistake by a pioneer set back women's efforts to be taken seriously not only as drivers but as human beings. Nor were animated females immune to these jokes. Socializing young children, the uplifting Disney film *Zootopia* ended with the lead character, an anthropomorphized female rabbit, driving away in an oversized Humvee-type vehicle. The male sidekick remarked to the movie's hero—who had overcome tremendous odds to graduate first in her police academy class, become the first rabbit added to the police force, and saved their community from being destroyed by vicious division—that he wondered if *she* could drive.[20]

The subject of women drivers historically elicited emotional, irrational responses. This is ironic because one of the central charges against women drivers was that women were too emotional to handle driving a car. What the evidence reveals, however, is a consistent, systematic effort to debunk a myth premised on an insulting, dismissive attitude toward women. Having to validate the erroneous presumptions' existence to disprove them ultimately served to perpetuate their shelf life. Acknowledging any differences in behavior or abilities leads to conclusions about relative superiority of the sexes, rather than an understanding that some women and some men can be excellent, safe drivers, while others may not be. Harping on perceived gender differences disguised the much greater violence men perpetrated behind the wheel and diverted critiques away from cell-phone companies that blinded us nationally to the terrifying costs of talking and texting on cell phones while driving.[21]

"Makes It Easy for a Woman to Park Like a Man"

For all of the scrutiny of women's driving abilities, jokes about women and parking proved to be a perennial critique. It was a common meme that women needed assistance, while men, as men, could handily park a car. Ads in the 1930s and 1940s suggested through text that "women particularly love the easy handling and parking" of their vehicles, while postwar ads frequently depicted women actually parking the car. Ads tended to use cityscapes or supermarket parking lots as prime examples of tough driving and parking situations. Women in the ads assured, as one did in 1952, "Parking is as easy as dialing a telephone!" A 1957 Ford ad disguised as a magazine feature titled "How to Park Your Car" featured a woman at the wheel, even though it was placed in periodicals such as *Boys' Life*.

Advertisers generally premised the ease of parking on either the power steering or the shorter size of the car. The Saginaw company promoted its "Safety power steering" in the mid-1950s, targeting women in magazines like *Good Housekeeping* and often using female movie stars to make their pitch. In one, actor Laraine Day, married at the time to the New York Giants manager Leo Durocher, proclaimed, "Now I can park just as well as Leo!" She conceded, "I used to take a lot of lip from Leo, and even little Chris laughed at my efforts." The embarrassment of having their children witness her struggles and indeed contribute to them was reflected in a number of ads. Another had actor Ella Raines describing how tense it made her to drive, "especially with my daughter Chrissie beside me. Parking always flustered and exhausted me, too." While Saginaw ads still did not make this an exclusively female issue, it was Saginaw's primary focus. One ad asked, "Wouldn't it be wonderful if you could have a nice muscular man handy to 'spell' you at the wheel . . . whenever you get arm-weary from fighting traffic, sharp turns, and *particularly* those skimpy parking spaces!" The ads assured women that having Saginaw power steering was "like having a 'co-pilot.'" Another promised Saginaw could help women "unpark," too, "with one finger! No aching arms. No split seams. No loss of breath or dignity! It's man's greatest gift to women drivers."[22]

Chrysler promised in a 1959 ad that its "Constant Control power steering . . . Supplies the extra muscle that makes it easy for a woman to park like a man." The following year, Chevrolet claimed that its car's handling "stretches parking spaces like rubber bands, just seems to make parking openings bigger and easier to get into." Studebaker opened one of the most patronizing ads, proclaiming: "Some men think all women are terrible drivers. But it isn't true. It's just that some cars are more difficult for them to drive than for men. Studebaker isn't. Here is a car so sensibly built a woman only 5 feet tall can survey all four fenders without sitting on a cushion." The ad concluded, "We know of one other passenger vehicle a woman can wheel, park and manuever as deftly as the 1965 Studebaker . . . but it's only a single seater." The featured "single seater" was a baby stroller, replete with a young child ready to go for a "drive."[23] Ultimately, ads premised on women's supposed inability to park were relatively short-lived.

Historian Lizabeth Cohen maintained that consumers in new post–World War II era shopping centers "found parking spaces wider than usual for the express purpose of making it easier for them—many of whom were new drivers—to park." To attract female consumers and workers, the shopping malls needed women to drive and their plans called for big spots for easy parking. However, this was not necessarily a prerequisite. From the 1920s to the present, parking garages helped solicit shoppers and demanded difficult maneuvering to park. No one ever reconciled the reputation of women as poor drivers with the installation of parking garages in shopping malls. Moreover, the suggestion that women were "new drivers" had always been, to some extent, true. The evidence reflects that while we culturally imagined the problem that existed for women parking to be ubiquitous, advertisers' emphasis on it only fell in the 1950s and 1960s, the exact time frame when these behemoth structures were being built and embraced. Even at the peak of the advertisers' expectation that ease of parking was a marketable point, most ads did not foreground or even allude to women needing help to park, some even had men at the wheel.[24]

Although there were occasional references to parking in ads in the last quarter of the century, as a marketing theme it largely died out. Just as they had before (and during) this period, automobile advertisers in later ads declined to suggest that women had unique parking problems. The ads promised that their cars would be easy to park and assured that drivers would not "hog" spots. Even when the advertisers' claims were not overtly gendered, the cultural expectation that women could not park persisted.[25]

"He Tried Ethyl in His Car Last Night"

One of the most concerted marketing efforts by gasoline companies centered on enticing women to their stations. Companies like Shell, Gulf, and Ethyl used two distinct approaches, each of which assumed a distinctive, feminine association. Early on, these companies sought to make their gas and oil products synonymous with women, with imagery and language that made women seem the embodiment of the brand. They also sought to make their stations destinations for women and their families. As car travel expanded people's horizons, it took them further and further from their homes and induced them to ask for car care and directions. To establish their brand as one that women could trust, some companies prioritized clean bathrooms and promotional giveaways.

Anxious to persuade the American public of the relative merits of its fuel, the Ethyl gasoline company relied on text-heavy ads that featured images embodying their brand—a young, attractive woman named Ethyl. The company associated its red gasoline, which featured the anti-knock ingredient tetraethyllead, with drawings of fresh-faced "Ethyls," with red hats atop their heads, frequently wearing bright red lipstick, red scarves, and either red coveralls or a red, fitted chauffeur's outfit. Ads appealed to consumers, as in a series of 1929 ads, with Ethyl suggesting: "Any car runs better if I'm in it" and "Give your car a treat—ask for me." A 1949 cartoon reflected the company's success: One woman asked another, "How come you're through with Jim?" Her friend replied, "I heard him say he tried Ethyl in his car last night."[26]

This early association of gasoline and women extended beyond Ethyl and appeared throughout the twentieth century. The yellow or clear appearance of most oils and gasolines also led many companies, such as Texaco and Gulf, to use women wearing yellow or white in their ads. Although not unique in their use of young, attractive women, gasoline companies did try to draw a parallel between their portrayals of the women as "clear. clean. pure." and the featured oil being poured for display. Ads also capitalized on sexuality, including showcasing women in some ads wearing bathing suits. The association continued into the twenty-first century, with Peak Motor Oil hiring racecar driver Danica Patrick as a spokesperson who consistently played up her sexuality in her advertising persona.[27]

Although most women featured in gasoline-station ads appeared to be single, white, and in their twenties, advertisers also recognized the value in reaching teens, wives, and mothers, and older women, and, by the late twentieth century, they included African American women, too. Across the century, most women appeared in gasoline ads in white (or light colors). Using white allowed companies to send two important messages: Their stations were clean, bright, and inviting; and their products were pure and unsoiled. Gulf brand gasoline had a number of these ads in the late 1950s, marked by the white clothing of the women (and some men) and the gleaming whiteness of the stations. Even for brands or ads that ventured into colors, white gloves lent themselves easily to establishing the quality of their brand by assuring that women could expect service that would not soil their clothing.[28]

Gas stations sought to capitalize on the growing market of families who vacationed by car throughout the century. Particularly in the post–World War II period, they ramped up their efforts to compete not just at

Mrs. Taxi-Driver

(A story of day-to-day progress in automotive research)

THERE'S no meter on her "cab," but she has plenty of regular customers. She is on call for trips to school, store, station and a dozen other places. Her children and her neighbors and their children are her "fares." She drives more miles than her husband—for the "taxi service" of the American housewife is a large part of her life.

Since women spend so much of their time behind the wheels of automobiles, they exert a strong influence upon trends in automotive design. Engineers strive not only to make cars more powerful and reliable, but to make them more beautiful, more comfortable, easier to drive. One has only to compare the present-day automobile with the car of ten years ago to realize the amazing progress that has been made.

But what of the next ten years? Engineers of the automotive and petroleum industries look forward to even greater progress than we have seen in the past decade. Progress will be accelerated because the technical men of both industries realize that the problems of engine, engine parts and fuel improvements are inseparable and that they must be solved by cooperative research effort.

To the solution of these problems Ethyl is providing both product and service. Our product, anti-knock fluid containing tetraethyl lead, is used by oil refiners to raise the anti-knock quality (octane number) of gasoline. Ethyl's research workers are cooperating with automotive engineers in steps to take advantage of better fuel. Our research laboratories in Detroit and San Bernardino are helping to coordinate the many individual lines of research engaged in by the technical men of both industries. And our field engineers are offering to commercial users of fuels and engines the practical application of the data we have developed.

The public benefits by every improvement in automobiles, trucks, buses, tractors and airplanes. Thus we believe by making our service available to the executives and technologists of the automotive and petroleum industries we are serving "everybody."

ETHYL
ETHYL GASOLINE CORPORATION
Chrysler Building
New York City

FIGURE 15. Advertisers frequently used women dressed in white and yellow clothing and accessories to symbolize the purity of gasoline and oil products. In its original color presentation, this 1941 Ethyl ad featured a woman in a white dress with a yellow jacket. She is referred to as a "taxi-driver," a common way that women's unpaid work was quietly acknowledged as work.

the pump but in the services they offered. Service stations, as early as the 1920s, recognized the importance of catering to women. Influencing every facet, from the architecture of the building to the flower gardens, from items on sale to the accessibility of the station, gas stations made most decisions with an eye toward women. In 1970, Citgo touted its "Good Neighbor Policy," which included making its stations "as attractive as good design, landscaping, and all-around neatness can make them," and jointly sponsored a "Business for Beauty" program with the General Federation of Women's Clubs. A 1979 article reported that "80 percent of all women choose a station by its cleanliness." Part of the sell also extended to the professionalization of the attendant, who increasingly moved away from informal, "greasy overalls" to uniforms with hats.[29]

One of the most important realizations for these companies was that people on the go needed to go to the bathroom. Just as the growing car culture and mobility of Americans transformed restaurants into fast-food delivery systems, gas stations learned that discerning consumers would spend their money at the pump if they could use the restroom and could also be tempted to come in to buy a refreshing drink and snack, too. Arguably, clean restrooms were not as high a priority for most men, who did not always need to sit down. Most companies instead recognized their greater importance to women and their children, and, aware of a national "growing anxiety over the transmission of venereal disease through the use of public facilities," as early as 1938 companies like Shell Oil advertised their "'Home Clean' restrooms in cooperation with *Good Housekeeping Magazine.*" Some companies, like the Moran Filling Station in Kansas, singled out women in announcing a "Ladies Rest Room," and in some upper Midwest states, some stations were even called Powder Puff stations. Transforming makeshift facilities into the more familiar rooms with "hot and cold running water, flush toilets, mirrors, paper towels, soap, and absorbent toilet paper" was seen as good business sense, raising the bar on what drivers expected stations to provide.[30]

Companies like Texaco went further and invested in the promise that they would have available a "rest room scrupulously neat." They assured Americans that their "spic-and-span cleanliness" would be maintained by a fleet of "White Patrol" cars that would "constantly check each of the *Registered* Rest Rooms." One early Texaco ad, appearing in 1939, suggested that Texaco stations were the "originators of *Registered* Rest Rooms." The ad had a mother and young daughter fixing their hair and makeup under the headline "Our 'Powder Room' on the Road." Alluding to Texaco's ability to provide a home away from home, the mother told her daughter: "You're lucky, Betty. . . . I remember when it was hard to find clean attractive rest rooms like this." Texaco relied heavily on images of young girls in its ads focused on restrooms, allowing them to emphasize that mothers would appreciate the opportunity to use a clean restroom and could fulfill her motherly duty in stopping at Texaco to get gas, by providing the most sanitary, domestic experience available for her children. As a stand-in for the mother, young girls, clutching their own baby dolls, walked confidently toward the restroom with the tag line, "Something a lady appreciates." Alluding to middle-of-the-night stops and featuring images of women holding their sleeping young daughters, ads sought to assure women that they could rely on Texaco to care for their families' needs. Even into the 1970s, when Texaco no longer tied their reputation to their restrooms, their commercials continued to highlight them.[31]

Competitors, however, did not concede their customers to Texaco. Phillips 66, later Union 76, and then the Gulf Company enacted similar programs but with a twist. The companies advertised their station attendants as professional women. Phillips 66 introduced registered nurses as spokespeople for their company, calling their team Highway Hostesses and expecting them to cover a territory of the United States and serve as a "combination of information bureau, saleslady, nurse, philosopher, and friend." Their program promised that the nurses would ensure the bathrooms were "hospital clean." Dressed in sharp uniforms, or occasionally in Florence Nightingale-esque capes and caps, the women were expected to be "couriers of comfort and protection." Proudly asserting the professionalism and capability of their female representatives, companies also used innuendo to ask questions like, "What can a 5′1″, 102 lb. girl like Susan Catt do to make your trip more enjoyable?" Ads like that one from 1966 promised consumers that Gulf's team of women, the Tourguard

Team, were "good lookers" who conducted a "49-point" inspection at each station, and advanced expectations of additional care, including medical care, ice water, and directions.[32]

The expectation that gas stations would offer restrooms was so entrenched that a 1986 *Los Angeles Times* article reported that cities in southern California, including Los Angeles, were debating whether to require gas stations to provide restrooms, because homeowners whose property adjoined gas stations frequently found people urinating on their lawns. Health concerns motivated the efforts to mandate clean public restrooms, while business owners fought back, arguing that maintaining a restroom was an expense they could ill afford, compounded by the financial costs resulting from vandalism. For many businesses, maintaining service at a standard that would appeal to women was no longer practical or desirable. Most businesses, however, still believed that they needed to offer restrooms, with one noting that when customers learned they lacked facilities, "they drive out and go across the street to the Texaco, which has restrooms." As with so many automotive amenities that businesses sought to feminize, gas-station restrooms were offered as a feminine concession, rather than a basic service to which all were entitled.[33]

The final way gas stations sought to appeal to women was by promising both service and guidance in their travels. In addition to gas and restrooms, companies strategized that the key ways to keep local customers and lure customers nationally was to offer car care and travel support. Early auto enthusiasts relied on mechanics and automotive supplies found in gas stations and, by the 1920s, companies formalized selling "secondary-market merchandise such as oil, tires, batteries, and mechanical equipment."[34]

Aware that women were increasingly tasked with car care, companies appealed directly to women to choose their brand and services. Efforts to sell merchandise and services ranged from insulting to supportive, with male authority invariably guiding the way. Ads used women to play the foil to tell all consumers about the benefits of visiting their stations. The services varied but often included, in addition to pumping gas, cleaning the windshield, checking the oil, and checking the air pressure in the tires.[35]

When you go on vacation, you'll find our Tourguard girls are good lookers.
Gulf
Gulf's Tourguard girls are professionally trained to give a Gulf service station a good looking over.
Every time one of them visits a station, it gets looked at in 49 different places. Rest rooms, sales racks, pumps, equipment. The works.
The result is neat, clean stations that make your vacation drive just a bit more enjoyable. It's a little thing, but...
We think everybody should get out for a vacation. So we do all we can to make it more pleasant.
Gulf Oil Corporation

FIGURE 16. To promote taking vacations by car, gas companies such as Gulf and Texaco ran ads like this one from 1967 to promote their national force of uniformed women who ensured sanitary bathroom services. Phillips 66 even required their Highway Hostesses to be certified nurses.

Another critical element of driving used to be the need to put chains on car tires in the winter. Service stations capitalized on their ability to easily put on the chains and by the 1930s it had become a standard service they provided. Companies frequently used women as the vulnerable driver they could rescue by providing or securing the chains. A 1960s Texaco ad credited a Knoxville, Tennessee, station with rescuing a woman embarked on a 1,000-mile trip with three young children. When bad weather hit, she pulled into the station—one Texaco service man drove out into the storm to find chains and put them on, while the other sheltered her family.[36]

Although gas and oil companies publicly sought women's approval, the pages of their industry journal, the *National Petroleum News*, told a different story. A series of cutting cartoons in 1970, for example, reflected the industry's ambivalence toward women. With thinly veiled animosity, one had the station attendant stretching the gas hose to its limit, unable to reach a car's fuel tank, as the woman at the wheel angrily protested, "What do you mean you can't reach it? You reached it last time I was here." Another disdainful cartoon had a woman confiding to another while their car was being fueled, "They don't pull anything on this old girl. No matter how often they raise the price of gasoline, I still buy only a dollar's worth." The industry seemed decidedly uneasy about the increasing number of women it served at the pump.[37]

In the 1970s and 1980s, as service levels declined nationally, a few companies continued to tout their exceptional "full service" attention. A 1970s Texaco ad used a woman at the wheel to state "you need service" and to encourage women to pay more by pulling into the Full Service islands. In a 1987 commercial, a teenage girl, with a day-old license, attempted to pump gas for the first time and the male attendant helped her by flipping up the mechanism to start the gas flowing: "That was easy" she declared, her youthful innocence allowing her to stand in for women's uncertainty.[38]

The expectation that women fundamentally did not know how to fuel their own cars never dissipated. Audi created a commercial for its 2014 TDI that had an upper-class white woman readying her car to be fueled . . . with diesel. Men (as well as other women and children) found themselves transfixed and horrified by her actions and male police officers, bystanders, and a station clerk all tried in vain to stop her. But the joke was on them . . . she was right. Her expensive car *was* fueled by diesel. An appreciative critic in *Car and Driver* believed the advertisers should have stopped there, and could not understand why an upper-class white man appeared at the very end of the commercial to give her a knowing look, as he too filled up his Audi with diesel. The advertisers could not make a commercial premised on women not knowing how to fuel their car and having a dozen men all think she was wrong, only to then have her be right. That would have upended gender expectations. They needed male authority to affirm that the female driver was right, to put things back in order.[39]

Companies hoped that, in addition to fueling their cars, women could be enticed to buy their products by serving as a source of guidance by providing maps, directions, and suggestions for local food and shelter options. By the 1940s, particularly with large numbers of men off at war, companies recognized that women made up an increasingly important consumer market and began to target them with travel information. Shell stood out for its efforts to reach female drivers. It first did so in 1944 with an "Alice in Wonderland" brochure. With a woman waving her handkerchief as she stood by her car watching a uniformed man walk away, the introductory text read, "We hope this little booklet will be helpful to the women who now have a new responsibility—the care of the family car." By 1961, industry analysts estimated that women accounted for half of all gas-station sales and believed that they prioritized service, convenience, and brand name in selecting their stations.[40]

Already by 1949, Shell's brochure for women "Travel a la Car" reflected a shifting understanding of the female market. Instead of detailing the ins and outs of how cars functioned and how best to care for them, the focus fell to travel. Written by their newly developed "Carol Lane" personality, Shell offered to help women shoulder what was apparently their responsibility, to plan their family's travels. They offered the use of Shell's service stations, maps, and touring service, which would help plan routes, send along hunting and fishing laws, and anticipate construction. Carol Lane promoted these services (and more) in an orchestrated media blitz, extending from speaking engagements at women's clubs to radio appearances, as well as placement in newspapers and magazines. Encouraging vacationing invariably meant encouraging car travel and a boon to gas stations across the country. The company estimated that women planned 80 percent of all trips and made decisions about where to stop. A subsequent brochure directed to Shell station managers asked bluntly, "Are Women Necessary?" by which they meant, should stations strive to value them as consumers? Carol Lane's resounding answer was "Yes, because women mean business . . . business for the Shell dealer." Courteous treatment and clean restrooms would go a long way in building customer loyalty. The company may not have taken women seriously as being car savvy, undermining the suggestion that mechanics clearly explain the work to be done by making the snide comment, "Women just like to think they understand," but the company did appear to value her as a consumer.[41]

Fairly consistently, the ads played upon the same trope seen elsewhere in the discourse, that men will not ask for directions but women will. One postwar Rand McNally map ad used a *New Yorker*–style cartoon, with a woman pulling up to a station attendant and declaring, "I want some water, some air, my windshield wiped, and a road map." Just as they believed women could more easily ask for assistance in car care, so too did gas stations see asking for directions as falling under her purview. A 1970 commercial featured a man who claimed the "pioneering spirit" would not allow him to stop and ask for directions. He complained to his wife, who suggested they stop at a Union 76 station, that she was giving up too easily and barked, "Confound it woman, I'm not stopping if I don't need gas." Having him nearly run out of gas and being forced to stop for gas, and thus directions, let Union 76 assure customers, by portraying the castigation of his wife as humorous, that they could meet the needs of all drivers.[42]

From at least the 1920s on, gas stations also strategized that they could lure in women with special attention, including promotional giveaways. A Wisconsin station gave away "free bouquets of fresh flowers with every five gallons of gas purchased on holidays." Station operators also discovered that they had, sitting in their cars, a captive audience for sales pitches, and began to promote household products. One of the earliest companies to sell to women at the pump may have been the Phillips gas company, which sold its furniture polish, glass cleaner, and insect spray in the 1930s. Those who followed did not limit themselves to gas or oil-based products; across the rest of the century, they promoted everything from knives and key fobs to silverplate serving pieces and car vacuums. Moreover, companies did not limit themselves to outdoor sales but also invited women into the station to consider the purchase of household appliances. Although gendered appeals faded in intensity, there was a long history of gas stations shaping women's driving experience. Pleasing and attracting women was central to their marketing strategies.[43]

"A Comfy Little Cocoon, but . . . at Risk"

A great deal of the mystique of driving a car rests on its transformative power. A car can literally and figuratively whisk people away, offering freedom and self-actualization to those adventurous enough to take the wheel. Less glamorous, but ever present for women, however, were the risks of driving. While both men and women were susceptible to breakdowns and accidents, advertisers and commentators seldom emphasized men's fears. Only for women did they emphasize a pronounced vulnerability as both drivers and passengers throughout the century.

Lost in the midst of celebrations of America's consumer identity in mall parking lots, urban ingenuity in parking garages, and cross-country adventures on the nation's highways were the constant cautions women received about the car's freedom. Into the twenty-first century, the expectation that women stay close to home shaped women's experiences as drivers. Advertising and articles in women's magazines, as well as the broader culture, persisted in both creating and responding to a belief that women should be hyperconscious about their travel patterns.[44]

The largest, most significant automobile club in the United States, the American Automobile Association (AAA), founded in 1902, played an important role in tying together women and vulnerability in their business model. While AAA's earlier efforts tended to be geared toward affirming and ensuring the ability of motorists to motor, supporting legislation for building highways, raising speed limits, and facilitating other measures across the country, as well as linking consumers to the goods and services they would need along the way, in the second half of the century, AAA began to solidify its role as drivers' preeminent safety net. The AAA archives reveal countless ads for its roadside assistance programs, most of which featured images of stranded women. Its journalistic stories touted the importance of men rescuing women drivers.[45]

One of AAA's early ads captured the themes to follow. A slim, young woman, shapely legs in full view, hailed a AAA Highway Patrol Service truck. The text of the 1933 ad that appeared in the *AAA Travel* magazine did not mention gender, assuring all that "When Your Car Won't Go AAA Service Will Go." While AAA ironed out whether to be called "triple A" or "The Three A" and built its clubs locally to create a national network, it consistently asserted visually that women needed help. One 1949 article even featured a woman dismayed, hands to face, as the AAA serviceman held out a small mouse. While it was an unlikely cause of her car trouble, it aptly captured the spirit of women's dismay and the chivalry of the AAA servicemen. Occasionally, ads featured the woman with a man and sometimes with her young children, but invariably the AAA ads showcased a younger woman, a "damsel in distress," frequently shown standing beside her car, revealing her legs below the knee. Only in the 1970s, did photographs and drawings in AAA materials feature women sitting in their cars. In the 1990s, the drivers appear to have gotten a little older, and one 1992 ad presented the woman as a businessperson, with formal dress and what appeared to be a Cadillac, but the focus on women in need persisted in the AAA ads.[46]

AAA was in a bind because although it used fear to encourage motorists to anticipate their needs and to engage AAA's services, AAA also needed women to be confident and want to travel. In the long-standing "Mademoiselle Motorist" column in its *American Motorist* magazine, AAA addressed the potential for a breakdown. Writing in 1958, the columnist opined, "American women today travel the highways alone with little concern for this relatively new freedom of mobility and independence, which the automobile and changed times have brought to them." In the case of a breakdown, women were counseled, "raise the hood . . . this is a recognized sign of trouble. . . . If your breakdown occurs at night, you may prefer to wait for a man who has a woman with him. . . . On the whole you should not be too suspicious; people who will stop for a woman in distress are generally sincere in wishing to offer assistance." In spite of some optimism, articles continued to promote the belief that women could not cope with even the most minor emergency, including a flat tire, and, by 1968, "Mademoiselle Motorist" warned women, "The flash of a diamond could be the trigger to trouble" and "You're most vulnerable when locking and unlocking the car."[47]

As telephone booths became more common, increasing numbers of ads showed women calling from them. In 1982, AAA launched its 1–800 "supernumber," so patrons across the country could call one number, wherever they were, and get help twenty-four hours a day. Promoting potential problems to sell goods and services, AAA kept scared women in their sights.[48]

Automobile and parts manufacturers also demonstrated a predilection for advertising that featured their products as the solution to problems they wanted women to anticipate. As AAA learned, being able to communicate was key. The first inklings of the mobile telephone appeared in 1910 in the *Ford Times.* Promoted by its inventor, C. Burr Forrest, the Auto Phone was a telephone set that could be attached to the dash of the car, and it enabled the driver to connect to any telephone wires "without even the necessity of leaving the car seat." While it would take many more decades for manufacturers to realize Forrest's car-phone vision, its perseverance clearly reflected a population keen to embrace these new technologies together.[49]

As early as 1966, the National car rental company advertised its cars as phone equipped, but it was really in the 1980s that advertisers truly began sustained campaigns to sell the public on portable communication. The products, advertised as solutions to emergencies and safety concerns, tended to include women and children with broken-down cars, as well as female senior citizens. These items included two-way radios and "SOS Phones," which did not feature number key pads but promoted their simple, reliable access to help.[50]

The target audience for the earliest phones, however, was male, particularly wealthy, white businessmen and men in trades. This paralleled the earliest target audience for cars, as well. Print and television ads featured men closing deals they would have missed if they had not had a phone in the car. While most of its conquests were financial, Centel's first television ad featured a handsome, successful businessman racing to relax with his attractive wife. Hyping both the phone's efficiency and its cachet for men, advertisers did not take the lead in promoting the phone as a business, homemaking, or safety tool for women. Occasionally, car phones and cell phones started to work their way into articles about women's safety, as with a 1991 *Texas Monthly* article that suggested calling the police on a cellular phone if a woman feared she was being followed. The threatening photos of women appearing vulnerable, waiting beside a broken-down car did exist for a host of products, including emergency-only phones, but in spite of evidence that consumers wanted cell phones for emergencies, advertisers consistently avoided that appeal.[51]

In contrast to the emergency car-phone companies, tire companies hewed to the traditional approach. Their ads proved to be some of the most threatening. While a car's malfunction might inconvenience men, the same problem jeopardized women's safety. A 1964 Goodyear ad made the specific, assertive claim, "When there's no man around . . . Goodyear should be." Another ad in the series featured a woman in heels, dress, pillbox hat, and white gloves just staring down at the flat tire in dismay. The copy made it clear. "She's stranded. Helpless." Even in an ad showcasing a woman changing a tire, the ads cautioned men, "You can't be with her every time she drives. So protect her with the safest tires ever built." Sometimes the campaign claimed that having Goodyear tires was "almost as good as having a man around." Ads even teased that using a Goodyear tire was actually more critical, as with one 1966 ad that told men, "It's almost as good as having you with her when she drives. Maybe better."[52]

The fundamental argument they made throughout the campaign was that men should ensure that women did not have to change a tire. Being broken down by the side of the road left women vulnerable not only to jeopardizing their femininity and class standing but also to sexual assault. A 1964 Studebaker driver's guide for women, "Going Steady with Studie," written by a woman who touted that "she has never changed a tire in her life" encouraged women to be more feminine in the case of a flat tire. She

When there's no man around... Goodyear should be.
She's stranded. Helpless.
A flat tire and no one in sight to change it.
But with the LifeGuard Safety Spare she won't have to change a tire.
Because the LifeGuard is not just a shield or tube, but a fully-inflated tire, with tread, cord and bead. Designed to keep her going even with a flat, puncture... or blowout.
The secret is two tires. One inside the other. The outside tire is the Double Eagle. It's made with exclusive Vytacord polyester ...the "dream cord" that's strong as nylon and smooth-riding as rayon...yet makes a cooler-running tire than both.
And like all Goodyear auto tires, the Double Eagle is made with Tufsyn rubber, that's 25% more durable.
In fact, the Double Eagle is the toughest, longest-wearing tire you can buy.
Add the optional LifeGuard Safety Spare and it becomes the safest tire in the world.
Chances are the Double Eagle will never let her down. But if it should, the LifeGuard Safety Spare takes over.
She won't have to stop to change tires... even with a blowout. It's almost as good as having a man around.

GO GO GOODYEAR
More People Ride On Goodyear Tires Than On Any Other Kind

FIGURE 17. In the late 1960s, Goodyear continually undermined men's and women's confidence in women's competence and threatened real danger for women with each flat tire, unless they had a man around or, better yet, Goodyear tires. This 1964 ad emphasized women's vulnerability.

"archly advised women what do in case of a flat: 'Put on some fresh lipstick, fluff up your hairdo . . . look helpless and feminine.' "[53]

Sometimes advertisers abandoned humor and allusion and introduced explicitly unsettling ads that featured women alone and forlorn. With the same taglines and similar copy, it is the women's uncertain look and isolation in two 1964 ads that set them apart. Set against a backdrop of dark woods, one 1964 Goodyear ad featured a woman gripping her coat tightly around her and looking over her shoulder. Another showed a woman with her young daughter broken down by the side of the road. Dark woods also dominated the upper two-thirds of this ad, along with the flat tire, the off-balance woman, and the tagline: "When there's no man around . . ." In the light background below sat the new tire and the clinching argument, "Goodyear should be." The ads did not feature menacing figures or weeping women, but the imagery spoke powerfully to a culture in which public life held the risk of sexual assault for women.[54]

Businesses did little to make things safer for women; instead, they created car and automotive-part ads that relied on male authority and female vulnerability. A commercial for Goodyear Polyglas tires aired during Monday Night Football in 1970. With ominous music pulsing through a seemingly treacherous drive, a woman navigated driving to the airport, contending with nighttime driving, changing lanes, a detour sign, a crosswalk, and a stop sign. As she slid over to the passenger seat after picking up her husband and the music mellowed out, the narrator intoned, "When a woman's at the wheel, Polyglas means more than mileage." They set up women as incapable of handling even the most mundane driving maneuvers: a stop sign! The ad tried to tell viewers that men and women should always assume their gendered roles, but for those rare occasions when they cannot, Goodyear's tires would be there to help women.[55]

While advertisers more commonly centered their ads on women's fears, or men's fears for women, they did occasionally create ads with men's cars breaking down. One significant difference was that ads with men rarely suggested vulnerabilities. Even when ads had men break down, generally the men were shown fixing a flat with their wives accompanying them, holding the flashlight or assisting in other ways, as men handled what one 1961 B.F. Goodrich tire ad characterized as "the nerve-jangling job of changing a flat tire with cars whizzing past your back at 60 miles per hour" or "The irritating struggle with a slippery jack." While certainly promoting their product as a way to avoid these unpleasantries, these ads stand in sharp contrast to the expectation that women broken down would be "stranded," "helpless," and potentially in danger, rather than irritated or inconvenienced. Moreover, the number of service clubs like AAA and Mobil Gas Club that emerged after World War II, promised that men, particularly white, middle- and upper-class men, would no longer be expected to change tires. Instead of fear, those ads tended to use humor to defuse the potential for men's vulnerability.[56]

As early as 1981, *Vogue* magazine reported that the Chrysler Women's Committee considered "car breakdown at night as a special fear of the woman driver" and companies believed female consumers prioritized security, so they introduced the "*illuminated entry system*. The minute you lift the handle of the outside door the interior lights go on back and front, before you even unlock the door." Following the same thread, automakers also developed the keyless entry system, which meant no fumbling for a key when there was danger lurking.[57]

In the 1990s, companies like Cadillac and Ford spearheaded efforts to cater to women's fears with twenty-four-hour automotive assistance, promising that they would be there for women "on any road . . . at any hour" and that their help was just "a phone call away." A brand manager for Cadillac claimed in 1996, "While customers in general seem pretty happy to have all the doors unlock when they go into park, women would prefer to have all the doors stay locked until they're ready to get out of the car." Sometimes the appeal to vulnerability justified fundamentals like strong horsepower and responsive handling, as with a marketing manager for Ford who claimed in 2010 that women said they liked those elements "because they can help her get out of a dangerous situation quickly and easily."[58]

Although advertisements played a significant role in shaping popular attitudes, so did magazines and newspapers. Two cartoons in the *New Yorker* in 1965 reflected male anxiety about women taking to the road. One had a strong man carry a woman through her front door, cleavage and bare legs exposed, as she proclaimed to her older, less attractive husband, "My car broke down, dear, and this gentleman was kind enough to give me a lift." Another had a woman in her sporty convertible stopped at a gas station. The male attendant leaned over to ask, "Anything else, Ma'am? Check your oil? Test your battery? Rob? Cheat? Lie? Kill?" The culture suggested that women drivers' expansive vulnerability existed amid endless dangers.[59]

Analysts found the fears engendered by these cultural narratives spread fairly evenly among different aged women. In one late twentieth-century survey, nearly half of the women reported being concerned about their safety while driving; these concerns included carjacking, intentional bumping to rob or steal a car, and phony accidents, staged to get unsuspecting women to stop. While it may be unsurprising that three-quarters of them feared driving through a crime-ridden neighborhood, about half also reported concerns about walking back to and unlocking their cars laden with bags and packages. Having children in the car also increased how unsafe they felt driving alone. Women interviewed about their driving experiences in the early 1990s described fear about stopping for gas at a convenience store and running red lights at night if they were driving alone, remarking, "I"m not going to sit there by myself and wait."[60]

In 2003, *Road & Travel*, a magazine created to serve women's automotive and travel needs, premised a story about women driving long distances alone on the "dire predictions" made by the author's mother. One of the first places young women learned to limit their driving patterns appears to have been from their parents. A largely positive reflection, the author laid out the care she took to undertake the trek and the pride she felt in accomplishing it. Subsequent articles in the magazine, however, did not emphasize women's successes. Instead, articles, even by the founder of the magazine, made common reference to women as sitting ducks and men as predators, and it even made references to action-crime films like *Taken*, to terrorize women's thoughts about traveling alone. The magazine, created for women who liked to travel, consistently undermined women's freedom, talking down to them about "stranger danger" and falsely reporting that "more than 100,000 women and children go missing in the United States alone every year many of whom are never found. The majority of predators seek out women or children who are alone."[61]

The popular women's magazine *Cosmopolitan* also ran sensationalized columns. The former head of New York City's Sex Crimes Unit, Assistant District Attorney Linda Fairstein, made the unsubstantiated argument in her "Need to Know" columns, as well as her brief booklets, that "thousands of women are attacked each year while in or near their cars: on long-distance trips, while stopping for gas or walking to or from a parking spot, or when their cars break down." Her 2010 article featured an allegedly true story about a cross-country trek that ended in the rape and murder of a young woman. She cautioned, "It feels great to head out on a long trip on your own, but it can also be risky." Even though she had two dogs with her and kept in phone contact, according to Fairstein, the motorist who stopped overnight at a rest stop brought on her death. Fairstein concluded her article with the following counsel: "Have roadside assistance available, and most important, never sleep in your car or take a break in any place that seems isolated. Avoid driving at night, splurge on a safe place to stay, and do all your shopping and gassing up in daylight." One appeal of driving long distances is its relatively low cost and the pleasure of covering a lot of territory. Arguing that women should only drive by daylight and spend excessive money for full service stations so that "you can stay in your car with the doors locked" and for all sleep breaks, and then compounding that advice with an expectation that women could not stop any place isolated, severely limited women's mobility.[62]

It was not just magazines targeted at women, though; the discourse consistently suggested that women really were not free. Popular travel guides counseled women drivers specifically. A 2001 guide to driving in Boston warned, "Single women should be especially careful driving in unfamiliar territory, day or night." *The Rough Guide to Florida* advised in 2012, "Raising the hood of your car is recognized as a call for assistance, though women traveling alone should, obviously, be wary of doing this." From sheriff's websites in Georgia to police department websites in Texas, advice from law-enforcement authorities about how women drivers could protect themselves proliferated.[63]

Fairstein argued that cars themselves and parking lots and garages were some of the most vulnerable locations for women. For her literary hook, she used a standard caution, a tale of horror, and then a concluding word of caution to emphasize that those women in their cars and walking to their cars were some of the most likely to get raped. Popular culture, too, placed sexual assault storylines in parking garages. A 1989 episode of the television show *Designing Women* used threats of sexual violence as the plot that drove the starring women to take self-defense classes and featured an incident in which a man followed the lead character, Mary Jo, into a parking garage. While that scenario ultimately served to showcase women's empowerment, the brutal rape of the Dr. Melfi character on the *Sopranos* in 2001 further underscored the terrors parking garages held.[64]

The evidence for parking garages as a site of violence for women does suggest it was not just imagined as a "dark, desolate, Stephen King designed" setting. Loath to see their industry as culpable, the parking industry published articles decrying their abusive portrayal in popular entertainment and sponsored a celebratory exhibition on the "House of Cars." The exhibit's heart-racing video montage of parking-garage chases and shootouts contained no suggestion of the sexual violence and fear that the garages portended for many women.[65]

Industry analysts confronted the fact that while exact figures on crimes committed in parking garages were not kept, they were sites of crime and fear. It is unclear, however, when garages assumed this identity. The first public parking garage in the United States was established in 1899, with the structure and function evolving across the century. Critical to its association with crime may have been the ability to reach skyward with them in the 1920s, as with the Hotel LaSalle parking garage in Chicago and the midcentury ability to dig underground; elevators and stairwells rose higher and dove deeper, offering more remote, isolated spaces. By the 1990s, the evidence revealed a close association between parking structures and crime. According to the U.S. Department of Justice, for those reporting rapes in 1993, 7.3 percent of victims indicated that the crime took place in a parking garage. Another study found that "of more than 1,000 premises lawsuits between 1992 and 2001 . . . in almost one-third of all cases reviewed, the basis for the lawsuit was a murder, rape, robbery or assault that occurred in a parking lot or garage." Even more sobering was the 2008 assertion by industry analyst Randy Atlas that "as many as 40% of rapes and assaults take place in parking lots." While these rates were likely exaggerated, particularly given the general reduction of violent crime nationally starting in the mid-1990s, a history of sexual assault informed a continued fear of parking lots. A 2012 article in the industry journal *Parking Today* critically explored "Why Women Fear the Parking Structure," and affirmed, "If you are a woman and you are alone and you are in a parking garage, you are afraid."[66]

The question of liability for these crimes was especially important to shopping centers and large hotel chains. In 1984, *New York* magazine noted that women had grown to comprise 30 percent of all business travelers and one of the responses from some hotels was to offer escorts in the parking garages on request. Nearly ten years later, a brief article in *Black Enterprise* found that the percentage of women business travelers had grown to nearly 40 percent and reported that hotels continued to focus on security, including better lighting in parking garages. A 2006 rape in the Stamford, Connecticut, Marriott hotel garage garnered the most significant attention on the point of accountability when the victim sued the hotel for failing to act when her assailant "had been in the hotel and garage acting suspiciously days before the attack, as well as the afternoon of the attack, and the hotel failed to notice him, apprehend him or make him leave." Instead of striving for better security and improving its accountability to female motorists, the Marriott chain countered that the woman, raped in the garage in front of her two young children, had "failed to exercise due care for her own safety and the safety of her children and proper use of her senses and facilities." Although Marriott eventually dropped its claim against the rape victim, Marriott's approach reflects a national, historical trend of companies maximizing profits from parking garages (and the consumers they ferry in) by refusing to invest in security or structural improvements for safety.[67]

Police Predators

The very forces that could have served to ensure women's personal safety in their cars played an active role in undermining women's freedom in society. In addition to fear of strangers, women learned to be wary of police officers as well. While newspaper and television reports recounted incidents of men posing as police officers to prey on unsuspecting female motorists, they also revealed a criminal pattern of police officers, including those on duty, abusing their power, sexually harassing and assaulting women across the country.[68]

Researchers began to question publicly police authority by investigating the practice termed police sexual violence (PSV) in the late twentieth and early twenty-first centuries. Police had a long history of misbehavior, however. As early as 1978, industry analyst Tom Barker characterized the police car as a "'traveling bedroom' because of the amount of sleeping and sex which takes place in the car." His study of police officers in one town found that nearly 32 percent of the forty-five officers questioned believed that their fellow officers had sex while on duty ("commonly referred to as under the color of law"), but they did not indicate whether the respondents understood the sex to be consensual, coerced, or forced.[69]

In seeking to understand the depth and breadth of the police sexual violence problem, researchers developed definitions of behavior that enabled them to analyze their findings more effectively. It is helpful to consider the definition established by researchers Peter Kraska and Victor Kappeler, naming it as "those situations in which a female citizen experiences a sexually degrading, humiliating, violating, damaging, or threatening act committed by a police officer through the use of force or police authority." In their analysis, Kraska and Kappeler categorized unobtrusive behaviors (invasions of privacy), obtrusive behaviors (body cavity searches, quid pro quo exchanges for sex), and criminal behavior (harassment, assault) that they discovered police officers committing. With access to women's personal information, officers also had the ability to stalk women. They called it "bimbo hunting." For example, in one 1988 account, officers waited in their cruisers outside of bars, and then ran the tag numbers for cars driven by women they targeted. When this practice was revealed, one observer claimed, "I don't think it's a flagrant occurrence," but the ability to run tags is a quiet, discreet process, and it is only exposed by an individual requesting to know if their tags have been run.[70]

One of the most effective ways researchers demonstrated that police sexual violence occurred was through analysis of media accounts. These reports generally described behavior ranging from lewd or suggestive

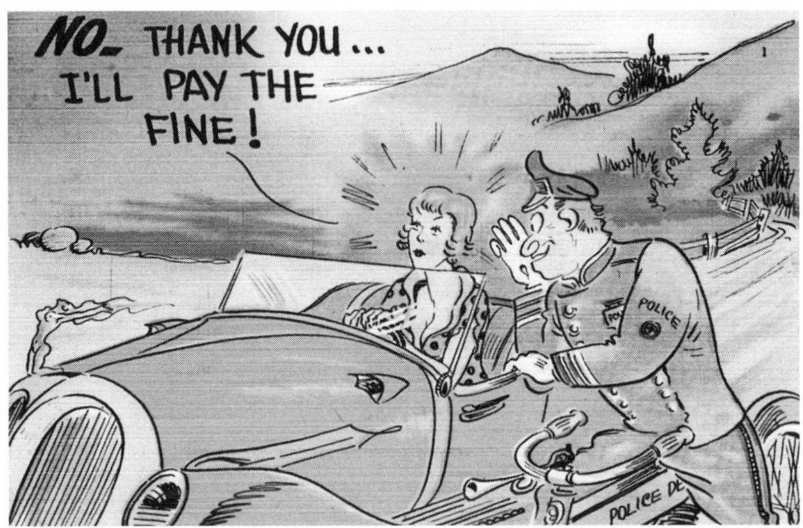

Figure 18. Analysts have found police sexual violence to be a pervasive national problem, but most police departments have abdicated their responsibility to create policies, train officers, or serve real, significant consequences to the thousands of officers committing these crimes against women. This undated (circa 1940s) postcard captures the desire of men in power to control women drivers; this series placed the police officers on motorcycles, which perhaps informed a resentment of women drivers. The artist also created a graphic, sexually free hood ornament to anthropomorphize the car as a woman.

comments, to demanding or forcibly disrobing, to sexual touching and groping, to outright sexual assault, including rape. These accounts revealed this to be a national problem for female motorists, from large cities like Chicago and Los Angeles to smaller towns and cities like Avon, New Jersey, and Gatlinburg, Tennessee. While certain states and departments occasionally seemed to register larger number of offenses, none seemed immune to the criminal behavior and most departments appeared to be complicit or flat-footed in response.[71]

A 2002 study analyzed 501 newspaper accounts of PSV between 1989 and 1997 and determined that of those that reported on the "victim's last activity before the police encounter, 40.5 percent (n = 83) of victims were either operating or the passenger in a motor vehicle immediately before encountering the offender." The types of locations for these encounters included traffic stops, and 59 percent of the victims reported that the initial meeting took place in "isolated or secluded areas." The authors of the study, Danielle McGurrin and Victor Kappeler, concluded that of the police charged with committing their sexual crime on duty, "36 percent (n = 72) assaulted victims inside their police vehicle. This is of particular importance when one considers that the police vehicle is the quintessetial personification of law enforcement. A woman who is assaulted in a police vehicle is not only being victimized physically and emotionally but also cognitively via the violent collision between police as protector and perpetrator." It is unclear how often officers got away with their misconduct toward women. The police harassment and assaults left women subject to the unwanted sexual advances by the police officers and then forced to report the misconduct to the same organizational, institutional structure that prioritized loyalty to each other, rather than a commitment to justice for its community's citizens.[72]

The most significant study of police misconduct toward women drivers concluded in 2002 that female motorists' vulnerability to police officers was comparable to that of African Americans. The police targeted women as easy marks, and cultural and institutional forces encouraged stereotyping of drivers and justified and protected the officers' outrageous, criminal behavior. Arguing that "Driving While Female" (DWF) was a parallel experience to "Driving While Black" (DWB), researchers Samuel Walker and Dawn Irlbeck contended that in both instances police stopped drivers based on their identity. They asserted that "officers engaged in racial profiling are usually acting in accord with department crime-fighting policies, while officers targeting female drivers represent the classic 'rogue' officers who are violating the law and department policy." Moreover, they maintained that a major reason for the "DWF problem is the failure of police departments to investigate allegations that come to their attention."[73]

Walker and Irlbeck followed up their scathing indictment the following year with an analysis of police sexual violence toward teenage girls, reflecting their findings that younger female drivers and passengers were especially vulnerable. In their earlier, broader research on female motorists they discovered that in addition to targeting girls with "their traffic enforcement powers," there was a clear, significant pattern of targeting girls, especially in "police department-sponsored Explorer programs designed to give teens an understanding of police work." Getting teenaged girls into their patrol cars provided police officers the opportunity to harass and assault them. With lackadaisical or completely absent policies and no oversight, these departments and programs allowed rogue officers extraordinary freedoms to commit their crimes. In a 1987 interview regarding the program in Ventura County, California, one Explorer executive provided insight into his organization's approach to such incidents. "This rarely happens, so we have no guidelines," he told the *Los Angeles Times*. "We can't have a policy that people will not meet and talk with each other when they are not in an Explorer activity. We can't stop people from being people." Ignoring the consistent use of automobiles by police officers for sexual coercion enabled further abuse to occur, particularly to young women.[74]

Reaching well beyond "pat downs" to determine if an individual had a weapon or contraband, twenty-first-century policies and unsanctioned practices of strip and body-cavity searches made female motorists vulnerable, including humiliating, public disrobing and vaginal probing by men and women alike. According to Kraska and Kappeler, "Human rights literature recognizes the police abuse of strip and body-cavity searches as a serious and prevalent form" of police sexual violence. In spite of a growing professional preference that anything lodged in the vagina be removed by a medical professional, offending officers seemingly relished the opportunity for state-sanctioned violence. And they did so in stark violation of the law. In one study of the federal litigation of police sexual violence cases, these searches made up nearly three-quarters of the cases—and the police lost nearly 70 percent of them.[75]

Seeking to better understand the significance of recidivism for those committing police sexual violence, researchers determined that "opportunity, power, authority, and isolation increases the likelihood of police sexual offending." More than thirty years after Barker's study, scholars continue to estimate "that more than 35% of all police engage in some form of sexual misconduct." A large number of the studies and those bringing scrutiny continue to rely on media accounts of charges and convictions for these crimes, instead of having access to a more complete data sample that might yield a greater understanding of the crimes and the criminals.[76]

Departments occasionally monitored the general behavior and performance of their officers in their cars. The first and most basic method used was an alignment of the clock with the odometer. Knowing where an officer was and for how long sometimes enabled their department to either refute or substantiate claims of wrongdoing by accusers. Departments also sometimes implemented stings or quality-control checks with officers suspected of wrongdoing. Finally, an element increasingly critical to monitoring behavior was the use of cameras—either footage shot by bystanders, security cameras on buildings, or, even more constantly, the camera mounted in the patrol car. While the cameras have captured misconduct outside the car, new technology could enable departments to require that officers also train the camera in the car so that female motorists could be better assured of their civil rights in the back seat of a police cruiser. The reality of the technology, however, was that it was frequently inoperable, freeing officers from scrutiny.[77]

Citizen advocates, including trainers who seek to reduce police misconduct, advocated in the twenty-first century that female motorists assert the right to not be isolated with a police officer. Suggestions ranged from using their cell phones to get a dispatcher on the line to indicating that they were complying with a request to pull over by driving to a better-lit and observable location—such as a gas station or even a police station. These strategies are also vulnerable to location, with poor cellular service or proximate, well-lit locations not necessarily available. While advocates, including law-enforcement officers who gave this advice to female family members and friends, maintained this should assuage women's fears, women's delayed responsiveness and challenge to authority invariably angered police, who not only already faced more dangerous nighttime stops but also were accustomed to the ability to control citizen behavior at will. A 2008 Missouri case involving Vanessa Kimery is illustrative of the myriad of issues. After seeing police lights on an unmarked police car come on as she was driving, Kimery put on her flashers and drove less than a mile to a nearby gas station where she was handcuffed and charged with resisting arrest. While the sheriff's department later dropped the charges, acknowledging, "We all have wives and daughters, and understand the heightened concerns people have when they travel at night," the contradiction between the advice given to female motorists and the policies governing traffic stops remained unresolved.[78]

Nor was it enough to offer defensive posturing to female motorists as a reasonable response to police criminal behavior. While the number of accounts reported in the news remained steady and constant, most departments appear to have abdicated their responsibility to both create policies and train their officers—by clearly delineating what the criminal behavior was and serving up real, significant consequences. Few districts across the nation enacted explicit sexual misconduct policies and whatever paltry training they offered generally was not supported with policies that had teeth. Periodically, individuals, organizations, or states did make headway in even acknowledging that a problem existed. Still, while citizen groups and police associations focused on criticisms of racial profiling and police brutality, few considered police sexual violence.[79]

Flying under the radar, officers exploited their power. Researchers for the 1997 ABC news program *20/20* used the Freedom of Information Act to request records for over a thousand police officers and "discovered cases of officers hired with criminal records, officers who were recidivist rapists, and officers who received 'a slap on the wrist' for brutal assaults." Officers who left a department rather than face criminal charges and even those who were fired found employment again, receiving recommendations "by the very department that forced their dismissal or resignation." In analyzing PSV offenders, a 2002 study contended that the problem was pervasive, stretching from the lowest ranking patrol officer to the police chiefs themselves, from newbies to those with extensive service in law enforcement.[80]

Several social, institutional, and legal variables allowed offending police officers to avoid prosecution. Police frequently targeted vulnerable women, including those who stood accused by the officer of some misdeed (drunk driving, speeding, driving without a license, etc.). In part, the ability to coerce sexual behavior from women rested on the women's desire to escape drawing attention to a real or perceived misdeed. In a 2008 review, a class of police trainees in Maryland "was engaged in a competition to get photos of women's breasts in exchange for not writing traffic tickets," but no complaints of police sexual violence had been filed with the U.S. Department of Justice Civil Rights Division. A 2016 verdict sent Daniel Holtzclaw, an Oklahoma City police officer, to prison for life after his case revealed that he preyed on African American female motorists, aged seventeen through fifty-seven.[81]

One important way women found justice was by seeking help in the courts. Bringing lawsuits effectively shined a light on a closed system. The financial costs also could potentially serve as a wake-up call for police departments that might otherwise have condoned or ignored misconduct by the officers on its force. In particular, the relative freedom from supervision that patrol officers enjoyed seemed to enable greater sexual misconduct. Lawsuits sought to litigate not just individual behavior but also broader institutional accountability.[82]

Still, in spite of lawsuits bringing both scrutiny and financial reckoning, most agencies lacked formal policies concerning sexual misconduct, they lacked effective training on delineating what sexual misconduct was and how to avoid doing it, and they lacked effective reporting opportunities for citizens who wished to bring forward complaints against officers. Fundamentally, this absence of concern is cyclical. With few studies done to evaluate the problem, it was difficult to substantiate the need for the policies, but if the agencies had implemented policies, training, and reporting procedures, it would have better determined the extent of the problem. Instead, the police nationally benefited from a complacent population willing to allow officers to sexually harass and assault female motorists, with only a rare handful of women bringing charges and seeking justice to effect change.[83]

Conclusion

The public response to women behind the wheel has always been skepticism. The sharpest critics fervently wished they could keep women off the roads and occasionally proposed bans on women drivers. Many found they could fuel anti-women sentiments by looking to the past. Starting in the 1930s and persisting into the 1970s, newspapers reported that in ancient times, the Romans rescinded women's right to drive chariots because women were poor drivers.[84]

A fuller history lesson reveals not only the absurdity of the modern claims but also the passions the right to drive elicited historically. When their government denied Roman women the right to drive, they protested in the streets. The historian Ovid claimed that the Roman women were incensed that men's driving privileges had already been reinstated, while theirs remained forbidden. "Angered by the loss of their carriages," he told the tale, "the Roman women retaliate by aborting their own babies." Historian Steven Green argues that Ovid uses this telling to capture how, as in Aristophanes' comedy *Lysistrata* "a similarly united female front uses its powers to force change." To this, it is also clear that women in ancient Rome well understood the power inherent in the ability to drive a chariot. Indeed, mobility (and status) was of such great importance in the lives of these women that they denied their husbands sex and refused to procreate in order to secure it.[85]

Still, the modern American obsession with proclaiming women to be poor drivers in these historical newspaper accounts motivated only the most distilled story: Rome had figured out the problem with driving and landed on the solution thousands of years ago—take women off the road. Although men lacked the patriarchal authority to ban women from driving, the popular culture was replete with humor, critiques, and fear that effectively served to deny women pride and freedom in their driving. Economic motivations inspired some efforts to cater to women by gas stations and roadside assistance programs, but many individuals and companies who yielded no economic gain seemed content to criticize women and accept their vulnerability to sexual predators. Perhaps the only area in which they were more critical of women came in efforts to maintain the car, the subject of the next chapter.

4

Caring for a Car

AUTOMOBILES NEED REGULAR MAINTENANCE and repair to stay operational, but historically car care guidance reflected traditional gender roles for both women and men. Auto manuals illustrated the consistent societal conundrum: Women were not supposed to know or want to know anything about caring for their cars, while men were assumed to have innate car expertise, including knowing what was wrong and what it would cost to repair the problem. Although many asserted that women could learn to care for their cars, advice to women frequently devolved into domestic analogies. In particular, those offering to teach women car care assured them that it would not strip them of their femininity. As the number of women who assumed responsibility for their car's care grew, so did an expectation that their devoted attention arose from their propensity for nurturing. While the car might seem inanimate, those dispensing advice asserted that under a woman's careful watch, the car would be healthy, well fed, and carefully maintained.[1]

The earliest car care advice dispensed to women drivers, found in newspapers, magazines, pamphlets, and guidebooks, reproduced the belief that women needed gender-specific instruction. Although gender-neutral advice manuals existed for drivers throughout the century, the notion that women needed directed assistance persisted. The car's introduction saw a burst of attention to women and car care, with pictographic stories directed at women.[2]

Chapter 4

Guidebooks for Women

As the number of women driving grew, publishers produced numerous books advising women about caring for their car. Female authors overwhelmingly wrote car-care guidebooks for women and did so within a framework of traditional gender roles. In the midst of the first and second waves of women's political activism, many authors made assertions of women's competence and arguments for women's empowerment. Authors advocated learning masculine technology but regularly tempered the messages with reassurances that women's increased technical abilities would not jeopardize their femininity.

Initially, automotive handbooks were rare. The first one written by a woman appeared in 1909 when Dorothy Levitt of England published *The Woman and the Car*. She offered women detailed instructions, including what clothing and accessories they would need, accompanied by pictures of women servicing their cars. The subtitle of her book, *A Chatty Little Handbook for All Women Who Motor or Who Want to Motor*, reflected not only its tone but also its openness. Cars were still evolving out of an intense period of competition and inventiveness, and Levitt underscored the necessity for women to understand and operate their vehicles. Her instruction that the reader would need to have an apron-like overall and "antioyl" soap to protect her clothes from grease makes clear that she expected women to be intimately acquainted with the car's mechanisms. She scoffed at the question asked of her, "Do you really understand all the horrid machinery of a motor, and could you mend it if it broke down?" by assuring the reader, "It really is not a very difficult matter. The details of the engine may sound complicated and may look 'horrid,' but an engine is easily mastered." She encouraged women to have the confidence that they could repair a car, and she assured them that car ownership was a worthwhile endeavor.[3]

Levitt acknowledged that women might have chauffeurs, as she was writing at a time when those who could afford a car tended to be wealthy, and conceded that she was advising women on the single-cylinder car. However, she maintained that women could undertake every aspect of caring for the car, from changing the oil to testing the brakes. Moreover, she asserted, "there is many a one whose keen eyes can detect, and whose deft fingers can remedy, a loose nut or a faulty electrical connection in half the time that the professional chauffeur would spend upon the work." Levitt couched her advice in both the class and gender constructions of the period. Whether women who sought to travel by car to extend their "civic housework" or women who claimed broadened freedoms behind the wheel with their bobbed hair and shortened dresses, the "New Woman" of the time was challenging the historically constricting roles. As they did with higher education and professions, cars could have been a way that women asserted their rights of ownership to public life.[4]

Thirty years later, in 1939, Priscilla Hovey Wright captured the spirit of her automotive advice by titling her chapter on car care, "The Right Service Station." Instead of offering advice on "how to," she asserted that "women should never attempt any repair work themselves, and, indeed, they seem to know instinctively that the inner workings of an automobile haven't the cosy intimacy about them that those of a vacuum cleaner or a waffle iron have." Wright cautioned against being knowledgeable, suggesting that women secure car care by "smiling graciously" and using words like "thingamajig."[5] Wright relied on humor to defuse the evident social tension inherent in women's responsibility for automobiles.

Wright was an exception, though, as earnest guidebooks proliferated. Although they featured young, attractive women behind the wheel or peering under the hood, their focus, harkening back to Levitt, was on women's automotive acumen. While some were hardbound books, most appeared in the cheaper, more accessible paperback version, and several took on the squatter, sideways format, to accommodate larger diagrams and photos, and to fit in the glove compartment. The women dispensing advice to other women asserted their expertise as former race-car drivers, auto mechanics, and professional writers.

Most authors tried to establish their credibility and motivation for the reader. Some women proudly attributed their automotive authority to the capable women in their lives. In 1966, for example, author Denise McCluggage thanked "the woman driver who can get the biggest car in and out of the smallest garage with the least trouble—my mother." Others who traced their knowledge as emanating from men in their lives positioned themselves as a capable guide, rather than asserting their expertise

Leslie's

Illustrated Weekly Newspaper

Jan 6th 1916 *Established in 1855* *Price 10 Cents*

KNOWLEDGE IS POWER

Figure 19. Women drivers appeared as stylish and competent on the covers of magazines in the early twentieth century. The caption for this 1916 cover depicting a woman fixing her car captured the early sentiment, later reclaimed in the second-wave women's movement, that "Knowledge Is Power."

as innate. These female authors asserted not just automotive knowledge but also contended that they were effectively translating from the male world to the female one.[6]

Many guidebooks took care to assure readers that an interest in cars did not erase their femininity. A 1974 book, *A Woman and Her Car*, announced about the author on its back cover, "Patty De Roulf has emerged as the Julia Child of automotive repair," suggesting that women could command both the kitchen and the garage. The language used to describe automotive care frequently drew on women's roles as caregivers. In fact, several books asserted that car care needed a woman's touch, including McCluggage's chapter titled "The Care and Feeding of your Car." An attractive photo of Ren Volpe posed over the engine with a prominent wedding ring assured women of her femininity, as did the title of her 1998 book: *The Lady Mechanic's Total Car Care for the Clueless*. She promised women that they would not forfeit being a lady if they attended to their car. In 2007, Courtney Hansen, named one of the one hundred sexiest women in the world, filled her book, *The Garage Girl's Guide to Everything You Need to Know About Your Car,* with photos of herself, creating the impression that changing filters and tooling under the hood could also make women sexy. In spite of the assertion by the women's movement that women could do it all, the social pressure persisted in qualifying women's dreams with exacting standards of appearance and behavior.[7]

Many authors, like Carmel Berman Reingold in 1973, made clear connections to domestic acumen to empower women. She maintained, "Well, the helpless type is just not in style today. Besides, if you can decipher a Julia Child recipe (and they're really complicated), do an intricate petit point, or sew a dress, you can learn what makes a car run." The emergence of the women's movement had Dorothy Jackson optimistically asserting in 1974, "With male chauvinism dying hard and women's liberation flourishing," it was high time women learned about the car. Still, the domestic analogies and the sense of the car as inherently male persisted. Lyn St. James, an acclaimed race-car driver, explained in 1984, "Men are frequently uncomfortable when setting foot in traditionally feminine territory—like the lingerie section of a department store—so there is

LIKE A MOTHER WITH A
BRAND NEW BABY

Figure 20. A page from a 1962 Studebaker Lark brochure conveyed some of the ways companies wanted women to see car care as just like attending to children. In this case, she's swaddled the car and is holding a bottle for it; the text assures women that breaking in a car is easier than changing a diaper.

nothing unusual about women not feeling comfortable in a auto repair shop."

Offering advice on how to contend with male mechanics on their turf, authors sought to fortify women with knowledge and confidence. Contending that garages operated in a world of their own, complete with language and etiquette, female authors tried to equip women with the correct language to help them avoid the constant threat of being deceived. Some, like Mary Jackson, who founded Women at the Wheel seminars in 1983, called the mechanics' language "garage-ese" and promised her readers that she would help them become more adept at understanding their car and in communicating with their mechanic. She approached the challenge by assuming that women were terrified and couched her advice in her own experiences of "vulnerability, frustration, and sense of powerlessness" in dealing with her car's maintenance.[8]

Most of the books embraced humor as a necessary element to ease women into the topic, using both the language and illustrations to convey information and levity. Particularly for books written in the 1960s and 1970s, the issue of the "woman driver" stereotype or identity was significant. McCluggage's *Are You a "Woman Driver"?* opened with a retelling of the discussion with her editor on how to title the book. "'You can't call a book that!' the editor tells me. '*Are You a "Woman Driver"?* is an insult.' I spot him immediately as a Typical Male Driver, his coolly superior attitude based solely on his maleness, not on his driving. 'And why is it an insult,' I ask calmly. 'If a woman drives, she's a woman driver—right?' 'Yes, but . . .' he stammers, 'when truck drivers yell it at her it's meant to be an insult.' 'But it shouldn't be,' I counter, 'and that's what this book is all about.'"[9]

She won the argument and got to use her title and approach, challenging the belief that women were bad drivers and that men were inevitably good ones, and Citgo sponsored her book. She also balanced her clear, accurate drawings of elements like the crankshaft and the fuel pump, with lighthearted cartoons of women and cars. Nearly ten years later, Dorothy Jackson was still battling the stereotype and used it to motivate her readers, "You know that in most men's estimation the woman driver is the low one on the totem pole." She challenged, "We know this isn't necessarily so and by quietly learning the subject we can then carry our own weight."[10]

Singling out women as drivers persisted in guidebooks throughout the century, consistently predicated on a belief that they were singularly incompetent. While economic and military disruptions affected women's relationship with the car, the messages they received about caring for their cars remained squarely grounded in a traditional gender framework.

"Chirping Under the Hood"

While some women sought out books, magazines offered women the opportunity to learn more about cars in automotive advice columns. The earliest male automotive columnists made no apologies for counseling women. However, as the century wore on, advice from men became more suspect. Following the Second World War, publishers seemed to believe that only women could dispense automotive advice to women, and they often turned to traditional female spaces, such as women's magazines, to encourage women to see the car as an extension of their housekeeping responsibilities. Even in trade paperbacks, the idea that women should turn to other women who spoke their language and understood their distinctive needs remained. Women giving and receiving the advice did not do so to subvert men's power, but instead they closely adhered to traditional gender roles as a model for their own identities as advisers and students.[11]

In October 1950, *Good Housekeeping* introduced automotive columnist Charlotte Montgomery. Soon thereafter, drawing on her monthly columns, she joined forces with petroleum giant Phillips 66 and issued the *Handbook for the Woman Driver*. Adopting the tone of a friend who also happens to be a knowledgeable expert, Montgomery offered advice on issues ranging from traveling with a dog to driving in winter, as well as "The What, When, Who, and Where of Car Service." She assumed that most women would not do their own car maintenance, with the possible exception of "not more than one in a million," so she organized her advice to highlight what needed attention and how women could secure it, as opposed to how to fix it themselves.[12]

Starting in 1965, *Woman's Day* also ran an automotive column. Its author, Julie Candler, also parlayed her columns into a book, *Woman at the Wheel.* The 1967 paperback cover proclaimed Candler "the foremost authority on women drivers, read by 7,000,000 readers of *Woman's Day.*" Her column and book shared the same tone and approach. She told her readers in the book's introduction, "Car-oriented though I am, I need [her book] as much as you do. . . . I intend to keep it always on hand in the glove compartment of my car." She somehow premised her automotive authority on her lack of knowledge and in her book offered an example of her using her own advice to investigate a "chirping under the hood." Candler, like so many of the guidebook authors, used arguments predicated on familiarity and common sense to make the case for women's competence. Drawing on a domestic analogy, she contended, "You wouldn't have a kitchen without a cookbook," and she likened searching for automotive solutions to looking up recipes.[13]

The magazine columns written by Montgomery and Candler reflected a belief that women needed car advice and would seek it out in the pages of women's magazines. The columns' placement up front in the magazines also suggests that this was a valued element; it was not filler but a consistent, significant part of the magazine's identity. The most surprising aspect of the columns' appearance, though, is that only *Good Housekeeping* regularly paired its 1950s automobile advice column with car advertisements targeting women. Frequently sharing the page or appearing alongside it, companies such as Chrysler and General Motors promoted their cars, and the Saginaw company encouraged the purchase of its "Safety Power Steering." Perhaps reflecting the purchasing power of its readers, *Good Housekeeping* attracted critical automotive advertising dollars. In contrast, the longevity of Candler's column appears to have done nothing to attract automobile advertisers to *Woman's Day*. Perhaps that is explained partly by the magazine's long-standing history as an inexpensive supermarket promotion, closely tied to food preparation, but it also makes the strength and endurance of Candler's column even more astounding.[14]

In the 1960s, automotive advice also found its way into fashion magazines, as *Vogue* successfully persuaded advertisers that its readers were both well-to-do and aspirational enough to justify the placement of ads. Car companies ran stylish ads focused on fashion and multipage fashion spreads, including models from upscale brands such as Mercedes and Cadillac. *Vogue* then made an even more concerted effort to attract advertising dollars in the 1970s and 1980s by running articles and a fairly regular column titled "Women & Cars." As the clothing advertised in the magazine became relatively more accessible and affordable, so too did the featured cars. By 1980, *Vogue* ran ads pairing the Ford Thunderbird and the Lilli Ann clothing line featured at the I. Magnin Department Store. Some car companies evidently felt assured enough about their products' appeal to *Vogue* readership that they also offered ads like an all-text one for GM, instructing women on "How and Why to Buy the Right Engine Oil." Fashion magazines tried to make cars and knowledge about them attractive and chic.[15]

With a more forthright approach, and signaling its importance to independent women's lives, the first stand-alone issue of *Ms.* magazine featured a column titled "Populist Mechanics" and set out to help women by "Demystifying Your Car." As was consistent, a woman wrote the article and relied on her experiences to relate the technical information. At its core, though, the author contended that knowledge was power, asserting, "There's a reason why men have kept cars an arcane secret all these years, and why women on campus are now demanding courses in auto mechanics as part of Women's Liberation. It's all very simple. To understand is to be free." Drawing on the rhetoric of the period, Elizabeth Hemmerdinger alleged that the mechanic told her not to "worry your pretty little head" and dismissed her outrage at the high cost by maintaining that "a man would know what's involved. Labor, parts, the works. He would just say, 'Fix it!' But a woman hollers." Empowering women with clear, simple drawings and explanations, she tried to explicate the cars' workings in three pages, so women could be "free of autophobia forever."[16]

"Just Like Feeding the Baby"

Several businesses also used a traditional gender framework to promote car advice for women and to sell their products. The Shell Oil Company produced one of the earliest efforts, in 1944, with the brochure "Alice in

Motorland: The Woman Behind the Wheel," for "women who now have a new responsibility—the care of the family car." Published during World War II, when many women had ably proved themselves in both the theater of war and on the home front, Shell recognized that many women had taken over jobs previously held by men. Noting that "we see our sisters doing new work with strange tools and complicated machinery . . . with complete understanding and skill," they still asserted that the best approach to women was to assure her that car care was "just like feeding the baby."[17]

Just as the U.S. government persuaded women to join the workforce by drawing parallels between operating home appliances and factory machinery, so too did automotive corporations explain that "the carburetor is a mixer" and "you can compare motor oil very well with the frying fats you use for French fried potatoes, onions or doughnuts . . . after a time, you must dispose of this once useful fat, and start over again with a clean batch."[18] Many women undoubtedly rejected these homemaking associations and the suggestion that women were incapable. One woman, interviewed decades later about gender attitudes during the war, recounted to Studs Terkel, "There was a letter column in which some woman wrote to her husband overseas: 'This is an exact picture of our dashboard. Do we need a quart of oil?' Showing how dependent we were upon our men. Those of us who read it said, This is pure and simple bullshit. 'Cause if you don't know if you need a quart of oil, drive the damn thing to the station and have the man show you and you'll learn if you need a quart of oil. But they still wanted women to be dependent, helpless."[19]

Responding to the growing numbers of women who needed to be independent, by choice or circumstance, companies asserted that women could depend on them for car-care counsel. Shell acknowledged, "A pretty booklet with dainty pictures can't begin to tell you how to service and repair a car yourself." Instead, Shell sought to demystify the dashboard by providing a descriptive guide. Beyond the hints the company offered, in order that women could "look at a car without fear and trembling," Shell also suggested that women use service station attendants and repair shop technicians to "do the dirty work."[20]

In 1956, the Champion Spark Plug Company produced a pamphlet titled "Car Talk in a Woman's Language: The Inside Story About Your Car and Its Engine—Written by Women Expressly for Women!" The company tried to tap into women's discomfort about their limited automotive knowledge. The women commiserated, "Perhaps we women deserve the WOMAN-DRIVER jokes and scorn we resent so bitterly? If we're honest, we'll have to admit that many of us *do* drive a car day after day, mile after mile, in blissful ignorance of what makes it tick." Champion claimed that ignorance of the car's maintenance could be expensive—"It can cost from $500 to $1,000 to replace an engine that burned out because *you* forgot to have the oil changed"—and put the responsibility for caring for the car on women. One woman proclaimed: "For the sake of our family's safety . . . for our ego's sake . . . and for the sake of our budgets . . . it's important for us to *know!*" Champion's simplistic visuals largely centered on stick-figure women imitating the functions of the engine (fanning, spinning like the drive shaft, etc.). The language in the text was targeted to women, too, explaining, "Just as the downstroke of your hand on an egg beater handle forces a series of connecting gears to turn the blades of your beater—so the powerful downstroke of the piston rotates a series of shafts and gears that eventually turn your car wheels."[21]

By 1967, some of the advice had been dressed up in psychedelic prints, like the California Harbor Service Stations' *A Woman's Guide to Car Care*, but the empowered tone predicated on ignorance remained consistent. They opened their booklet by reminiscing, "There was a time when a woman just had to stand there, looking helpless and frustrated, and three men rushed to her rescue. Now a woman must be more practical, more competitive. . . . This is a guide for the thousands of women who have no one but themselves to rely on for those oh-so-important details of car care." It also reminded women who thought that marriage would spare them the responsibility, that "even the most thoughtful of husbands" have forgotten to change the oil or have the tires rotated. As men abdicated caring for the car, advertisers tried to suggest women had responsibility for car care. They maintained that women should not *do* the work but must learn what had to be done and when.[22]

In *Tire Talk for Women*, the Women's Service Bureau of the Goodyear Tire & Rubber Company offered women an opportunity to "better understand the 'care' and 'feeding' of tires—those important down-under doughnuts on which so much depends." In addition to explaining where the tire got its name ("originally considered 'attire,' or covering, for a wheel"), booklets appearing in the late 1960s and early 1970s featured two confused and worried-looking women in their segments on the "Do's" and "Don'ts" of tire care. In the "Do's," the booklets featured the woman with her head spinning from trying to understand phrases such as "gradual stops" and "check regularly." The "Don'ts" had a man's large hand shaking its finger at the woman, while she put her finger on her chin . . . the words "squeal" and "bumps" filling her head. Although they ostensibly valued women as consumers by creating a Women's Service Bureau and believed women capable of changing a tire, Goodyear still concluded their booklet in the same vein as it began, hoping that women would consider its tires because, "We women can take pride in our influence on the design of tires that are attractive as well as functional." Goodyear's approach to women rested on a supposition of women's ignorance.[23]

Partnering with the Citgo gas station, Charlotte Montgomery resurfaced in 1971 with *Car Talk for Women Drivers*, which assured women that her advice would "appeal to every woman's natural desire to be a smart shopper." She drove home the importance of picking the best service station and encouraged women to "use your woman's good sense and judgment—just as you would in picking a butcher or a dry cleaner." She concluded, "There's no question how much any driver (male or female!) depends on a trustworthy, well-trained mechanic. To a woman, he's one of the most important men in her life." This proclamation tied directly to the company's advertising tagline: "There's a Car Man for Every Woman at . . . CITGO."[24]

Businesses imagined women as consumers and hoped they could integrate car care into the presumed "natural" scheduling that had women maintaining dentist appointments, haircuts, and new shoes for their families. Instead of truly enabling an understanding of the car's inner workings, businesses hoped they could persuade women to entrust cars to male professionals. Professionalization and automation meant that growing numbers of men no longer could care for their cars, but those same downward pressures meant that women did not either. Local and national businesses emerged to provide mechanics, and these men assured both women and men that the "right man" was on the job.

"Powder Puff Mechanics"

There were, however, exceptions. Women did train as mechanics and it is remarkable how quickly and clearly an argument was made for women to acquire technological skills through formal instruction.[25] Many observers in the early twentieth century saw "Women as Auto Mechanics" as a logical outgrowth of their broader participation in, and engagement with, the public world. Others understood that in order to drive a car, one needed to be able to care for it. The 1910 *Boston Daily Globe* article "When Women Take to Motoring" acknowledged that some women disliked machines and feared getting dirty. It concluded, "But the time has come when the ambition of the woman autoist is to be able intelligently to understand the mechanical features of her car" so that she may be able to drive it herself and not rely on a chauffeur.[26]

In addition to publishing brochures, organizations and businesses tried to teach women how to do car care by providing hands-on training. Promoters strategized that explaining basic car care to the small but growing numbers of women drivers was an opportunity to create brand recognition and loyalty. The advertised classes, usually offered for free a couple of hours a week for a period of eight to sixteen weeks, promised to be a foray into learning how to take care of automobiles, "make minor repairs and take care of trouble on the road."[27]

Most of the earliest classes had a seriousness of purpose because they wanted to enjoin women as motorists and mechanics in World War I. In a larger sense, women understood that they relied on others to service their cars or had to develop their own abilities to enjoy fully the freedom the car offered. The war forcefully punctuated this lesson. American women's automotive contributions to the war effort included not only sending over their own automobiles but also ensuring their ability to maintain the vehicles. Many garage instructors observed that women did not lack ability as mechanics; they simply lacked training and experience.

Some women did serve as volunteers driving in Europe, and the importance of mechanical aptitude was quickly evident. The experience of women like Mrs. Bartlett Boder of Whitestone, New York, who volunteered for the British as a driver in 1915, served as an important lesson. Boder, who drove a three-ton truck in France, recalled, "Once when I was driving the truck near a place called Ardois the rear wheel came off and I just sat down by the roadside and cried because I could do nothing with it." Recognizing that women could be more helpful if they did not depend on male mechanics, those organizing formal training mandated car maintenance and repair as part of the curriculum.[28]

Volunteer organizations such as the Red Cross and the National League for Women's Service teamed up with automobile schools, like those offered by the Young Men's Christian Association (YMCA) and other private companies, to offer both driving instruction and classes to help women understand the "principle and construction of the automobile."[29] By 1918, *American Motorist* reported that more than six thousand women served in the Red Cross Motor Service alone. Press stories covering these courses and women drivers often included photos of women gathered around an automobile engine or dressed in their sharp, masculine uniforms.[30] As the United States increasingly sought to aid Great Britain and France, and anticipating America's direct involvement in the conflict, the efforts to coordinate training for women escalated and led to the formation of many varied Women's Motor Corps.[31]

A glowing *New York Times* article on female motoring volunteers in the United States that appeared in the months before the war ended, asserted that "Women Show Skill as Auto Drivers." It praised women's dexterity and sureness, and their care in driving in U.S. cities, claiming that the police had "golden opinions" of their comportment. It also recognized their skill under the hood: "Before the advent of the corps, there were few women who could disarticulate the bones of the cars, but there are now many of them who are doing well as mechanics." Being able to drive took on increasing value during the war, as women could not only drive ambulances but also transport goods, individuals, and even the vehicles themselves, freeing men to serve in other capacities.[32]

With the end of the war, however, many of those who had embraced women's capable car care reverted to an expectation that it was not women's work. Beyond those few who prided themselves on their deft ability to change spark plugs or tinker with the engine, most women did not look under the hood. Ultimately, the war years primarily proved to be an exception to the rule that women could not and, indeed, should not care for cars.[33]

For a select few, though, car care remained a significant domestic concern following the war, and the Girl Scouts offered the opportunity to earn a Motorist badge, first introduced in 1916 as a badge in Automobility and symbolized by a winged wheel. The 1920 regulations, in keeping with the national trend toward professionalization and bureaucratization, stipulated that girls had to have a physical exam, earn a badge in first aid, successfully attend a certified training school, procure a driver's license from her state, and take an oath of allegiance. By 1930, the badge looked the same, but the requirements to earn it had grown even more stringent. The expectation of girls' automotive competence had grown even higher. The first line of questioning for the Automobile Examination asked girls to "Show what six important things should always be assured before leaving garage" and required them to change a tire. The expectation that girls be independent actors behind the wheel reigned through 1940, but after that the organization's interest in girls' automotive acumen went dormant for about seventy years.[34]

Nationally, the intermittent attention to women drivers and their automotive knowledge intensified as the United States geared up for war in 1940; growing numbers of volunteer organizations addressed what would be the crucial service of women behind the wheel. Many early volunteer efforts paralleled those of World War I, with women organizing efforts to aid Britain and assist in national defense. Promoting the training as a means "to make them competent 'trouble shooters' should their vehicles break down," classes offered certificates "qualifying them as emergency motor repair technicians."[35]

The U.S. declaration of war in December 1941 accelerated women's military service as drivers and mechanics, as well as their need to be largely responsible for maintaining cars on the home front. Early efforts focused on emergency training at the "double quick," and, as the war stretched on, magazines and newspapers participated in educating women, maintaining that it was important for women to care for the car properly. One 1943 reflection on women's housework in the *New York Times* suggested that auto mechanics constituted part of the skill set required of the homemaker. The cover of composer Kay Swift's score for "Fighting on the Home Front Wins!" featured a mother and young daughter in coveralls changing a tire, while her lyrics proclaimed, "This is our war too, and we're there with you, Fighting on the Home Front Wins." By situating women's efforts to fight the war at home, it also broadened societal expectations about where and how women might work. Social propaganda encouraged women to see their work in a similar vein, as with one ad that had a woman working as a gas-station attendant: "Giving your car the same care she used in keeping house and not a bit afraid of soiling her pretty hands." No matter the setting, magazines encouraged women to see themselves as feminine homemakers doing their part for the country, and car care was one of their responsibilities.[36]

For many women, learning to service a car was their patriotic duty, not a lifelong dream. Many undoubtedly questioned their role under the hood, as did a woman featured in a 1943 *Ford Times* article that reflected on a couple's gender role reversals. In the military, her husband became a cook and dishwasher and she trained to work with engines and machinery. He eventually trained as a machinist's mate and someone suggested that after the war they "could open a garage, and work together." She responded, "God forbid! I'm willing to do my part now, because we're at war. But when this war is over, I want to stay home. . . . No more engines for me—the nearest thing I want to machinery is an egg beater or a baby carriage!'" As Maureen Honey, a historian of propaganda, noted of women during and after World War II, "The normative image of the full-time homemaker did not disappear during the recruitment period." Instead, by assuring Americans that the demands on women to do waged work were temporary, it helped reinforce the traditional ideals.[37]

Of course, in the postwar era, some women did find that the war had given them an opportunity to pursue a trade for which they were suited but for which they would not have been encouraged. Such was the case for at least one woman, although the caption to the story "The Mechanic Is a Lady," assured readers of the *Ford Times*, "Pretty Yvonne Kay is as handy with that carburetor as she is with a lipstick brush." Trained in Assembly and Repair while she was in the WAVES (Navy), a Ford dealership hired her as a mechanic. The coverage vacillated between emphasizing that she was "a downright eyeful" and that she "could take an airplane motor apart and put it together again with [her] eyes closed." She claimed to be "just a mechanic's helper. I fuss with carburetors and fuel pumps," but then she acknowledged that she spent her weekends taking apart and reassembling her '37 Ford sedan.[38]

The conclusion of the war did not end women's curiosity about the car, it just shifted the justification for their involvement from a defense imperative to one based on finance and safety. A 1954 article about women studying automotive maintenance at City College of New York suggested that "a lot of wives are beginning to doubt their husbands' mechanical ability as their cars run up repair bills." The author of a 1955 *Saturday Evening Post* article, "Don't Tell Me Women Are Helpless!" reported on his realization that car-maintenance decisions rested with women who did not know very much about the car. Eddie Abbott's garage attracted hundreds of applicants to its first six-week program, "Gas, Gaskets, and Glamour." The cutesy names would continue, the most condescending of which were the "Powder Puff" names, but the seriousness of purpose with which women approached their education suggests that they believed the knowledge they gleaned to be of great importance.[39]

The use of "Powder Puff" to describe women's participation in men's sporting activities began in the 1920s when humorist Will Rogers referred to a women's aviation race as a "Powder Puff Derby." The term served to denigrate women by explicitly conveying their principal interest in makeup, and thus appearance, rather than prioritizing their performance in whatever athletic endeavor they sought to compete. Organizations and businesses used the qualifier to assure women that learning about the car's mechanics would not transform them into men. The "Powder Puff" cover assured them they would maintain their feminine identity. Although concerns about women getting dirty appeared in most discussions of women's automotive training, none of the reports on the courses revealed anything other than grease being a means to an end. Women did not indicate it was a problem and frequently commented on the cleanliness of the garages in which they trained; while they might get oil or grease on themselves, wearing protective clothing and caps and maintaining a clean work space made it a manageable process. Occasionally writers suggested, as Abbott did, "In coveralls and monkey caps, with dirty hands and smudged faces, their own husbands wouldn't have known them." The sense that women working on a car made them unrecognizable and ungendered pervaded the coverage of women's car-care classes. Reassuring "ladies," found regularly in the automotive guidebooks, appeared in coverage of the car-care clinics, too. One 1974 article described how "very proper" women "removed their white gloves and poked curiously at carburetors and transmissions" and an ad the next month assured women, "We won't make a mechanic out of you."[40]

To attract women and dispel concerns about them usurping men's power, companies offering these courses emphasized that they were not training women as mechanics but merely trying to help them do basic maintenance and know better how to communicate with the repair shop. Frequently setting up the most naïve women as foils, newspaper coverage of classes included women giggling at being introduced to the motor, including one who proclaimed that a voltage regulator "looks like a toaster!" and another who screamed "when an instructor handed her a transmission gear. 'I thought it was a spider.'" Even in 2008, this persisted; in one class a woman who could not figure out how to use the oil dipstick discovered that "she was pouring oil down the wrong pipe." The reporter had another woman saying to the male mechanic at the end of the class, "'Woo-hoo!' she purred. . . . 'You answered questions I didn't even know I had.'"[41]

Accounts of women's automotive classes also frequently justified women's quest for knowledge because their husbands were serving overseas, they were widows, or they wanted to save their family from fraudulent, overpriced repairs. Even though some advertising and reporting included stereotypically silly coverage of women as unsophisticated motorists, such as a woman with her hand to her mouth dismayed over the overheated engine and the admonition "Don't panic!" most representations of women's interest and performance were more serious. One 1975 instructor reported that not only did he expect all the women in his class to graduate from his four-week course, but he also believed that they would do so "magna cum laude."[42]

More commonly, women's value as consumers granted them the most authority. Organizations and private individuals called on service stations to be more transparent in their dealings with the public. Jeanne Wertz, the creator of the Automotive Council for Women, believed that eventually garages would be required to post prices for car parts and labor charges, and challenged, "Why does all this have to be kept secret?"[43]

A long-standing expectation that only men were born knowing what was wrong with a car and what was a reasonable cost to repair it enabled the industry's secrecy. Believed ignorant of the language and the significance of the problems, women could comfortably say they did not know, but the standard line that they would check with their husbands before approving repairs meant that a second person who did not know was signing off. In spite of all the "puff" talk, a 1964 study by two automotive organizations recognized that women had responsibility for the family's budget and stretching their money, and were unwilling to hand over car care and costs to service operators they distrusted. Women lost no ego in demanding that mechanics start at the beginning in explaining the alleged problems. For men to admit their ignorance was unmanly, so the auto industry banked on men's discomfort in confessing their limited automotive knowledge.[44]

Occasionally there were exceptions when companies took a more empowering approach and challenged the traditional messages that dominated guidebooks and coverage of automotive workshops for women. A 1973 "Grease and Glamour Clinic" ad empathized with women, "Ever since you were a girl, you were taught that women cope with mechanical problems by going to pieces over them. With your help, we're going to prove that's nonsense." The ad concluded, "A woman's problems with cars aren't biological, they're only educational." An automotive workshop jointly sponsored by a Chevrolet dealership and the Connecticut chapter of the National Organization for Women, even suggested by their partnership that car repair was a feminist undertaking. One teacher noted in 1977 that a lot of "women wanted to become independent, not dependent on husbands or boyfriends to take care of their cars." A student expounded, "We want to save a few dollars, not be talked down to in a gas station, improve our consumer awareness and gain self-assurance." Some women clearly sought independence and understood it to be within their reach to achieve it automotively.[45]

Almost all courses offered to women were free or inexpensive and did not depend on being a customer of the dealership, station, company, or organization. The expectation that providing this knowledge would entice existing customers to bring in their cars more often for repairs and win new customers fueled businesses' willingness to run the courses as a public relations investment. Chrysler initiated their Women on Wheels (WOW) program in 1971, and by 1978 the number of participants had grown to 133,000. Countless other local and national programs cropped up to attract this market of women drivers as well in this period.[46]

Many of their instructors claimed that they really connected with the women when they emphasized beauty, money, and cooking. One instructor, Leo Johns, thought he connected best by comparing carburetors to cooking; it "mixes the proper amounts of air and fuel." Teaching women for the YWCA in 1977, Robert Gallo likened "radial tires to jello, the size of pistons to the size of soup cans."[47]

Still, some took a more straightforward, nongendered approach. Reg Melling was training eight women; he showed them a diagram, told them what to do, and walked away. Working in teams of four, they had to keep at it until they figured out the repair. Instead of seeing their automobile education as a parallel to their female experiences, he contended, "They're making up for what they missed in their teens. That's the age when almost every boy goes through a hot-rod period and learns about engines." Occasionally, too, corporations shifted, as Goodyear did, from Women's Car Care Clinics to the unisex Car Care Clinics.[48]

In the late 1970s, perhaps inspired by the women's movement, female mechanics regularly began to offer car care classes. Deanna Sclar, who wrote *Auto Repair for Dummies*, "deliberately didn't call it 'Auto Repair for Women.' That implies that women require special language, and that's not true. Men need it just as much. But men are closet dummies. They can't admit they don't know anything about cars." In 1977, her classes attracted about equal numbers of women and men. Another mechanic, Ren Volpe, noticed in assisting her male boss that women deferred to the men or would not roll up their sleeves. She ended up teaching hundreds of women in classes exclusively for women, "where they could ask anything and not be embarrassed by what they didn't know." After previously running classes for women only, the woman-owned Chicago Auto of Cambridge, Massachusetts, offered its first free car care seminar for men in 1986.[49]

Nearly twenty years later, Pat Lazzaro, a race-car driver and mechanic who taught for the Firestone Tire & Service Centers' Women's Education Program, joked, "Cars are built and designed by men. They can't be that complicated." Disparaging men to assure women that car repair was easy, she used the same kind of condescension usually applied to women. Although Lazzaro asserted women as capable, in her case she traced her knowledge to her "tomboy" identity, which enabled her to gender her car care identity as masculine.[50]

Into the twenty-first century, automotive companies and organizations continued to embrace a gendered approach to girls and women, forever imagining them as a new, valuable market. Drawing on the same rationale that inspired the earliest Girl Scouts, girls in troops learned about car care, even if they did not yet drive or own a car. In 2001, one troop got its automotive instruction from Sarah Fisher, who would go on to compete in the Indianapolis 500 later that year. The Girl Scouts teamed up with Fisher and the Firestone Tire and Service Centers because they believed girls were suffering from " 'autophobia'—a fear of anything having to do with servicing automobiles." In 2006, the Girl Scouts of America and General Motors teamed up to offer a Car Care Clinic for girls. Ranging from exposure to experience, badges for girls at each age encouraged them to become familiar and comfortable with the car and its inner workings. News accounts promoted the programs as new, innovative, and timely, and presumed that it was a first for girls, even though the Girl Scouts had encouraged this knowledge nearly one hundred years earlier.[51]

There were occasional popular culture moments in the late twentieth and early twenty-first centuries that suggested women who understood cars were sexy. Characters in movies like *My Cousin Vinny* used car talk as a sexual turn-on, with Marisa Tomei's character Mona Lisa Vito exciting her fiancé Vinny Gambini (played by Joe Pesci) and an entire courtroom with her surprising, encyclopedic automotive knowledge, including the climactic scene in which she wins the case as the star witness with her authoritative testimony about slip differentials, rear suspension, and the years General Motors made the car model under scrutiny. *Ebony* magazine began a 2004 article titled "What Every Woman (and Man) Should Know About Cars" with the story of a woman who told a date to "pop the hood," began inspecting his car, and "six weeks later they got married." Although popular media sometimes promised women that car knowledge would make them sexually attractive and desirable to men, the expectation rode on women already being sexually attractive and desirable, with their specialized knowledge only used to create allure rather than undermine men's masculinity.[52]

Much more common was the fear that radiated throughout the culture that women who knew too much about cars would be de-sexed. Mechanical know-how threatened to strip a woman of her gender identity because it threatened the male preserve on what was supposed to be "natural" automotive wisdom. Occasionally, assurances that "ladies" could learn some basics emerged, but primarily served as a sell to convince them to trust and use a particular garage or dealership. For women to emerge as mechanics in their own right, however, and to get positive cultural recognition for their deviance generally necessitated attributes that pushed beyond the traditional female-male binary.

Over the car's history, the gendered expectation of women as different from men continued to pervade car care. Not only did this difference mean that women generally did not serve as their own mechanics, but also it meant that businesses approached them differently as consumers. The overriding message to women was that their education should come in selecting a good (i.e., male) mechanic and in being able to communicate the problem to him effectively.[53]

Grandmothers, Nuns, and Topless Mechanics

While the automotive industry spent most of the twentieth century reassuring women that if they bought specialized products and services they would not need to understand how cars worked, a small percentage of women took matters into their own hands and trained as mechanics. While their numbers were small, their gender transgression drew the attention of visual artists and newspaper columnists eager to explore why a woman would willingly work on cars. Very little coverage of women's automotive exploits occurred during the 1930s, when the economic crisis made employment of women the subject of much acrimony and laws in most states prohibited the employment of married women. The positive coverage during the 1940s focused entirely on women's war efforts as "Mary Jo Mechanics." However, in the other decades, recurring stories of lone women, husband/wife teams, and entire garages staffed by women appeared. The novelty of these unusual actors primarily served to reinforce the oddity of their action, rather than providing a road map for other women to follow.[54]

Across the century, it was necessity that led women to embrace this male-dominated craft. In the car's early years, the limited number of garages and mechanics forced owners and drivers to learn how to care for their own cars. As we have seen, women advised other women to learn how best to maintain their vehicles from mechanics. One independent woman confidently asserted, " 'I take entire care of my machine, allowing no one else to touch it." Some advertisers promoted their car the way Hudson Motors did in 1916: "This Year Choose a Car That Won't Require Repair Men." Trying to buy a reliable car makes good sense, but as the ad reminded readers, "The Best Mechanics Have Gone to War," and women may need to learn to care for it. Economic austerity and military conflicts likewise made car care something women had to perform themselves.[55]

Some women, though, chose to service cars. That they were able to get dirty, work with machines, and fix things was appealing. For those who served in a military or volunteer capacity, it might have been thrilling and liberating to find work that demanded pants and other masculine attire. This would have been particularly true in the first decades of the century, when some women challenged their prescribed gender identity through transgressive acts such as adopting androgynous or masculine styles of clothing.[56]

One of the earliest women to train as a mechanic, and certainly one of the most politically motivated of her generation, suffragist Rosalie Jones decided to pursue automobile repair training on principle. She believed that understanding the car was critical to women's entry into the business and political worlds long dominated by men. In 1915, she asserted, "Repairing motors is not dainty work, but it is intensely interesting and there is greater need for women in the manufacturing business today than ever before." Correctly prophesying that women would win suffrage within five years, she challenged, "If we are not capable of earning our own living then we are not capable of properly using the franchise." Maintaining that the work was not hard, she encouraged women to go into it as a lucrative growth industry. With her wealth and connections, however, she only anticipated training for six weeks and then planned to sell automobiles instead. She hoped to lead the way, however, and that other women would begin to work in the field.[57]

In a chapter on "Women as Drivers," the 1918 *Putnam's Automobile Handbook* assured readers, "So far as mastering the mechanical and technical details of a car, women seem to be just as apt as most men, if they take it seriously enough." It noted that since 1915, the 400 graduates of the YMCA Automobile School ranged "from the society debutante to the mature matron, chorus girl, actress, and a few who desired to become professional chauffeurs." The *Handbook* also acknowledged male skepticism and distrust of women as mechanics:

> When the first applicant came, it caused some of the instructors to gasp:
>
> "Why, a woman cannot understand an engine."
>
> "Only because they have never tried," was the response. "Give me a chance—I'll show you."

> "But you would get all dirty. The men have to crawl under the cars and get covered with grease and grime," was objected.
>
> "If they get any dirtier than I did this morning when I had to clean out the kitchen stovepipe," was the comeback, "then I'll give up; grease has no fearsomeness for a housewife."[58]

In keeping with other parallels between homemaking and auto mechanics, the *Handbook* also noted, "It is just a bit odd to see a woman patching an inner tube as handily and daintily as though she were embroidering a bit of Christmas frumpery; but really she handles the shears to cut the patch a lot more readily than most men, and she puts the patch in place as carefully as though she were mending the seat of her young hopeful's rompers." The clear message in their storytelling was that women not only were capable but were already doing similar work in the home and it would translate seamlessly into the garage.

It is not so much that women lost credibility after this early success as the fact that the male identity of the mechanic was rarely challenged. There were some notable exceptions, however, and they fell into three categories of women. From coast to coast, accounts of rare female mechanics addressed not just their work under the hood but also their appearance and marital status. Always central to the coverage was a consideration of *how* this gender deviance came about. While some reports of female mechanics took their subjects and their endeavor seriously, newspaper accounts regularly used the woman's identity as a hook, emphasizing that she was topless, a grandmother, or a nun.[59]

Gas companies flirted with the idea of using women as lures when hiring attendants, which the *National Petroleum News* mocked with a 1970 cartoon. It featured an older, overweight man pumping gas and a male customer in his car angrily denouncing, "I'm going to call the Better Business Bureau." Presumably he was not calling to complain that the station announced "Topless Attendants!" but rather that the attendants were topless men. Industry publications also described gas stations that employed sexy female attendants, hoping to outfox male consumers as the stations struggled.[60]

Bringing together car care and female sexuality helped define the automobile garage as über-masculine; companies occasionally employed female mechanics. This allowed garages to exploit these associations in three dimensions, bringing to life the fantasies encouraged through their promotional matchbooks, playing cards, and calendars. *Playboy* winked at this in a 1969 cartoon with the caption: "You expect more from Standard—and you get it!" The image of a naked woman getting into a man's car as he stopped for gas suggested men could win naked women as a prize for stopping at the gas station. Those embracing the most base of these gimmicks hired scantily clad women to do "light" work, such as checking the oil and cleaning the windows. For example, in 1986, Darrell's Grease and Go, in Des Moines, Iowa, hired women to work topless at their garage. Even stations that did not make bikinis or tight sweaters de rigueur still promoted their female employees as "mechanics," even if their jobs involved only car washing and moving vehicles for the mechanics.[61]

More common, the press highlighted legitimate female mechanics who were unusual in some other way. For example, they often featured grandmothers or nuns whose presumed asexuality served as a juxtaposition to the overt sexuality of having a young woman in the garage. Presumably not interested in the men in the shop or the male customers, these female mechanics stood out as quirky. Their presence was novel and not threatening because their age and devout faith made them un-sexed in a space predicated on hypermasculinity.

Lucille Treganowan, the most renowned grandmother mechanic, started out working on cars long before she was a grandmother. Much as historical figures remain frozen in memory at a certain age, what interested reporters about women like Treganowan was that they were grandmothers. Most accounts acknowledged, however, that these grandmothers had been working under the hood since they were much younger women. Divorced in 1960 and raising three children, Treganowan, for example, did bookkeeping by day in an auto repair shop and studied repair manuals at night. She was promoted to mechanic in 1962, but the early coverage of her invasion of the "World of the Grease Monkey" made no mention of her marital status or her children. A 1964 story in the *Pittsburgh Press* featured her as a "rare creature, a woman who understands autos." Four years later, reports again skirted the issue, still calling her Mrs. Treganowan and describing her as "an immaculately groomed blonde mother of three who started out to be a school teacher." While touting her femininity and attractiveness, the articles focused on her ethical business practices. They assuaged fears about her sexuality by quoting her proclaiming, "My first love is automatic transmissions." The articles stood out, nestled as they often were in the women's pages of the paper, amid the wedding announcements.[62]

Sister Joan Marese, a Catholic nun, told a reporter in 1977 that her automotive work "increases my faith in God," and that "there are times I pray when I'm under a car." Nicknamed by her religious sisters "Sister Fixit," she suggested that her thousands of hours of automotive training brought her into contact with "a lot of men who wanted to talk about religion and God and I feel I was some help." In addition to repairing cars for her convent, the Sisters of St. Joseph, which saved them the costly repair bills, she also shared her automotive knowledge with girls at St. Angela Hall High School in Brooklyn, New York. While focused on faith, Sister Joan also sought to empower women automotively. Her message was, "I wish women could realize they can do it. All they need is a little confidence, and the owner's manual can be very informative."[63]

Mechanics who worked on cars along with their husbands also assuaged fears of women's loose sexuality or lack of femininity, and press coverage of these women frequently featured the wife-husband team. The accounts often emphasized that women started by assisting their husbands but became mechanics outright, as in the 1970 case of Betty Edmonds. Her family's service station needed a certified inspector, so she trained as one and worked seven days a week pumping gas and doing all kinds of car repairs. Frequently falling into what one *San Francisco Chronicle* article hailed as the "over-40 wonder women" category, married mechanics had already secured husbands and, as one proclaimed, underscoring that she was not in the job seeking sexual attention, "'It's great—I don't have to worry about my wardrobe or manicures.'"[64]

There were also growing numbers of self-identified lesbians who worked as mechanics and created repair shops, such as Wrenchwomen in Washington, D.C., and Chicago Auto in Cambridge, Massachusetts. While not able to serve openly until 2011, there is evidence that the military historically offered lesbians, and women generally, the opportunity to

Figure 21. Lori and Valerie at Wrenchwomen, an all-women auto-repair shop in Washington, D.C., 1978. ©2016 JEB (Joan E. Biren).

work as automotive mechanics in the services. Regardless of how they got their training, a growing number of women after the 1970s touted their woman-owned garages, and increasingly more of those also touted that they were lesbian businesses, as well. Boomer Kennedy, the owner of Chicago Auto, openly promoted her shop as woman-owned and usually included a woman's silhouette in her ads, even when she did not expressly use gendered language. She claimed in 1984, for example, that hers was Boston's first woman-owned garage, listing her shop's assets: quality, honesty, integrity. She challenged readers in a local newspaper, "Wouldn't your car prefer a woman mechanic?" In the same era, she also occasionally touted her shop as "gay owned."[65]

Historically, some women found that operating a garage by and for women only gave them more confidence and removed them from the "cynical eyes" of men. In 1921, Pauline Leiner planned to open such a garage, fresh from her experience training at a YMCA automobile school. She learned that a large number of women not only drove but also gained independence and automotive skills during the First World War. She reflected, "There's something, apparently, in the sight of a woman tinkering with an automobile that arouses what some Englishwomen would call a 'fair old devil' in men who seem to feel their superiority overmuch in the oil-laden atmosphere of a garage." She feared that "a stray male helper or two, obscure in position, would surely spoil the whole effect," so she settled on a woman-only business model that she termed an "Adam-less Eden, where there won't be any gimlet-eyed males staring superciliously and exclaiming, 'That ain't th' way you do it, ma'am.' " Asked if she thought there would be enough women mechanics to sustain her business, she concluded, "There are too many women, just like me, who became skilled mechanicians during the war."[66]

This early account found many parallels in the second half of the century, with women ready to deploy their skills both on their own vehicles and in local garages. Not having the tools or an appropriate space to work stymied many of these mechanically minded women. However, starting in the 1970s, a growing number of garages rented stalls to do-it-yourself car mechanics who wanted to perform their own brake jobs and tune-ups.[67]

Some women wanted to do more than just repair or care for their own cars; they wanted to make a career out of being a mechanic. Of course, the number who did so was always very small. As Lillian Borgeson observed in the 1980s in *Vogue*, "Only fatherhood has been more exclusively male." Even at the height of women's automotive training in World War II, the number of women mechanics nationally never exceeded 1 percent. One woman called her 1985 training "gruesome," describing the male students' hostile behavior: spitting at her feet, kicking her tools, and generally making her unwelcome. Persevering, she landed her first job in a San Francisco shop that advertised "men and women" mechanics, and she believed that being a female mechanic was a "selling point" in a city famed for its more open attitudes toward gays and lesbians. Still, even with local, federal, and corporate encouragement, the number of women working as automotive service technicians and mechanics in 2013 was 1.4 percent. Even when combined with the women making up 1.6 percent of the automotive body and related repairers, these occupations remained two of the most nontraditional jobs for women in the twenty-first century.[68]

Despite the odds, thousands of women developed strong mechanical skills as teenagers. The first woman to drive coast-to-coast, Alice Huyler

Ramsey, "claimed that she was 'born mechanical.'" Yet many expressed discomfort with women's mechanical skills, fearing that they revealed a less feminine and more masculine woman. A 1955 article about Betty Siddell, who "tinkered with engines ever since she can remember," rebuilding jalopies and motorcycles, and opening her own auto repair shop, assured the reader that this thirty-four-year-old "isn't a big, husky Amazon. Betty's a trim 120-pounder with terrific drive and plenty of courage." She concluded about her own acumen, "It's like any other job, some do it well, some don't. Sex makes no difference." One story she recounted captured men's discomfort with her prowess, noting that when she fixed a "flat tire on a date, it killed the romance right then and there," and simultaneously assured readers of her interest in dating men. Other women pointed to their long-standing experience, learning at the feet of fathers, as the incentive to pursue this unusual line of work. In 1979, Judy Wels found that while "some customers did double takes" when they saw her, the quality of her work had won them over.[69]

Some women opened shops believing that a woman-owned and -operated shop could be successful because other repair shops ignored or took advantage of women. Believing their gender to be an asset, some shops used names like Sisters' Automotive and Women's Garage, to encourage women to use their services. Others risked less by having generic names but traded on the promise of fair, honest work. Lora Iaconis suggested that the trust was implicit: "If I say the serpentine belt is cracked or worn, they automatically agree and want the repair done immediately. They usually don't even ask to see the belt." Nor were women the only ones who thought they would get service that was more trustworthy. Karen Valenti, owner of North Hollywood Discount Muffler & Brake, noted that although 75 percent of her clients were women, she believed men comprised 25 percent because they considered hers more trustworthy than a male-owned shop.[70]

Navigating these gendered interpretations of their work, some women discovered that technological improvements enabled them to reconcile their bodies to the car and the garage. A 1979 *Working Woman* article encouraged women to pursue a lucrative career as auto mechanics and assured them that diagnostic equipment made the job much less grimy and that air-operated tools meant that women did not need to be "burly." Margie Seals opened her garage, "My Favorite Mechanic . . . Is a Woman," in 1992 and later contended that women were ideally suited as mechanics because they tended to be "detail oriented, and their smaller hands" let them maneuver around the car's engine. Mae Harper carved out a career in automotive diagnostics and a reporter emphasized her appearance, clearly assuring readers that she had not become masculine when they noted, she "looks like she should be at home baking pies and taking care of the grandchildren." Many women, like men, used their experience as they aged to move out from under the car and to secure work as supervisors, technicians, and instructors.[71]

An emphasis on the cleanliness of both workers and the shop always underscored discussions of what women brought to car garages. Of course, men also began to realize that as women's market share as decision makers grew, they could profit more by offering clean, accommodating waiting areas. These reminders dated back to the 1920s, at least. An editorial in the *Tacoma Tribune*, reprinted in the *Ford News*, suggested that women "felt a real affection for their cars" and would select a garage that was "fastidious rather than that which was slovenly." One 1932 study chastised those two-thirds of auto businesses that did not "cater to the woman on service," with either no waiting room or one only rated as "fair." Many observers thought making women feel comfortable in a historically male space was important to attract female customers. By 1961, *American Motorist* reported the numbers of women bringing in repair jobs had nearly doubled, and "almost half of all women drivers make some of the vital decisions about car servicing and maintenance."[72]

Some companies' appeals to women rested entirely on perceived gender differences. In 1966, Nationwide Safti-Brake trained employees to explain repairs to women, offered a waiting room, and planned to locate new shops near shopping areas. Some women used the décor of their shops to demonstrate a woman's touch, such as Los Angeles' Lace-n-Armor garage's teal and grey paint job or the bright pink door and signs at Rosemary's Repairs in Marlborough, Massachusetts. In 2002, the Great American paired with Nordstrom for the sexually suggestive "Lipstick and a Lube" promotion. Even though companies occasionally focused ad campaigns on quality care, the consistent embrace of gender difference remained a staple of most auto-shop business models.[73]

"My Husband Is *So* Pleased That the Car Man Is Helping Me"

Women occasionally maintained their own cars and frequently oversaw the maintenance of the family cars, but representations of female mechanics in movies, art prints, comics, and advertising usually relied on images of women bent over, with exposed breasts, and under cars with their legs spread open. Moreover, as with so much of women's lives, the portrayals consistently prioritized women's sexualization vis-à-vis the car, as opposed to the quality of the work they did. In all instances, the male gaze informed the readings of these women's work.[74]

One of the most prevalent sexual fantasies advertised in the late twentieth century was the scantily clad woman washing a man's car. *The Bikini Carwash* offered a soft-porn vision of topless women working at the carwash. One Chicago-area businessman tried to bring this fantasy to life with his Bikini Carwash in 1995, but he faced local opposition. Authorities forced him to close shop and apply for an entertainment license when he charged customers $20 for bikini-wearing women to wash and dry their cars. Capturing their multiple roles as caregivers, cleaners, and sex objects, women in these kinds of promotions typically caressed the car and rubbed it down. A television commercial teased out the tension one man faced in deciding between two car-wash options: one option was youthful, attractive cheerleaders dressed in white; the other was older, dour nuns who used the best cleaning product. By having him choose the nuns and their product, the company suggested how clearly superior it must be to trump the sexy fantasy of cheerleaders washing his car.[75]

The early twenty-first century saw actor Megan Fox in two popular *Transformers* movies in which she played a mechanic, but as a National Public Radio critic noted, her more important role was to be on display, "an arrangement of plump breasts, bee-stung lips and submissive/seductive postures." Yet this suggestion of female mechanics as sexy and desirable was not new. Movies like *Heat Lightning* (1934), *Urban Cowboy* (1980), and *My*

Figure 22. This undated postcard captures the expectation that a garage that chose to employ female mechanics would only capture prurient men, as opposed to legitimate automotive customers.

Cousin Vinny (1992) historically suggested that the distinctive role of a female mechanic was a sexy one and frequently tempered her deviance by suggesting that her knowledge emanated from her family's business.[76]

The sexual suggestions of the garage and car care stretched back to the earliest cars, as with a 1906 postcard that featured a woman putting oil in the engine. Titled *Lubri-Kate*, the artist cut away the woman's driving coat to the knee to reveal her shapely leg and foot. Another postcard, from the mid-twentieth century, had a man sitting in his car staring down at the woman's legs splayed open below him. The text read, "Yes—I know that's the third time you have adjusted it—but its not just right yet," letting the viewer know that her work was irrelevant to why he was interested in a female mechanic. Even the car's hood ornament was a man leering down at her. The garage sign promised "We employ only lady mechanics," and an advertisement featured phallic "Lug Plugs," while another female mechanic strode away, wrench in hand, and a promise of more sensuality.[77]

Sultry women and cars also captured the imagination of pinup artists like Gil Elvgren at midcentury. In "Quick Change Artist," with a woman changing a tire and "Help Wanted (Pretty Perplexed)," which had a woman posed astride the engine and holding a wrench, the women, as in most of his images, wore tight-fitting dresses, stockings with garters, and high heels with thighs exposed. A similar motif appeared on postcards as well. One by a Dutch photographer featured a topless woman, face covered by her crossed arms, with a wrench in each hand. While some women had automotive knowledge, most artists represented female mechanics as objects not workers. This held true for representations of female mechanics in music videos, such as the pop group Bananarama's 1983 video for "Cruel Summer," Rihanna's "Shut Up and Drive" in 2007, and Beyoncé's 2010 "Why Don't You Love Me?"[78]

Into the twenty-first century, female mechanics in the comics offered a powerful foil to men and challenged gender norms in appearance and behavior. The *Monty* strip had the namesake character's masculinity called into question by a tough-talking, female mechanic in overalls and a backward baseball cap. Cartoonists also drew on the female mechanic to disrupt perceptions of women and men, as Robb Armstrong did in his November 2004 *Jumpstart* strip, when he had Joe's best friend Clarence's wife, Charlene, star as a "Master Auto Mechanic." Armstrong presented the men comfortable in, and oblivious to, their lack of automotive knowledge but still maintaining that "usually a female knows absolutely nothing about how a car works." Positioning the star Charlene as a "Master Auto Mechanic" enabled Armstrong to use Joe as a foil for those still harboring sexist ideas about women's automotive capabilities and to share a laugh over the normalization of men with no motor knowledge.[79]

The cartoon form also offered the opportunity to laugh at anonymous men and women who knew nothing about car care, and their amusing exchanges. In one of Greg Cravens's *The Buckets* strips, Larry Bucket confessed to his wife Sarah Bucket that he was a failure as a man, in part because he was helpless around cars, but she affirmed his masculinity by having him take out the garbage. Cartoonist Jimmy Johnson had the title characters in his strip *Arlo and Janis* clueless about their car woes in 2000, with Arlo wondering if the "funny noise" was "funny ha-ha or funny peculiar?" He then conceded and explained his joke, "Well, you know I'm not much of a mechanic." Cartoons enabled society to laugh at the entrenched expectation that occasionally men failed in their automotive knowledge and served to reinforce the sense that car care was not a woman's concern.[80]

Another way that men shaped women's relationship with the car was in an expectation that they oversaw their wives' and daughters' car care. Many women relayed verbatim instructions from men and checked with them before approving service recommended by a garage. Just as many expected that male grocery shoppers were doing the bidding of their wives, not independently selecting items on their own, so too did many believe that women were just the messengers at the garage. Yet, as many men conceded and many garages hoped, men frequently did not know any more than women did about their cars. Still, men retained the voice of authority within the family, vouching for the relative merit of companies, services, and products.

In the last third of the twentieth century, men and women increasingly capitalized on transformations in the economy and the culture that allowed them to pay others to do work, rather than learning how to do it themselves. They discarded handicraft skills passed on from generation to generation that stretched and repaired household items in favor of a consumer culture that enabled people to buy new or pay someone else to repair items. It became as antiquated as darning socks for a middle-class man (or woman) to fix the car in the driveway. As cars became more sophisticated in the late twentieth century, even knowledgeable individuals could not compete with the accuracy and speed that computers introduced into car care.[81]

Ads began to reflect a growing reality: While cars continued to affirm men's masculine identity, neither women nor men knew very much about cars. Ads showed men vouching for the credibility of the company's auto technicians, rather than being the ones to seek the service themselves. In 1971, the Citgo company introduced "a Car Man for every woman" campaign. In one ad, a young woman bent over the car coyly announced, with three laughing men in the background, "There's a new man in my life. And even Daddy likes him." She quickly assured the reader, "Oh, he's not one of my boy friends. He's the Car Man at my Citgo station. He's a whole new idea for cars . . . and for girls." In these ads, it was not just the women who sought the assistance but approving fathers and husbands who needed it. Another ad in the campaign featured a woman proclaiming, "My husband is *so* pleased that the Car Man is helping me. But then, he thinks that everyone should look after me." Unspoken, but self-evident, was that husbands could no longer look after their wives' car care. The companies could not easily feature men who did not know what the shock absorbers did or how to tune an engine, but they did so by showcasing ignorant women and authoritative men. Citgo even made the mechanic an object of affection, with one ad promoting their campaign pronouncing, "All of these women are in love with one man."[82]

An unusual 1971 ad depicted a woman (in white) working under the hood of her Mercury Comet GT and a Quaker State Motor Oil ad that same year assured women that they needed to use Quaker State's products to "take care of your husband's baby." Advertisers knew that many women had primary responsibility for their own car, at least, and assured them of "simple maintenance" and "peace of mind." The service and care promised by these companies frequently came with an assurance of male expertise, with Mr. Goodwrench, the Pep Boys (Manny, Mo, and Jack), the Citgo Man, and Texaco's "Man Who Wears the Star" just some of the fictional men who assured quality care.[83]

In 1981, Goodwrench predicated its advertising campaign on caring about the consumer, but some ads still highlighted women's lack of knowledge, like the 1983 ad that had a woman pumping her gas, saying, "I know where the gas goes. And that's all I care to know. Mr. Goodwrench knows how to keep my car running right." In general, there was a growing expectation that both women and men had limited automotive knowledge, and that their knowledge, or lack thereof, was comparable. In addition, increasingly sophisticated technological developments meant that no longer did men lord their expertise over women, or even pretend to know what was wrong with the car, but both of them knew that if something was wrong with the car it needed to go to a professional.[84]

Another business that, like Mr. Goodwrench, grew out of the decline of full-service gas stations in the 1970s was Jiffy Lube. It built its car-maintenance business on speed and efficiency. Its ads assured consumers, "whether you drive a big expensive foreign car or a subcompact, Jiffy Lube has the correct oil, the correct lubricants, and the correct filters." In ten minutes, Jiffy Lube promised to check and fill all of the fluids in the car, as well as check wiper blades and tire pressure in its fourteen-point inspection. The company's assurance that its technicians would take responsibility for checking all critical elements freed the driver from having to remember to ask someone to look at each of those things. A plastic decal on the windshield meant that consumers did not even have to guess when their car was due for another appointment. Many earlier articles foreshadowed this need, chiding women for not following through on the important work to be done and featuring laundry lists of things to check. They often noted that many women did not like to ask for help in investigating each of the concerns, so companies that took care of it all tapped into a freedom for women. No longer did they need to learn to service their own cars or even remember what work needed to be done or when; taking it to an all-in-one place let them adhere to their gender roles by caring enough to have a man do the work.[85]

Ads for car care increasingly featured men with their cars, starting in the 1970s. Although the ads evaded the issue of having another man maintaining their cars, Jiffy Lube, in particular, mocked men who did not know enough about cars to choose Jiffy Lube for their care. One billboard ad threatened that if men did not use Jiffy Lube's service they would end up riding to work on a little girl's bike. Another billboard ad used sexuality to appeal suggestively, "Get a Quickie after the beach," with a bikini top dangling from the word *Quickie*. They embraced this emphasis on speed and sex with the corporate tagline, too: "You're in. You're out. On your way." Although soliciting men's business became acceptable, the ads continued to premise their appeals on traditional gendered expectations. Jiffy Lube suggested that men who used its business to care for their cars were more masculine, even as the company stripped away men's fundamental need to be capable of the work themselves.[86]

On a larger scale, late twentieth-century car manufacturers began to promise comprehensive care with the purchase of an automobile. Historian Sally H. Clarke traced the efforts of corporations to build trust with consumers while maximizing profits, noting in particular the evolution of responses to the shoddy production of automobiles. One outcome was that corporations began to offer a number of options to consumers. The first line of attack was to argue to consumers that their cars were easy to care for; according to one 1966 ad, "Ford says that even a secretary can perform certain service functions simply by following the instructions in the service manual." A 1987 Toyota ad promised that its Corolla was "One of the most trouble-free cars you can own." Fundamentally, Toyota sought to assure car buyers that all their concerns would be moot if they bought its brand. Second, automobile companies staked their confidence in their cars by pairing them with a safety net, such as Volvo's 1980s "24-hour roadside assistance" or General Motors' OnStar services built into the car. Finally, companies began to offer warranties or a promise that all maintenance would be covered for a set period of time. Some companies, like American Motors, believed that women cared more about warranty provisions and dealer service than men did and thought they should promote them to women.[87]

Corporations also tried to keep customers loyal with service maintenance programs and the quality of cars generally improved, so the number of emergency repairs declined. Being at a remove from the physical workings of the car returned to being a sign of class status, reminiscent of the 1920s—when those who could, hired chauffeurs to handle their car's upkeep and repairs. Advertisements promised that people could buy or lease cars with warranties and, when necessary, pay someone else to do the dirty work in a garage.[88]

Conclusion

In spite of the expectation that automobiles were unknowable to women, women found themselves responsible for securing car care for their family. Aware of this market, businesses appealed to women with assurances that their services not only would be quality but also would be clean. Even as businesses expanded their gendered messages to include men, they continued to hold tight to an expectation that male authority was the bottom line in choosing a business for car care. Women had responsibility for securing it but not for knowing anything about the car. Those few women who did transgress their gender roles to work competently with cars carefully assured others that they would not violate any other gender norms: Car care was the limit of their transgression. Indeed, some women in bikinis or tight sweaters winked at the idea that feminine women could make legitimate mechanics. In spite of the many challenges to gender roles across the twentieth century, car care retained its male identity and left women to navigate it in strictly gendered terms.

5

The Car and Identity

HISTORICALLY, AMERICANS UNDERSTOOD that different makes, models, and colors of cars could help identify individuals. Gender and sexuality, in particular, played a fundamental role in shaping the identities of both cars and the people who drove them. Across the century, companies and individuals went beyond connecting automobiles to a driver's gender and sexuality to suggesting that cars themselves had discrete, knowable identities. An example that typifies this pattern occurred when politician Newt Gingrich claimed in 2010 that the reason he abandoned his wife for his mistress was that he could not "handle a Jaguar"; all he could take on was a Chevrolet. Characterizing his wife and his mistress of six years by car brand allowed him to quickly contrast their identity to a public familiar with automobile brands and their reputation (in this case, high maintenance versus ordinary). The facility with which a man could convey his relationships with women by conflating them with a car speaks to the power of automobiles in helping to define gender roles in modern America.[1]

The human predilection to anthropomorphize facilitated the ability to blur the identities between women and cars. Psychologists, anthropologists, and marketing researchers have all sought to understand the significance of people's tendency to see the "human in non-human forms and events." Anthropologist Stewart Guthrie observed that we often "animate and anthropomorphize" at the same time, and offered the car as an example. "We animate but do not anthropomorphize, for example, if we say an automobile purrs like a kitten, and anthropomorphize but do not animate if we speak to our pet turtle. If we speak to the automobile, however, we both animate and anthropomorphize."[2]

Americans have enthusiastically both animated and anthropomorphized automobiles, imagining that cars have "faces," made up of "headlights for eyes, grille for a mouth and the bumper as jaws." Those faces and (car) body shapes combined in the minds of many to convey human identity. In 1984, the Renault company was so intent on capturing this connection that it spent $500,000 to make a commercial at the George Lucas studios; the thirty-second commercial transformed a man, frame-by-frame, into an Encore car.[3]

Drawing on the finding of developmental psychologists that infants can "recognize faces even in inanimate objects arranged in the pattern of eyes and mouth," carmakers into the twenty-first century weighed this interpretation. They consciously decided whether to keep their "doelike headlights" (Mini Cooper) or develop their front grille to look like a "snarl," which combined with cutting off the top of the headlights to create a "sinister eyelid" "looks like it will bite your head off" (Ford Mustang). Regardless of what motivated this interpretive behavior, that people did so suggests a key way that Americans gave meaning to their own lives, not only to establish their identities but also to perform their gender.[4]

It appears that many Americans partially anthropomorphized cars to "make better sense of the world," believing that cars have "some important human traits but do not consider the entity as a whole to be human." Of course, occasionally individuals anthropomorphized cars and acted as though a car actually was a person, but, by and large, most people embraced their vehicles as humanized machines that they could talk to, understand to have personalities, and give a kiss to on occasion. Of all the ways that people imagined their cars as human, the most significant stands out as its gender because it was the car's ability to perform gender that allowed individuals to affirm their own gender roles and engage in a largely unexamined intimate relationship.[5]

Cars as Female

The cultural tendency to prescribe fixed gender identities to cars persisted from the introduction of cars all the way into the twenty-first century. People quickly began to name cars and assign their gender identity; this analysis will focus primarily on cars' female association. Ford's dominant place in early automotive history yielded the first of many female names for cars, along with establishing the idea that cars were female. Lizzie, a popular nickname for the Model T, affirmed a female association that persisted. In 1908, the year the Model T appeared, Elizabeth was the seventh most popular girl's name in the country, and Lizzie was a familiar female nickname. This early appearance of the female name for a car is remarkable, given the male identity so often ascribed to cars in general and to the Model T in particular.[6]

Giving cars a female name persisted for over one hundred years. Popular culture and private recollections revealed that it was understood as self-evident. Soldiers in World War I penned poems to Tin Lizzie and the Model T's war efforts, while those in World War II named Jeeps for their girlfriends, with military units voting on names like Stella and Susie. A 1950 commercial featured Marilyn Monroe seductively calling for gas-station attendants to put Royal Triton in her car Cynthia's "little tummy." Into the twenty-first century, people continued to gender their cars and give them nicknames. Individuals reflecting on the reason they named their cars noted, "They're faithful companions, like pets" and claimed that they were "extensions of ourselves." Naming cars, according to one psychological study, gives "them personalities which reflect the nature of our relationships with them." One 2014 study found that Baby, Betsy, and Bessie rounded out the top three names for cars. To the extent we can document the tendency to refer to cars by gender, they have been predominantly female.[7]

Male identities for cars existed but tended to be exceptions. Occasionally ads deployed the car itself or a particular car feature, such as the emergency brake, as a phallic symbol. A 1965 Volkswagen ad, for example, blurred the visual form of the penis and the car's stickshift and asked, "Does the stickshift scare your wife?" "Muscle cars," too, assumed a macho identity, as with ads for the Mercury in 1966, which contended,

"Every model looks like a man's car, feels like a man's car, and acts like a man's car—because it is." In a 1974 reflection on the Pontiac GTO that appeared in *Playboy*, an industry observer proclaimed, "Buying a GTO is like getting two inches added to your cock." The strategy of making cars appear masculine to affirm men's masculinity seemed to be a perceived antidote for car models unpopular with men.[8]

Chevrolet tried to stake a claim that its Camaro was not just a man's car but also explicitly a heterosexual man's car. Its 1997 ad campaign targeted white, heterosexual men with its bravado, "If everyone owned one, maybe we could have prevented disco." Historian Gillian Frank, in his exploration of "discophobia," found some white men in the late 1970s and early 1980s were angry that their preferred music, "rock and roll," had been usurped by disco on the radio and in the broader culture. Tapping into that historic homophobic and racial animosity, Chevrolet charged in the ad that disco was "A pimple on the face of music history" and asserted the Camaro as a car for "real men." Not content just to put men in the driver's seat and suggest the car's sacrosanct masculine identity, some ads asserted an antifeminine identity that promised to keep women and effeminate men out.[9]

Most commonly, however, the culture revealed a funhouse mirror that reflected quirky, gendered associations of cars as female. Quips connecting cars and women appeared soon after the broad introduction of the car, with one in 1913 opining, "The Ford is like a sweet-tempered woman—mighty agreeable to have around," while another warned, "The finest of automobiles, like the finest of women, are ugly when they are slovenly and ill-kept." Modernist artist Francis Picabia drew his *Portrait of a Young American Woman in a State of Nudity* (1915) as a spark plug, inviting the interpretation that young women and cars "ignite flames of passion." The parallel between women and cars, defined by their beauty and sensuality, persisted in men's appreciation of them, as well as in their desire to possess them.[10]

The successful mid-century market researcher Ernest Dichter, who premised his work on all objects having an identity and even a soul, concluded in his work for Chrysler that the company should position its Plymouths as types of women. He drew national attention when he suggested that dealers should feature the convertible in showrooms because men associated it with the freedom of a mistress . . . even though men generally bought the sedan, which they conflated with their wife. In the late century, Chevrolet ran commercials for its Geo brand with the song, "Getting to Know You," showing the cars being lovingly attended to by their owners. Across the century, the descriptions of cars' human qualities blurred the distinction between the two.[11]

The description of the cars' bodies often suggested a parallel to women's bodies. Sometimes, as with a 1941 Ford ad, the words did not expressly say "female," but describing the car as a "lean, lissome beauty" left little question of her gender. In one of his novels, William Faulkner proclaimed the automobile "our national sex symbol" and described men "spending all Sunday morning washing and polishing and waxing it because in doing that he is caressing the body of the woman who has long since now denied him her bed." The postwar discontinuation of the Lincoln-Continental, a car renowned for its luxurious aesthetics, inspired hundreds of letters, including one by author John Steinbeck. He wrote in 1948 to "beg to be high on the list" when they produced them again. He claimed, "I had many cars in my life, but none that so satisfied my soul as the Continental. She was a real lady."[12]

One way that people blurred the line between women and cars was by dressing them both up, particularly for early twentieth-century parades. Celebrating events like World's Fairs, competing in floral parades, and attracting attention to issues like suffrage, women decorated cars with flowers and often used flowers to adorn themselves as well. The color of the car sent a gendered message, with pink and purple likely signals of a female owner, as did covers for the steering wheel and seats, floor mats, and other decorative touches. Artist Phyllis Yes applied paint and lace to a Porsche in 1985, transforming it into a Por-she named Portia. The devotion men paid to their cars, decorating them with eye-catching rims, outfitting them with subwoofers, and even dangling dice did not serve to feminize the men or the cars but instead signaled a masculine style. In 2010, when Dodge chose a historically "feminine" color for the Challenger, which they claimed men purchased 85 percent of the time, they declared it to be a "new tough-guy color: Furious Fuchsia." Women's

Figure 23. Disregarding the women who loved the new VW Beetle (1998–2009), the company sought to masculinize its car, which meant bigger wheels and "tougher" colors. Volkswagen announced the change with this 2011 ad.

accessorizing, in contrast, affirmed their feminine identity and that of their car. One early twenty-first-century trend, in particular, suggested that the car and driver were both feminine and even flirty. Just as women attached fake eyelashes to their eyes, so too, they applied "carlashes" to their car's headlights.[13]

As for the cars themselves, sometimes the accessories served to be an exclamation point on femininity, exemplified by the twenty-first-century's hyped new Volkswagen Beetle shape. Volkswagen believed that nearly 70 percent of their new "bug" sales went to women. The cars came with a vase in the dashboard, bringing the accessorizing with flowers full circle and tapping in to an old tradition of vases that attached to the vents or mounted in the car (for pleasant smell in the days before air conditioning). To try to reclaim more men in 2011, the company brought in Porsche designers to develop a more masculine look to the car, introduced a Fender audio system and bigger wheels, "toughened up" the color palette, and removed the flower vases. They proclaimed, "It's a boy!"[14]

Fashion giant Miuccia Prada took inspiration for her Spring/Summer 2012 collection from cars, offering women the opportunity to become a car, with pieces aligning the female frame with the designs of 1950s-era cars, replete with high-heeled shoes sporting taillights and protruding flames. Seeking to capitalize on this idea, General Motors enlisted journalist Andrea Silvuni and festooned him with the title "Italian writer and shoe design analyst" to write "Fashion and Cars: The Matching of Soles and Souls," the pretense of which was to analyze cars and shoes together because they "can provide a window into secrets of personality." Ranging from innocuous to ludicrous, these efforts to merge women and cars persisted.[15]

One of the longest-standing suggestions was that the electric car was female. There was an early battle to determine which cars would take hold in America—steam, electric, or gasoline. In addition, there was a short-lived possibility, advanced by some, that there would be different cars for women and men. Automotive writer Ryland Madison, for example, claimed that by 1912, "The time has gone by when motor cars had sex—when the gasolene car was preeminently for the man, and the electric, because of its simplicity, for the women." The presumption, therefore, was that men primarily preferred gasoline cars and women electric. Certainly, ads for electric cars in *Country Living in America* did sometimes focus on the car as designed for women, as with an Ohio Electric ad that designated theirs as for "a woman of refinement." Historian Michael Berger contends that the electric cars helped female drivers maintain their femininity. Yet ads also appeared, like one in May 1913 for a Detroit Electric car, that targeted men, assuring them it was perfect for city life and leisure. In a subsequent issue, following an article discussing the importance of automobiles for developing character in both men and women, an ad had a man at the wheel of an electric car, touting its significance for business and pleasure.[16]

Scholar Gijs Mom's gender analysis of the evolutionary development process of electric vehicles reveals that electric cars competed with the steam- and gasoline-powered cars in the first years of the twentieth century and concludes that men bought a large number of electric cars. In a 1900 accounting of the national production, for example, of the 4,192 cars produced, the largest number of cars manufactured were steam-powered: 1,681. The next largest number of cars manufactured, 1,575, were electric; gasoline-fueled cars trailed, with 936 produced. The evidence suggests that it belies logic to assume that electrics were understood to be "feminine." Mom found that the number of female owners of electric cars was dramatically lower than we might have imagined. Filtering our expectations through an electric-equals-female lens and limiting our analysis to advertising alone has resulted in the erroneous assumption that men did not buy or drive electric cars and that women preferred electric vehicles over gasoline ones, completely ignoring the initially most popular steam-powered cars. Using women in ads to convey ease, safety, and refinement is a long-standing technique and does not serve as evidence of women as drivers of electric cars. In fact, drawing on statistics culled from southwestern cities, such as Tuscon, Arizona, and Houston, Texas, as well as the state of New Hampshire, Mom found in most of the country there were negligible numbers of electric- or gasoline-powered cars registered to women. His findings are supported by a historical reflection in *American Motorist* magazine, that held, "In 1900 there were only about 65 women in the entire country who could drive an automobile," including two or three in Philadelphia, a dozen in Chicago, and two dozen in New York. It may well be that the numbers were slightly higher than this rhetorical assessment, perhaps including larger numbers in Detroit, Michigan, and Washington, D.C., but it does not stand to reason that women were the force behind sales of electric cars. Mom found that electric car companies offered substantive, real attention to men in popular magazines and trade journals by 1913. In the *Electric Vehicle* journal that year, for example, an editorial maintained that the electric was now "chiefly characterized by its 'manliness.'" It is probably impossible to know the extent to which the small number of registrations truly reflected how many women drove or what women thought about the competing automobile technologies, but it is clear thereafter that American culture asserted a connection between electric cars and women. While the rhetoric may have resonated on a small scale between 1900 and 1912, this association appears to have existed outside of any substantive reality.[17]

Following their early competitiveness, steam and electric cars faded quickly against the dominant gasoline-engine market. It was not until the twenty-first century that electric cars re-emerged when Toyota spearheaded a successful effort to sell hybrid and electric cars to American consumers. American companies proved unwilling to commit comparable resources to innovate cars that could compete with traditional gas- and oil-dependent ones. Toyota's introduction of the Prius built on its established, dominant market position and its decades-long efforts to appeal to women.[18]

While some Americans understood the cars to be revolutionary and sought to align their identities with what they considered progressive environmental and economical practices, many continued to embrace a negative, inviolable connection between women and hybrid/electric cars. The 2010 buddy-cop movie *The Other Guys* reflects some of this hostility, with one character disdainfully reflecting as he rode in a Prius, "I feel like we're literally driving around in a vagina." Another man affirmed this fear when he approached the duo in the Prius, chortling, "I didn't know they put tampons on wheels." There was no public outcry or anger at this negative association, nor was this comedy the only one to make it. The following year, two more movies used the Prius to make gendered jokes. The lead male character in *No Strings Attached*, jealous of a male rival, admired his Prius, but then made his dig, "It's kind of girly." Having already established the car as feminine, the film also sought to foreshadow the rivals' identity, later revealed to be gay. The feminine identity of the Prius was also later asserted in the controversial trailer for the Ron Howard comedy *The Dilemma.* Had Howard contented himself to use the "joke" only in the film, as the other two films did, it probably would not have elicited such objections, but Howard's trailer opened with Vince Vaughn's character proclaiming, "Ladies and gentlemen, the electric car . . . is totally gay." Aggressively banking on the association of electric cars as feminine, popular comedies helped entrench the century-old connection.[19]

"It Depends on the Kind of Woman You Are"

Just as popular culture persisted in affirming electric cars as feminine, another trope asserted that women riding in cars with men risked their reputations. Ranging from sexual innuendo to pregnancies to allusions of sexual assaults, the cultural discourse that merged women and cars commonly reflected vulnerability. For most girls and women, getting into a car driven by a boy or man had the potential to jeopardize their reputations and transform their identities. A 1941 cartoon postcard had a woman pushing a baby in a pram and the header read, "Scram! I've learned my lesson, no more thumbing rides for me!" as a man in a red convertible raised his hat in greeting. As Sidonie Smith described it in her analysis of Beverly Donofrio's narrative *Riding in Cars with Boys*, "To climb into the driver's seat, for a young boy, has been to get an identity as manly and desirable. To get into an auto, for a young girl, has often been to get into trouble." The risks and consequences for girls and women, including sexual assault and pregnancy, can also be understood by considering the alternative. When someone controls an automobile, it suggests independence. Lack of control—not having a car or not being the driver—enforced a cultural dependence. Even women who regularly drove, and drove well, knew to toss the keys to a male companion. Even more limiting, their lack of private transportation severely limited women's mobility and affected their ability to work outside the home, care for their children, and provide for their home. Women's automotive powerlessness served to further define and empower men's control of cars.[20]

Several female singers have built songs around women's desire to take the wheel. Chrissie Hynde crafted "Thumbelina" about a woman and child who leave behind "the thunder and rain" of a relationship and take refuge in "the broken line on the highway." Singer-songwriter Tracy Chapman sang in 1988 about a young woman who initially dreamt of using her lover's car to escape the heartbreaking cycle of poverty she faced in the Grammy-winning "Fast Car," while Melissa Etheridge also used the metaphor of driving to escape in her 1995, "You Can Sleep While I Drive." These singers stand out against the dominant discourse of male artists, particularly New Jersey's rock 'n' roll legend, Bruce Springsteen, who helped assure the centrality of the automobile to the development of masculine identity. His music empowered men as drivers and made women passengers.[21]

For women who drove trucks or practical cars, their effort to seek out reliable transportation called into question their femininity and, for some, their sexual orientation. Perhaps it was a fear that disclosing her stint as a "Truck-Driving Marine" would call her sexual identity into question that kept actor Bea Arthur from disclosing her military service. Although in England, the young Princess Elizabeth publicly announced her training as a mechanic and truck driver, the exceptional nature of war encouraged acceptance. With the end of war, however, fears of being perceived as masculine for driving a truck existed with no counterweight of honor or necessity.[22]

Advertisements for the SUVs that emerged late in the century were careful to assure women, as one 1983 Chevy ad did, that "The kind of Blazer it is depends on the kind of woman you are." The images and language of the ad, even with no visible men, suggested that the women were unquestionably feminine and heterosexual. Similarly, a 1985 GMC ad featured two refined women with their van and shopping bags on swanky Rodeo Drive in Beverly Hills, California. Still, the social risk of being perceived as a lesbian for driving a rugged car persisted for many women. One woman maintained in a 2007 *Los Angeles Times* op-ed that a man lost interest in her after one date because he discovered she drove a Subaru Outback and suspected she was a lesbian. The kind of car a woman drove had the potential to define her sexuality to others.[23]

One surprising benefit of the lesbian stereotype was that it encouraged a limited number of automakers to acknowledge lesbian consumers and try to market to them. Most discussions of gay consumer power in the early 1980s focused on the male market. The responsiveness of Mazda and Subaru to their lesbian consumers was remarkable, therefore, not only for standing out as companies that marketed to homosexuals, but also because they were two of the few national companies that marketed directly to lesbians.[24]

Automakers also risked overt criticism and boycotts to create positive associations for women who did not choose their cars to attract men. Conservatives waged a letter-writing campaign in 1994 because Mazda sponsored the *Roseanne* episode in which the lead actor shared a kiss with Mariel Hemingway on national television. The Mazda Miata had become a favorite among lesbians, with one woman terming it the "official lesbian vehicle." When Ellen's character came out as a lesbian in her TV show *Ellen* in 1997, companies such as Chrysler and Mazda (owned by Ford) withdrew their ads, fearing consumers would associate their cars with gay people. Even when companies supported homosexuals, they often did so with "gay-vague" spots, usually with two men. According to a 2007 accounting, "Subaru has been the most prominent company to embrace the gay market. As long ago as 2000, the automaker created advertising campaigns around Martina Navratilova, the gay tennis star, and also used a sales slogan that was a subtle gay-rights message: 'It's not a choice. It's the way we're built.' Little wonder that many lesbians refer to their Outbacks as 'Lesbarus.' "[25]

In this case, the car not only became identified with gay women, for some, it *became* gay. Just as cars were sometimes understood to be female, sometimes the cars assmed a sexual identity, too. For some, this branding jeopardized their own identities, for others, it proved to be an unusual opportunity to affirm themselves. With concerted, overt efforts to reach lesbians, Subaru's marketing enabled some women to affirm their gender and sexual identity with the purchase of their cars.

Similar opportunities and limitations appeared for a stereotyped heterosexual, familial-focused female in the guise of the "soccer mom." Enmeshed in a national discourse deploying coded language, advertisers and women used their vehicles to affirm their maternal identity: cautious, focused on the safety and comfort of their family, and caring. From its introduction in the mid-1980s, the minivan usurped the station wagon as *the* matronly, domesticated vehicle. Fearing that they would be unable to extricate themselves from the car's identity, many women and men shunned the vehicle.[26]

"May We Pronounce You 'Man and Mustang?' "

Cars occasionally appeared as sentimental, maternal caregivers or took the form of a human baby. In the mid-1960s, the CBS network aired a sitcom premised on the idea that the mother of Jerry Van Dyke's character had been reincarnated as a car. *My Mother the Car*, while unusual (and critically panned), succinctly captured the idea of cars as dependable, female caregivers. The theme song appreciatively crooned, "She helps me through everything I do and I'm so glad she's here."[27] Conversely, the periodic suggestion that the car was a baby enabled advertisers to play on owners' devoted attention to their "baby." "Like 'one of the family,'" professed one couple of their "baby" and how they cared for it with Mobil Oil in a 1941 ad. A 1971 article chronicled the "new to motherhood" author and her husband who had "adopted" an eight-year-old that was "running a temperature" and lethargic. Describing their journey to their local automobile diagnostic center, they approached their experience "as proud parents" of a Volkswagen. A 2013 Nationwide Insurance commercial centered entirely on the loving devotion a father gave to his baby, washing it, protecting it from shopping carts in a parking lot, and weeping when it hit a fire hydrant. Tapping into people's protective approach to their cars, the commercial sought to tap into their figurative devotion.[28]

Although there were exceptions of mothers and babies, cars anthropomorphizing as female romantic and sexual partners predominated. These examples were not mere suggestions that a car was "known as a woman's car" and therefore assumed a female identity. Instead, the language and imagery indicate that the car was both female and animate. Historian Beth Bailey contends that this equation of women and cars was common in mid-century America: "Both were property, both expensive; cars and women came in different styles or models, and both could be judged on performance. The women he escorted, just as the car he drove, publicly defined both a man's taste and his means."[29] "It has a twinkle in its eye. It flirts with you ," professed a 1964 Chevy Corvair ad that described the car as having "come-hither looks." Companies embraced this blurring, as it served to humanize, and indeed individualize, their cars, enabling them to use romance and sensuality to make their sale.

Singers used this approach for the same reasons; and for almost as long as there have been cars, there have been songs about cars as women. Singer Chuck Berry's first famous hit, appearing in 1955, imagined a male protagonist in his Ford V8 chasing his unfaithful female partner, "Maybellene," in a Cadillac Coupe de Ville. As cultural critic Grant McCracken noted, "The emotional, visceral, interactive nature of [driving] blurred the boundary between the driver and the car. Unable (or unwilling) to see exactly where driver leaves off and car begins, drivers were inclined to take credit for properties that belonged to the car. *They* were now large, gleaming, and formidable. The speed, grace, and power of the car now belonged to them." Berry's

This baby won't keep you up nights.
Alas, not every car is born a Volkswagen.
But of the lucky ones that are, it's hard to find a trouble-maker.
Of course, by the time a new Volkswagen comes into the family it's been doted upon by 1,007 inspectors.
So it's not surprising that the skin is blemish free.
That the steel bottom is sealed tight against annoying moisture.
That what's inside is just as perfect as what's outside. (Many parts are inspected 2 or 3 times.)
And just to give you an extra feeling of security, VWs are covered by an extra year of warranty.*
Not just any warranty.
This one includes four free check-ups by our famous diagnosis system—a system renowned for spotting trouble. Before it's trouble. (A comforting thought.)
But if we find any and it's under warranty, we'll fix it for free. (Another comforting thought.)
As good as our baby is, however, the day will come when you'll decide to part.
But it's consoling to know that after 3 or 4 years it's been known to bring home more dollars than any other economy car.†
Pleasant dreams.
*If an owner maintains and services his vehicle in accordance with the Volkswagen maintenance schedule any factory part found to be defective in material or workmanship within 24 months or 24,000 miles, whichever comes first (except normal wear and tear and service items) will be repaired or replaced by any U.S. or Canadian Volkswagen Dealer. And this will be done free of charge. See your dealer for details. †SOURCE: 1969 Manufacturers' Suggested Retail Prices and 1972 Average Used Car Lot Retail Prices as quoted in NADA Official Used Car Guide, East. Ed., Oct. 1972, Kelley Blue Book, West. Ed., Sept.-Oct. 1972. © Volkswagen of America Inc.
Few things in life work as well as a Volkswagen.

FIGURE 24. Advertisers sometimes referred to cars as babies, and the text of this 1974 ad included a promise that "the steel bottom is sealed tight against annoying moisture."

car's ability to compete for Maybellene parallels the human experience. Frequently signified as female in the lyrics, cars also appeared as sexual women. In the 1980s, Bruce Springsteen sang of a woman as a "Pink Cadillac" with her "crushed velvet seats," while Aretha Franklin's version of "Freeway of Love" imagined herself as a pink Cadillac, "So jump in. It ain't no sin. Take a ride in my machine." Franklin controlled the car . . . and was the car.[30]

While the Cadillac may have proved to be the most common lyrical stand in for women, other models were used, too, including Mustangs (Wilson Pickett) and Corvettes (Prince). The metaphors exploited by singers generally portrayed women's mobility and independence in a way that suggested loose sexual morality. For a "car" to have many "jockeys" suggested a woman who has "got to slow down," their freedom to drive fast crushing their identity as a respectable girl or woman. In "Little Red Corvette," Prince sang to a woman that he was going to try to tame her "little red love machine." This admonition for women/female cars to be more constrained appeared frequently; the popular imagination could not abide by their fast moves.[31]

Romantic pitches also pervaded the culture. The text and companionate images dramatically illustrated the fine line that existed between literally and figuratively loving one's car. Cars' purported female identity helped rationalize and normalize this behavior in the culture. If men love women (and their bodies), then a man falling in love with this particular "type" of woman could be seen as normal, and even adorable. Belief in men's romantic commitments to their female automobiles, including the proclamation of marriage, appeared across the century. An author writing in *American Motorist* in 1930 professed his love for his car. The cartoon drawing reflected the narrative, with the groom down on one knee before the car's "face," declaring, "I love you enough to satisfy the most jealous and exacting motor." An ad for Valvoline appeared during World War II with a man's car proclaiming, "A Wife has *some* rights . . . even if she is only a Machine." Echoing the drama of human relationships, the car protested, "I'm your automobile—the car you 'married' a year or two ago. Maybe I'm not as sweet and fresh as I was then, but whose fault is it? I spent the best miles of my life slaving for you over a hot road!"[32] "She" then threatened, "But don't go thinking about deserting me! The Government says that we have to stay 'married' a long time. So treat me right—

we'll *both* be happier!" Companies encouraged the loving association men brought to their cars.

A public service announcement by Dow Chemical appearing in 1958 encouraged men to care for their cars and it also explicitly gendered cars as female. Beyond the requisite eyelashes, the car sported lipstick, and the voiceover for the cartoon-style animation intoned a clear relationship between men and cars they defined as women. About thirty seconds into the announcement, the narrator observed, as a man and a car looked lovingly at each other: "There's something special between a man and his car. The man offers his tender devotion, and loving care. The car responds by being willing, agreeable, and dependable. Just like any attractive, but temperamental female. Yes, a car is a woman."[33]

As the short film reflected on the man's car as an extension of his own personality and his chivalrous defense and care of her (the car), it affirmed that they were true to each other, as the plentiful pink hearts attested. After the film explicated the importance of cooling systems, the car batted her eyelashes and the man said, as he hugged her, "We'll take good care of each other from now on."

The idea of men's love for cars fit easily into the cultural discourse, particularly, it seems, for the more expensive makes. An Austin Healey ad assured men in 1960 that they "would fall head over heels in love" with their cars. The Lotus car company also tapped into the belief that men *truly* loved their cars. A 1961 ad featured a priest marrying a tuxedoed man and his Lotus; the headline pronounced, "I do!" *Life* magazine ran a story about men's love affair with cars, claiming that American men, after "cooling off a long-standing romance with his glossy American mistress," had taken up with a string of "little floozies from Germany, England, or Italy." However, the author asserted, after the daliance "he's back, panting like the exhaust of a 325-horsepower Cadillac for the same old sweetheart, the American automobile." Having sent the American car to the "beauty parlor and the masseuse," the author hoped the "errant Romeo will stay devoted—at least through 1963" and they faced the dilemma of how to "keep him faithful." Ford hoped men would fall hard for its latest model; a 1966 ad asked, "May we pronounce you 'Man and Mustang?'" A huge hit for the band Queen in 1975 professed men's passion with "I'm in Love with My Car." At the height of passion for American cars, language of love and loyalty for female cars pervaded the culture.[34]

Men's love and devotion to female cars persisted across the rest of the century and into the twenty-first. Humorist Erma Bombeck speculated that men's relationship with their cars was "perhaps the most possessive, protective, paternal" one you would ever encounter, with their love and affection transferred to each subsequent model they owned. She cautioned, "And if Detroit ever turns out a model that sews on buttons and laughs at his jokes, ladies, we're in trouble!" A 1986 Honda ad assured male buyers that they could "Fall in love without paying the price." Paralleling the human experience, Honda promised its car would not make a lot of demands; its fine engineering meant the car would not need a lot of attention, and its low cost meant it would not take a lot of resources. A 1988 *New Yorker* cartoon had a woman standing in the doorway of the bedroom, confronting a man and a car peering out from under the covers, and proclaiming, "I *knew* you were having an affair with your car!" A lot of people took the joke seriously. Forty-one percent of female respondents to a Firestone survey in 1994 contended that "men's real affair was with a car." Although 62 percent of men did contend that "they loved women more than their vehicles," that left 38 percent of men who presumably loved their cars more than women. Country singer Shania Twain dismissed a car-loving man as a potential mate, knowingly crooning of his true love, "You're one of those guys who likes to shine his machine, You make me take off my shoes before you let me in; I can't believe you kiss your car good night." A 2013 Firestone personalized mailer, decorated with a handwritten script, proclaimed, "I can't go on without you!" Inside, Firestone suggested the customer's car had written a letter to its owner, "I sit here, parked, my mind reflecting like a rearview mirror, remembering the way we used to be." Pleading for a return to their "shared excitement," it suggested "with a little work, I know I can still make you happy." Signed with "XOXOXOXO," Firestone wanted people to "Show your car some love."[35]

Many ads suggested, either rhetorically or in a light-hearted manner, that consumers loved their cars. Ads like one for Buick in 1979, for example, claimed its car would elicit "The difference between a car you like and a car you love," with a man down on his knees cleaning the car's whitewall

I do!
He found it appalling just to go out and buy it! So, it was practically a marriage. Lotus Elite stands on ceremony. It's not just a car to be taken up with lightly. Lotus Elite demands that certain type of man characteristic of nobility. In a word, the union must have 'taste'. Lotus Elite is a $6,000* Grand Touring English sports car of excellence. The blood line is racing! The breed is speed! The dowry: four cylinders, disc brakes and independent suspension all the way around. Built to get there quicker, ride surer, with tremendous fuel economy.
LOTUS
LOTUS ELITE
For an introduction wherever you may be and/or full particulars write. If the car fits drive it! Prolonged try-out called leasing, $135 to $150 a month, socially acceptable.
*Equipped ready to roll with slight freight variances.
(About That Mask—He has a very jealous wife aw-ready!)
WESTERN DISTRIBUTORS, INC.
317 NORTH VICTORY BOULEVARD
THORNWALL 2-2326 VICTORIA 9-6418
BURBANK, CALIFORNIA

Figure 25. Advertisers and consumers applied anthropomorphism and imagined some cars as human beings, seeking to seduce men into wanting them. This ad for the 1961 Lotus Elite imagined a man marrying his car because "It's not just a car to be taken up with lightly."

THE NEW 2003 JAGUAR S-TYPE Beneath its classic, sultry curves, lie the latest advances in technology and performance. We've transformed this stunner into a technological marvel, with a first-in-class 6-speed automatic transmission, refined suspension and Dynamic Stability Control. What that means to you is silky, smooth shifts, precise handling and a confident ride, even in the most extreme conditions. The new incredibly well-rounded S-TYPE. Beyond beautiful. Exceptional at $44,975.*
jaguar.com/us 1-800-4-JAGUAR
SEDUCTRESS ON THE OUTSIDE.
STARK RAVING TECHNOLOGICAL MANIAC ON THE INSIDE.
THE NEW S-TYPE
The art of performance
JAGUAR

Figure 26. In this 2003 Jaguar ad, the car is a "stunner" that is a "seductress" with "classic, sultry curves," enticing men with connections to the female body and sexuality.

tires. A 2003 Jaguar ad suggested that discovering its new car was like "a sexy date that you discover is also a gourmet cook, a massage therapist and a brain surgeon." The ads confidently asserted that the S-Type car would make men "fall in love with its looks," but it would offer so much more that it could "keep the relationship going." Offering loving care to a car was predicated explicitly on the love a man felt for a woman, and the expectation that the car could reciprocate the feeling.[36]

While marrying cars remained fantastical, in 1999 a man tried to marry his Mustang GT. He remarked, "Well, in California they are doing same-sex marriages . . . So we are in Tennessee. Why can't we do the good ol' boy thing and marry our cars and trucks?" He filled out his marriage application, listing his wife's place of birth as Detroit, her father as Henry Ford, and her blood type as 10W-40, before being flatly told that he could not marry his car.[37]

At times, men's commitment to their vehicles seemed overshadowed by the trope of men betraying their human girlfriends or wives with female mistresses in the form of a car, which accelerated in the late twentieth and early twenty-first centuries. Perhaps in response to the greater freedoms and rights women sought at home and at work, advertisers strategized that a car that catered to men's needs was more appealing than ever. A 1970 Oldsmobile ad promised that its car would be the perfect caregiver; the ad assured men that the car "Cradles you ever so gently. . . . Pampers you. . . . And caters to your sense of style with magnificent interiors." A 1996 commercial toyed with viewers when they had two elegant, middle-aged women lunching, and one remarked while touching her wedding band, "He told me he needed more space. . . . Said he needs to feel more power and control in his life." The friend responded, worried, "Well, what's he want to do?" Instead of the terrible, expected answer, "He wants a divorce," the woman smiled to reveal, "He wants a Cadillac DeVille." Cars offered love and unselfish devotion that women could not or would not deliver.[38]

The culture also celebrated the purposeful destruction of a car as a surefire way for women to convey their heartache and anger to men who betrayed them. Women tapped into an awareness that men loved their cars passionately and saw it as an opportunity to hurt "her" as a stand in for the man and other woman involved. Women intended the cost of the destruction to measure far beyond the auto repair shop.

Many betrayed women in popular media wrought their anger in the destruction of vehicles. Left without money or a ride for her abortion, Stacy's friend Linda spray-painted "Prick" on the car of the boy who abandoned her in the 1982 film *Fast Times at Ridgemont High*. Julia Roberts in the 1988 movie *Mystic Pizza* vented her fury at what she believed was a cheating boyfriend by dumping fish garbage into his pristine, red convertible Porsche. The torching of a cheating lover's BMW in *Waiting to Exhale* inspired other women to "go Angela Bassett" on their men's cars. Other women sang about punishing men with imagined violence. Country singer Carrie Underwood may have been the first to turn this kind of vengeance into the chorus of a song, as she did in her 2006 hit "Before He Cheats." Discovering her lover's infidelity, she keyed his car, carved her name into his leather seats, and "took a Louisville slugger to both headlights, slashed a hole in all 4 tires. . . . Maybe next time he'll think before he cheats," she crooned. Philadelphia soul singer Jazmine Sullivan sang "Bust Your Windows" in 2008. She also marked the car, using a crowbar to write her initials, and concluded that he was lucky she did not do more damage: "You broke my heart, so I broke your car. You caused me pain, so I did the same." Trying to inflict some degree of the pain she was feeling, Sullivan's jilted protagonist lashed out at her lover's car, knowing full well it would convey her wrath and despair. Anecdotal evidence suggests that the singers were not just imagining this kind of retribution. A 2013 radio-station poll showed the list of reasons people gave for vandalizing someone's car weighed heavily toward unfaithful boyfriends. Beyoncé's artistic film rendition of her 2016 *Lemonade* album featured her taking a baseball bat to parked cars and then, at the wheel of a monster truck, crushing a row of cars, while the lyrics she sang spoke to her rage at infidelity and betrayal.[39]

"He's Definitely Excited"

While love remained a central focus of people's relationship with cars, lust, too, proved to be a recurring theme. In particular, companies objectified women by suggesting a sensual link between their shape and the form of cars. Advertisements abounded with subtle signifiers, as with a 1924 one for the Auburn car that described the "Curved sides" enhanced "by a high European waistline." Depicted with the silhouette of a shapely woman, the language easily applied to both the woman and the car.[40]

Playfully blurring the duality of the English language, E. E. Cummings crafted a poem to describe a man's "painstaking, delicate, and bittersweet technique of breaking in a new car as an analogy for making love to a virgin." He wrote:

she being Brand

-new;and you
know consequently a
little stiff i was
careful of her and(having

thoroughly oiled the universal
joint tested my gas felt of
her radiator made sure her springs were O.

K.)i went right to it flooded-the-carburetor cranked her

up,slipped the
clutch(and then somehow got into reverse she
kicked what
the hell)next
minute i was back in neutral tried and

again slo-wly;bare,ly nudg. ing(my

lev-er Right-
oh and her gears being in
A 1 shape passed
from low through

second-in-to-high like
greasedlightning)just as we turned the corner of Divinity
avenue i touched the accelerator and give
her the juice,good [41]

In his modern storytelling, particularly by calling the car "she" and "her," it was easy for Cummings to transpose the car and the woman. The Fisher autobody company built its brand around the allusion that its automotive bodies could be "read" as sensual and female. Fisher's tagline, Body by Fisher, encouraged viewers to "Look to the Body." So direct was its invitation to men to gaze upon the woman that some of Fisher's ads did not even include an image of a car. In the 1931 film *Big Business Girl* the lead character learned that she was getting promoted because, "A girl with a chassis like that can be a half wit and get by." Cartoons and comics also used the double entendre. One postcard suggested, "You auto come down . . . And see the new streamlined models," contrasting images of a thin and full-figured woman, with the cars as the backdrop. Others had mechanics proclaiming, "Lady—I don't see nothing wrong with your rear end," as a shapely woman stood with her backside to him. These appeals, made by men to men, appear to have fallen short with women. Scholar Deborah Clarke notes, "Overall, women seem less concerned about the car's relation to sexuality, a topic of far greater interest to men"; this finding is consistent in the broader cultural discourse as well.[42]

Starting in the 1930s, companies also began to use sexualized images to market their products. A series of Simoniz wax ads in the 1930s featured nude women with breasts exposed. In one ad, a naked woman covered in a clear, plastic poncho ostensibly symbolized how wax would protect the car. With unparalleled explicitness, companies conflated cars and women, and used naked female bodies to arouse men's sexual attention.[43]

Trying to excite men by luring them to their cars, Fiat and other brands built on the observations of anthropologist Grant McCracken, who observed of men and their cars, they "expressed toughness, virulence, power, and style. They expressed mastery of the world, mobility, independence. They were about potency and sexuality." Seeking to further exploit

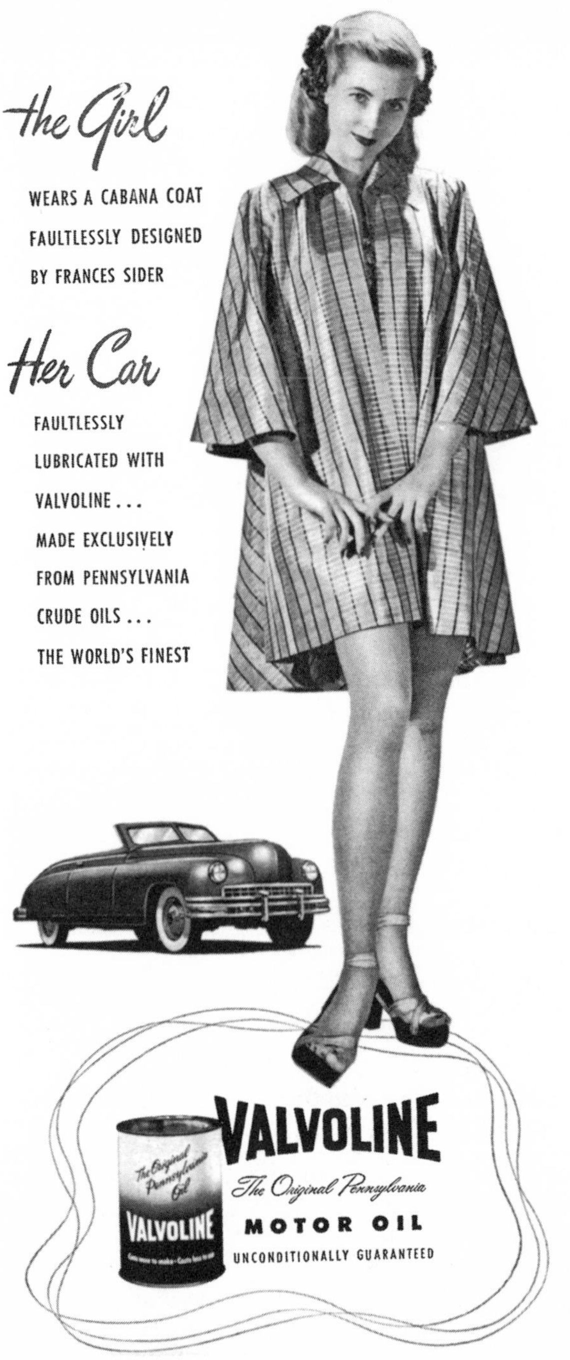

the Girl
WEARS A CABANA COAT
FAULTLESSLY DESIGNED
BY FRANCES SIDER
Her Car
FAULTLESSLY
LUBRICATED WITH
VALVOLINE . . .
MADE EXCLUSIVELY
FROM PENNSYLVANIA
CRUDE OILS . . .
THE WORLD'S FINEST
The Original Pennsylvania Oil
VALVOLINE
VALVOLINE
The Original Pennsylvania
MOTOR OIL
UNCONDITIONALLY GUARANTEED

Figure 27. With unparalleled explicitness, companies conflated cars and women, and used scantily clad female bodies and suggestive language to arouse men's sexual attention, like they did in this 1941 ad for Valvoline oil.

this objectification of cars as women, Ernest Dichter suggested marketers tap into the memory of men's first sexual encounter with "a slogan along the lines of: 'We're sorry we can't bring back your first car, but if you try the Plymouth it will be that same feeling.'" *Time* magazine believed Dichter's analysis of cars as sexual conquests of virgins, wives, and mistresses was a "gold mine for Chrysler." Another company that explicitly capitalized on sexuality was Fiat, which introduced its cars to the United States in the 1960s. It assured buyers that "because Italians regard their cars almost as highly as they do their women," their cars offered "immediate responsiveness. The sweet, even disposition." The ads flattered men that they knew a man recognized, "a beautiful thing when he sees it—and what to do with it. A man loaded with red blood cells that glow brighter when adventure's in the wind."[44]

Keying in to men's desire, comedian Mort Sahl joked in a 1970 review for *Playboy*, "If someone were to ask me for a short cut to sensuality, I would suggest he go shopping for a used 427 Shelby-Cobra. But it is only fair to warn you that of the 300 guys who switched to them in 1966, only two went back to women." Subaru placed an ad in *Playboy* in 1973 claiming that its new GL Coupe was "Like a spirited woman who yearns to be tamed." The suggestive text of the ad contended that a woman wanted a man to control her, forcibly, sexually: "The sculptured lines of the one piece body invite you in. With front wheel drive she's different. . . . Let her cradle you in the softness of her highback reclining bucket seats. Surround yourself with the lushness of her interior appointments. The GL Coupe is ready. Now. Turn her on. . . . Control the Coupe's every movement—her every twist and turn—as you take hold of her rack and pinion steering."[45]

Continually propping women on the car hood, next to the car, near the car, ads encouraged men to "feel great all over when you look at one," intending men to shop for both cars and women. Sometimes ads referred to her whole body, while others focused on specific body parts; the double entendre of words like rear end, chassis, and "rack and pinion" further entrenched the connection between the bodies of cars and the bodies of women.[46]

Car companies even went so far as to hire "girls" to represent their brands. In breathless press releases in 1968, Joan Parker replaced Pam

The Subaru GL Coupe. Like a spirited woman who yearns to be tamed.

Perhaps you're a man who grabs life by the cuff. You live life your way. And it shows... in the clothes you wear...in the women you love...and in the car you drive.

The Subaru GL Coupe is waiting for you.

Sleek. Agile. The sculptured lines of the one piece body invite you in. With front wheel drive she's different. A step ahead of the others. Go to her. Let her cradle you in the softness of her highback reclining bucket seats. Surround yourself with the lushness of her interior appointments. The GL Coupe is ready.

Now. Turn her on.

Lead her to the open road. This is where the Subaru GL Coupe wants to be. Unleash the relentless power of her 1400cc quadrozontal engine. Control the Coupe's every movement – her every twist and turn – as you take hold of her rack and pinion steering. She'll make it smooth with her four wheel independent suspension. She'll carry you away as she peaks to the red line of her tach.

The Subaru GL Coupe is yours. Waiting for you.
And one more good thing, she costs so little to keep happy.

Front Drive
Subaru

Subaru
SUBARU
For your nearest dealer call 800-447-4700. In Illinois, 800-322-4400. Subaru automobiles, priced from $2,196. Plus dealer prep., freight, state and local taxes, if any. Manufactured by Fuji Heavy Industries, Tokyo, Japan. Imported by Subaru of America, Inc., Pennsauken, New Jersey

FIGURE 28. Subaru's explicit 1973 ad used sexual imagery to suggest that its GL Coupe was a woman who wanted to be controlled and would be sexually responsive to men.

Austin as the "Dodge Rebellion Girl" and "Dodge Fever Girl." Noting not just her measurements and petite height, they included a photo of Parker in her go-go boots. Pontiac hired Natalie Carroll to be their "Firebird Girl," using her image alongside their car to convince buyers that they "Sell Excitement." An automotive writer asked Carroll if she was being used as a sex symbol, but she denied it. A Pontiac advertising manager conceded that they were using Carroll because she had a "savage graceful look, a wild look about her which we think fits the image of the Firebird," suggesting that her "tight leather clothing . . . is high fashion right now."[47]

Many Japanese and European automakers, in particular, deployed sexuality to lure men. This positioning of women with the car was expertly exploited in a 1970 ad introducing the Toyota Corolla to America. A woman in a minidress with a plunging neckline leaned against the car's window that contained the detailed pricing; the ad claimed, "Some people find the left rear window its most beautiful feature." Using the word *beautiful* four times, it suggested that the price of the car and the woman were both beautiful and concluded, "We can't blame you for being attracted to the left rear window." In 1987, Honda suggested that its engineers, striving to re-engineer the Prelude, "arrived at a very sensual conclusion," and then described the changes they made to the body of the car.[48]

These intermittent suggestions intensified in frequency heading into the twenty-first century. A 1996 Hyundai ad had its new Elantra promising more shoulder and leg room and more "hip room" as the car drove up the curve of a woman's reclined body, her navel visible, her groin just out of view. A 2011 commercial for Nissan, titled "Model vs. Model, played on the "analysis" of airflow over the streamlined bodies of the Juke model and the supermodel Brooklyn Decker. Like others in this campaign, the ad sold the idea that the bodies of Decker and the car were comparably sexy. Fiat tried to break into the American market again, running a 2012 Super Bowl ad that had a man checking out a beautiful woman and discovering after she entranced him, including speaking to him seductively in Italian, that she represented the car, each dressed in black with red accents and tattooed with Fiat's scorpion logo.[49]

Appearing as both props and subjects, cars and women also blurred the line sensually in twenty-first-century music videos, TV commercials,

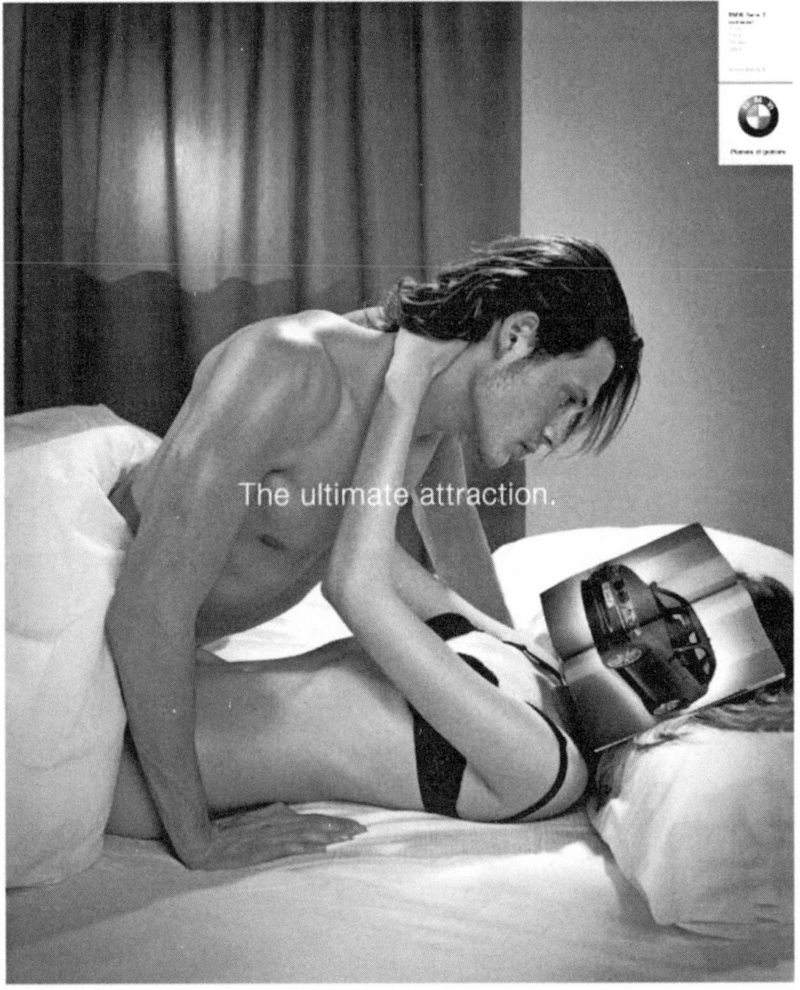
The ultimate attraction.

FIGURE 29. BMW's 2003 ad did not need text to convey the message that "The Ultimate Attraction" for men's sexual desire was their car.

and print advertisements. Perhaps one ad did so most crassly, with its 2003 print ad depicting a heterosexual couple having sex. The man on top stared passionately at a magazine spread showcasing the newest BMW model. The magazine fully covered the woman's face, blond tresses emerging from underneath. Singer Rihanna drove a red Ferrari in her

2007 music video and suggestively sang that she was a "fine-tuned supersonic lean machine" looking for a driver because her "engine is ready to explode." A 2012 Scion TV commercial had four bikini-clad women in clear plastic heels doing doughnuts (tight circles) in their IQ model, while eating cream-filled doughnuts and drinking milk. Another ad paired model Kate Upton and a car wash in a Super Bowl spot, using male voyeurism to ogle the Mercedes and the supermodel.[50]

Some early twentieth-century cars featured crafted hood ornaments of nude women, often with wings for arms and long, flowing hair, to symbolize flight. As society shifted its emphasis from expensive ornamental design to inexpensive opportunities to assert individuality, people adorned their cars with stickers and magnets. The trucker mud-flap silhouette that epitomized this cultural representation and inspired the wrath of *Thelma and Louise* back in 1991 did not disappear but instead expanded into a stable of female body "types." Companies produced female silhouettes to affix to cars, including one that was full-figured and another with visible nipples, high heels, and the body arched up in a sexually prone position, leading the police to consider the First Amendment right to affix it to a car in Great Falls, Montana. Aggressive assertions of male fantasies proliferated and included a sticker stating "4 doors for more whores," which adorned the back window of a car in a New Jersey parking lot in 2014.[51]

In the twenty-first century, a few men publicly professed that they took the suggestion of a car's sensuality to climax. Encouraged to love and lust after their cars by the culture, they found their attraction to the car's physical body to be so powerful as to equal or even trump human sexual contact. One man, Edward Smith, filmed for a Barcroft TV documentary, professed to having had sex with over 1,000 cars. Captured on film caressing, kissing, and ejaculating on cars, the documentary suggested that he was unusual but not alone in his predilection for motor loving. More popularly, many Americans learned of this limited phenomenon when the TV show *My Strange Addiction* featured a man in a five-year "committed relationship" with his car. One company sought to capitalize on this idea as well. In 2013, the Long Island City Hyundai dealer ran an ad with a woman discussing a man (off screen) with a medical doctor. The physician concluded, "He's definitely excited," while she confirmed that the symptoms had lasted for more than four hours and that he was holding "it" with both hands, and then cut to the man gripping the steering wheel. With this over-the-top commercial, the company received national attention for suggesting that owning their cars would stimulate the same sexual "euphoria" as Viagra. Whether termed mechanophilia or autoeroticism, it appears borne out of a discourse that encouraged "mechanical lovers."[52]

Beyond identifying with a car based on love and lust, Americans also identified the car as a place that afforded opportunities to pursue both with other people. Away from watchful eyes, the intimacy and privacy that cars provided made the automobile a popular site for both marriage proposals and sexual encounters. In the 1920s, Americans tried to legislate an end to automotive couplings, limiting automobiles on college campuses and passing state laws that made "stopping and parking" constitute "reckless driving." Critics of "necking" and "petting" focused their concern on morality, as well as road safety. One letter writer to the *New York Times* acknowledged the historical context, noting, "The one-armed buggy driver has been the butt of jokers from time immemorial," but he was fearful that "careful drivers are constantly being menaced by meeting cars driven by boys whose necks are encircled by flapper arms and whose shoulders are furnished with frowsy flapper heads." Researchers Robert and Helen Lynd also discovered in their study of Muncie, Indiana, that sex in the automobile landed some young women in juvenile court, with one judge decrying it as "a house of prostitution on wheels."[53]

In the 1930s, the evidence suggests that the car accelerated acceptance of dating nationally, and it served as a preferred location for couples to have sex. A student publication at the University of Chicago "recommended the automobile 'whenever possible.'" Historian Beth Bailey concluded, "Cars were generally considered the best and most private option for sexual privacy."[54]

The *Chicago Tribune*'s research department did a study in 1953 on the meaning of automobiles and found, "Cars certainly play a vital part in our mating and dating customs. Any youngster who thinks of a date automatically thinks of a car." They concluded with a portion they underlined for emphasis: "A major part of the car's intense value is providing socially acceptable outlets for these basic human drives, while at the same time concretely symbolizing our control of these fundamental impulses." Even when they were parked, cars had the potential to transport people sexually.[55]

A 1962 Ames, Iowa, newspaper identified the car as the most successful site for proposals, ranking it ahead of a woman's home or a public place. While this may seem foreign to modern readers, it reveals the longstanding importance of the car. In addition to providing refuge for sexuality, cars closed off the outside world and gave people the opportunity for private conversations. For all people, and especially couples, the quiet of the car allowed for focused conversations. As one woman reflected, "There's a different kind of intimacy in the car than there is anywhere else." By the twenty-first century, the emphasis on public spectacles dominated the cultural value placed on engagement stories, and cars faded to an auxiliary role, with one recipient of a popular flash-mob proposal sitting in the open back of a SUV, while sixty people helped her questioner ask, "Will you marry me?"[56]

While automobiles afforded couples sexual opportunities, some couples did not seek them out. Although difficult to capture, it is evident that some women tried to limit or deny sexual advances made in cars. A 1930s postcard depicted a man angrily confronting the driver of his car. The chauffeur protested that he "heard the lady say stop!" while the accused man insisted it was not the driver's place to interfere. Chuck Berry in his 1966 song "No Particular Place to Go" laments that a woman thwarted his sexual advances, claiming, "All the way home I held a grudge, but the safety belt, it wouldn't budge!" Beyond allusions to thwarted sexual endeavors, the evidence also reveals sexual violence in cars. Some men asserted that by consenting to ride in their car, women were consenting to sex. Women found themselves subjected to sexual assault when they accepted rides from men.[57]

Yet, in spite of women's vulnerability, consensual sex was a common, sought-out feature of cars. A 1953 study found that a whopping 18 percent of those born before 1900 "reported that they had engaged in premarital sex in cars." Historian James Flink charted the ways automakers sought "to facilitate lovemaking in cars," from "fold-down bed" and "bed conversion" options for cars in the 1920s and 1930s to the 1970s van as "the height

"WHAT HAVE YOU STOPPED FOR?"
"WHY, I HEARD THE LADY SAY STOP!"
"WELL, YOU STICK TO YOUR JOB, SHE WASN'T TALKING TO YOU!"

Figure 30. Most people in the twentieth century did not have chauffeurs, so there would have been no one to hear any objections to unwanted sexual advances or assaults. This undated postcard captured a man attempting to come to a woman's defense, as she cried out "Stop!"

of accommodation to sexual drive in automobile design." One 1970 study estimated that about 75 percent of cars had bench seating in back, with its bed-like qualities conducive to having sex in the car. In a national study in 2001, one- third of the women surveyed reported that sex was one of their top activities in a car. Still, by the twenty-first century, with bench-style seating long gone, and along with it the comfortable ability to use the car for sex, as well as an increase in the number of smaller cars, the percentage of people having sex in cars appears to have declined. While there may have been other factors pulling people out of the car, including fewer housing shortages; crackdowns on "lover lanes;" and more people working outside the home, leaving homes available for rendezvous, the discomfort of bucket seats and seat belts undoubtedly contributed to a shift in the car's appeal in this regard. Many have speculated about the twenty-first-century decline in the appeal of cars to young people, with fewer young people seeking their licenses and buying cars. Perhaps this shift can be attributed, in part, to the shrinking number driven to do so by sexual drive.[58]

This is not to say that the desire or practice disappeared. Vanessa Carlton imagined a woman's first time having sexual intercourse in her 2004 song "White Houses," reflecting on the cracked leather seat of the man she now considered "her first mistake." A 2011 study of "sexual spaces in everyday life" found the car played "an important role in delimited, usually male-centered sexual behavior (fellatio or male genital stimulation)." Respondents reported that they had never "had vaginal sex in the car, primarily due to the vehicle's physical constraints." College-age respondents suggested that men continued to receive sexual pleasure in the car, which sometimes served as foreplay to intercourse in a bedroom.[59]

The power of the car for men to lure women also pervaded the culture. The women who fell for the car, and subsequently for the man who owned it, underscored the importance of men having a car to attract a mate at all. According to the cultural narrative, in weighing suitors, having a set of wheels proved to be an important quality most women sought. A 1984 ad for Gulf Oil showcased the value of a man's car that he had used a dozen years earlier to catch the girl he later married. Sometimes, however, the suggestions were more creepy than cute, as with a 2000 Volkswagen Golf ad that promoted the car's remote-control side-view mirrors, which the male driver was using to scope out women. Whether playful or aggressive, the fundamental importance of a car for men to pursue women remained throughout the century.[60]

Identifying with one's car took on significant meaning across the century, attesting to the power not only to define oneself by a particular brand or model but also to assuredly categorize others along the lines of gender, age, race, sexual orientation, and class. Beyond those sociological parameters, consumers and the marketers who catered to them, also tried to avow that cars reflected and shaped one's personality. Naming one's car, personalizing one's relationship, loving and even lusting after a trusted companion, cars integrated themselves into the fabric of American life in ways that inspired artwork, poetry, and literature. Forged in the shared experiences and the dependence that unfolded, the car took on a meaningful role in people's lives. For women, the anthropomorphized car frequently served as a female rival, while, for men, it drew their amorous affection. While occasionally humorous, the inclination to objectify and embrace cars as women ultimately served as a disappointing development in the quest for greater equality in American gender relations. As with Internet brides imported from countries with much higher expectations of women's servitude to men, enabling men's love for inanimate vehicles allowed them to command the object of their affection to do their bidding, and rationalized passion for a car as a legitimate, mature choice. This associative pattern focused on meeting men's desires contributed to a greater polarizing of gender roles, and further affirmed men's automotive power.[61]

EPILOGUE

Nouveau Riche Pretenders

CARS HAVE LONG HELD incredible importance, as objects in their own right as well as by helping to define American gender identity. The experience of learning to drive, buying a car, driving a car, and maintaining a car has largely been understood from the perspective of a male driver. Cars and their mastery have long afforded men a patina of social standing. This aura and credibility extended even to men who did not own a car, did not know how to repair a car, or did not even know how to drive one. Men's status as arbiters of all things automotive accorded them tremendous social power. Women rarely could overcome their outsider standing. Women's visibility, as they changed a tire or drove a car, exposed them as nouveau riche pretenders.[1]

Cultural analysts regularly recounted the tendency of American men to ascribe particular importance to their cars' ability to convey power. America's pervasive car culture provided men ample opportunities to assert their social muscles. In spite of twentieth-century American women gaining greater independence and more power, the patina still served to affirm that, culturally, women and cars persisted in being a secondary relationship. Men did not even have to be in possession of cars; the cars themselves were believed to be the rightful property of men. Women who began to rail against their outsider status in the last quarter of the twentieth century did not even get to the car as they contended with injustices in both their personal and professional lives. Poor treatment on the sales lot or derogatory assessments of their driving typified the discourse that persistently shut women out of the car's social power.[2]

Into the twenty-first century, even depictions of women as drivers remained fairly unusual. A politely worded request in a letter to the editor of *Popular Mechanics* in 2004 revealed the entrenched attitudes. A female reader asked, "Just once in a while could you show a woman driving a boat or a truck?" The editor included his response to her letter: "I could, but I won't. You'll have to read *Cosmo* or *Redbook* to see women driving. Our readers are almost all men, so we'll be in the driver's seat for the foreseeable future at *PM* (*Popular Mechanics*)." Whether they persisted in belittling women as drivers in general or lashed out at women driving the newest Porsche SUVs, because it ruined the brand's masculine identity, men claimed control of automobiles.[3]

Taking a gendered lens to cars also illuminates the long-standing power of patriarchy. The broader American society and its car culture in particular persisted in being patriarchal into the twenty-first century. Men and women have found themselves perpetuating it, if only by continuing to socialize others to its ideology. The power of cars is a largely heretofore unexamined force that has contributed to a polarizing of gender roles and the imbalance of power between women and men.[4]

An understanding of men's social and cultural control of cars does not deny the agency and power that women had in commanding their own cars, knowing how to repair them, or how to shop for them. Instead, it challenges the expectation that women have had the same experience as men, and emphasizes that after more than one hundred years, women are still understood to be *poseurs* when they are at the wheel.

ABBREVIATIONS

AA	*Advertising Age*
AAA	American Automobile Association Archive, Heathrow, Florida.
AAC	Library and Research Center, Antique Automobile Club of America, Hershey, Pennsylvania.
AES	Arthur and Elizabeth Schlesinger Library on the History of Women in America, Cambridge, Massachusetts
ALE	*Albert Lea Evening Tribune* (Minnesota)
AM	*American Motorist*
AMW	Alice Marshall Women's History Collection, Archives and Special Collections at the Penn State Harrisburg Library, Pennsylvania State University Libraries, Harrisburg.
BAA	*Baltimore Afro-American*
BDG	*Boston Daily Globe* (until 1960)
BFR	Ford Motor Company Records, Benson Ford Research Center, the Henry Ford, Dearborn, Michigan
BG	*Boston Globe* (1960 and after)
BHG	*Better Homes and Garden*
BL	*Boys' Life*
CLA	*Country Life in America*
CN	*Courthouse News*
CT	*Chicago Tribune*
DP	*Denver Post*
EDP	Ernest Dichter Papers, Hagley Museum and Library, Wilmington, Delaware
ESQ	*Esquire*
FN	*Ford News*
FT	*Ford Times*

FLS	*Free Lance-Star* (Fredericksburg, Virginia)
GH	*Good Housekeeping*
GMA	General Motors Archive, GM Heritage Center, Sterling Heights, Michigan
GTR	Goodyear Tire and Rubber Company Records, University of Akron, Akron, Ohio.
GU	*Guardian* (UK)
HBS	Baker Library Historical Collections, Harvard Business School, Cambridge, Massachusetts
HC	*Hartford Courant*
HCD	J. Walter Thompson and Baden Records, Hartman Center, Duke University, Durham, North Carolina
HOU	*Houston Chronicle*
IAP	Print ad (original or copy) in author's possession
JWT	*J. Walter Thompson News Bulletin*
LAT	*Los Angeles Times*
LD	*Literary Digest*
LHJ	*Ladies' Home Journal*
MA	*Motor Age*
MN	*Marketing News*
MTW	*Marketing to Women*
NG	*National Geographic*
NPN	*National Petroleum News*
NY	*New Yorker*
NYM	*New York* magazine
NYT	*New York Times*
PI	*Printers' Ink*
PM	*Popular Mechanics*
PP	*Pittsburgh Press*
PT	*Parking Today*
RD	*Readers' Digest*
RE	*Reading Eagle*
RT	*Road & Travel*
SCR	*Scribner's Magazine*
SD	*Science Digest*

SEP	*Saturday Evening Post*
SFC	*San Francisco Chronicle*
SM	*Southeast Missourian*
SW	*Spokesman-Review* (Spokane, Washington)
TB	*Toledo Blade*
TG	*Gazette* (Cedar Rapids, Iowa)
TP	*Times-Picayune*
USA	*USA Today*
VF	*Vanity Fair*
WHC	*Woman's Home Companion*
WP	*Washington Post*
WSJ	*Wall Street Journal*
WW	*Working Woman*

NOTES

Preface

1. Betty Friedan, *The Feminine Mystique,* 50th Anniversary Edition (New York: W. W. Norton, 2013), 515; Daniel Horowitz, *Betty Friedan and the Making of the Feminine Mystique* (Amherst: University of Massachusetts Press, 1998), 170; email correspondence with Daniel Horowitz, 24 October 2012, and Daniel Friedan (son), 19 November 2012; Michele Kort, "Portrait of the Feminist as an Old Woman," *LAT*, 10 October 1993; Ruth Schwartz Cowan, *More Work for Mother: The Ironies of Household Technology from the Open Hearth to the Microwave* (New York: Basic Books, 1985), 85; Virginia Scharff, *Taking the Wheel: Women and the Coming of the Motor Age* (Albuquerque: University of New Mexico Press, 1992), 146–51, 163; Virginia Scharff, "Putting Wheels on Women's Sphere," in *Technology and Women's Voices: Keeping in Touch*, ed. Cheris Kramarae (New York: Routledge, 1988), 136; Margaret Walsh, "Gender and Automobility: Selling Cars to American Women After the Second World War," *Journal of Macromarketing* 31(1) (March 2011): 59–61; Deborah Clarke, *Driving Women: Fiction and Automobile Culture in Twentieth-Century America* (Baltimore: Johns Hopkins University Press, 2007), 37; Cotton Seiler, *Republic of Drivers: A Cultural History of Automobility in America* (Chicago: University of Chicago Press, 2008), 50–52; Margaret Walsh, *At Home at the Wheel? The Woman and Her Automobile in the 1950s* (British Library, 2006), https://www.bl.uk/eccles/pdf/baas2006.pdf; Carol Sanger, "Girls and the Getaway: Cars, Culture, and the Predicament of Gendered Space," *University of Pennsylvania Law Review* 44(2) (December 1995): 707, 715, 727.

Sanger coined the expression "simultaneous shift" to capture the additional work women did "using the time wisely by working in one's car while waiting near the school, next to the practice field, or outside the swim club" (720). Sanger also described the British "Ladycabs" that used only women as drivers; in 1992, "forty percent of the company's passengers [were] children being picked up from school" (737).

2. Christine McGaffey Frederick, "The Commuter's Wife and the Motor Car," *Suburban Life* 15 (July 1912): 13–14, 46; Fisk ad, *SCR*, October 1919; Chevrolet ad, 15 October 1927, Baden, Box 3, HCD; Ford ad, *FN* 18(8) (1938): 192; Dorothy Dignam, "It Takes Nerve and Verge," *FN* 20(3) (1940): 63; Ford ad, *Life*, 15 July 1945; Charlotte Montgomery, "School Car Pools," *GH*, January 1955, 26; Pontiac ad, *Life*, 10 March 1958; *Life* ad, 9 March 1959; Cadillac ad, *Sunset*, 1963; Cadillac ad, *Texas Monthly*, April 1976, 13;

Cowan, *More Work for Mother*; Scharff, *Taking the Wheel*, 151, 171; Seiler, *Republic of Drivers*, 56; Clarke, *Driving Women*, 10–11, 14; Clay McShane, *Down the Asphalt Path: The Automobile and the American City* (New York: Columbia University Press, 1994), 151, 164–67.

3. McShane, *Down the Asphalt*, 151; Seiler, *Republic of Drivers*, 87.

4. Kathy Peiss, *Cheap Amusements: Working Women and Leisure in Turn-of-the-Century New York* (Philadelphia: Temple University Press, 1986); Beth Bailey, *From Front Porch to Back Seat: Courtship in Twentieth-Century America* (Baltimore: Johns Hopkins University Press, 1989); McShane, *Down the Asphalt*, 157, 167–68; James Flink, *The Automobile Age* (Cambridge, Mass.: MIT Press, 2001), 158–62.

5. Ed Janicki, "Autos," *BL*, May 1970, 15; McShane, *Down the Asphalt*, 151, 156, "devil wagon," 166; Clarke, *Driving Women*, 14; Scharff, *Taking the Wheel*, 33; Nancy Tillman Romalov, "Mobile Heroines: Early Twentieth-Century Girls' Automobile Series," *Journal of Popular Culture* (Spring 1995): 236.

6. John B. Rae, *The American Automobile: A Brief History* (Chicago: University of Chicago Press, 1965), 8–15; Clarke, *Driving Women*, 3–4, 10–11; Bonnie Remsberg, "Women Behind the Wheel," *Redbook*, September 1973, cited in Scharff, *Taking the Wheel*, 37, 182; W. C. Madden, *Haynes-Apperson and America's First Practical Automobile: A History* (Jefferson, N.C.: McFarland, 2003), 1–4; McShane, *Down the Asphalt*, 131; Romalov, "Mobile Heroines," 234.

7. Clarke, *Driving Women*, 15–18; "Elkhart Lady First in Land to Drive a Car," *Hammond Lake County Times* (Indiana), 28 June 1928, 12.

Landon's identity as the only female employee in an automobile company stands out as an anomaly. Delving into her background, however, reveals that Mary Landon was a cousin of Haynes's business partners and fellow innovators, Elmer and Edgar Apperson. Like most other examples of early women drivers, such as Bertha Benz, the car industry tended to be a family affair (*Automotive Industries* 15 [1906]: 825). The promotion of seventeen-year-old Florence Woods securing the first license granted to a woman to drive in Central Park in 1900 is in keeping with this tradition as well, as her father was an inventor and car salesman (McShane, *Down the Asphalt*, 157; "Auto-Permit for a Woman," *NYT*, 3 January 1900; Gijs Mom, *The Electric Vehicle: Technology and Expectations in the Automobile Age* [Baltimore: Johns Hopkins University Press, 2004], 29–30).

Historian Virginia Scharff credits Genevra Delphine Mudge of New York as the first woman to drive, in 1898. Mudge is also heralded as the first woman to race and the first to have an accident, careening into five pedestrians during a race (*Taking the Wheel*, 37). The acclaim, however, is sourced to 1973 in Remsberg, "Women Behind the Wheel." Similarly, the first woman Scharff indicates was licensed in 1899, Mrs. John Howell Phillips from Chicago, is cited from a 1974 motor-vehicle-industry publication (25 and 182). One report on Mudge refers to women drivers as "Mudge followers" (Motor Vehicle Manufacturers Association, "Automobile Facts and Figures," 1973, in Bob Broderick, "Across the Desk," *Uniontown Morning Herald* (Pennsylvania), 24 February 1973).

8. Milton Lehman, "The First Woman Driver," *Life*, 8 September 1952, 82–95; Scharff, *Taking the Wheel*, 16–17, 23–25.

9. "1st Woman Driver Invited to Kokomo," *Kokomo Morning Times* (Indiana), 16 April 1965.

10. "Her Own Mechanic on Drive to 'Frisco," *NYT*, 6 June 1909; "Women Automobilists on a Cross Continent Tour," *Fort Wayne Sentinel*, 15 June 1909; "Woman Driver Makes Coast in Maxwell," *Boston Sunday Post*, 15 August 1909; W. H. B. Fowler, "Pretty Women Motorists Arrive After Trip Across the Continent," and Maxwell ad, *SFC*, 8 August 1909; Maxwell ad, *The Standard* (Ogden, Utah), 24 August 1909, 8; Alice Ramsey, *Veil, Duster and Tire Iron* (Covina, Calif.: Castle Press, 1961); Tom Mahoney, "Alice Huyler Ramsey: First of the 'Weaker Sex' to Show Driving Superiority," *Cars & Parts*, June 1979; David Holmstrom, "Come Rain or Mud or Broken Axle," *Christian Science Monitor*, 18 and 19 September 1990; Marcella Vig Baldwin, "In the Early Days of Motoring," *NYT*, 26 June 1994; Cheryl Jenson, "American Women at the Wheel: By Blazing a Coast-to-Coast Trail, She Helped Put a Nation on the Road," *NYT*, 6 June 1999; Marina Koestler Ruben, "Alice Ramsey's Historic Cross-Country Drive," Smithsonian.com, 4 June 2009, http://www.smithsonianmag.com/history/alice-ramseys-historic-cross-country-drive-29114570/?no-ist; Robert Peele, "History That's More Than the Sum of Its Parts," *NYT*, 28 March 2010; Megan Turchi, "The Story of the First Cross-Country Road Trip by a Woman," boston.com, 9 June 2015, http://archive.boston.com/cars/news-and-reviews/2015/06/09/the-story-the-first-cross-country-road-trip-woman/UrXnAbdkfy1YVlUTvKRuNM/story.html; "America on the Move" exhibit, Smithsonian, http://amhistory.si.edu/onthemove/exhibition/exhibition_7_3.html (accessed 9 September 2016); McShane, *Down the Asphalt*, 157.

11. "Mrs. Emerson Carey" obituary, *Hutchinson News* (Kansas), 18 April 1961, 3; "Alice Ramsey Is Both! 'First Lady of Automotive Travel' and 'Woman Motorist of the Century,'" *Fairborn Daily Herald* (Ohio), 5 January 1971; "Gertrude Krazer" obituary, *Syracuse Post Standard* (New York), 31 May 1990; Clarke, *Driving Women*, 17.

12. Rubin, *Alice Ramsey's Historic Cross-Country Drive*; Seiler, *Republic of Drivers*; Clarke, *Driving Women*, 111–13, 132, 166, 175, 194, 201–2 (notes 1 and 2); John Jakle and Keith Sculle, *Motoring: The Highway Experience in America* (Athens: University of Georgia Press, 2008); Jennifer Parchesky, "Women in the Driver's Seat: The Auto-Erotics of Early Women's Films," *Film History* (2006): 178; Sanger, "Girls and the Getaway," 708; McShane, *Down the Asphalt*, 150–51, 153; Chris Lezotte, "Born to Take the Highway: Women, the Automobile, and Rock 'n' Roll," *Journal of American Culture* 36(3) (2013): 161–76; Scharff, *Taking the Wheel*, 22–23, 26, 107.

13. Clarke, *Driving Women*, 1, 3, 5, 8–9, 11, 166, 175; Scharff, *Taking the Wheel*, 112, 117; David Gartman, *Auto Opium: A Social History of American Automobile Design* (New York: Routledge, 1994), 54–58; Marie T. Farr, "Freedom and Control: Automobiles in American Women's Fiction of the 70s and 80s," *Journal of Popular Culture* (Fall 1995): 157; Mary Walton, *Car: A Drama of the American Workplace* (New York: W. W. Norton, 1997), 224; Hasia Diner interview about Henry Ford's anti-Semitism, http://www.pbs.org/wgbh/americanexperience/features/interview/henryford-antisemitism/. The power to read and convey individual identity was fully understood to be evident in a car's make, model, and adornment. Sherry Christiansen, "Is Your Car a Republican or a Democrat?" Autoshopper.com, http://blog.autoshopper.com/articles/536/Is-Your-Car-a-Republican-or-a-Democrat/; David Harris, "Driving While Black: Racial Profiling on Our Nation's Highways," 7 June 1999, https://www.aclu.org/report/driving-while-black-racial-profiling-our

-nations-highways?redirect = racial-justice/driving-while-black-racial-profiling-our-nations-highways; the President's Task Force on 21st Century Policing, *Final Report of the President's Task Force on 21st Century Policing* (Washington, D.C.: Office of Community Oriented Policing Services, May 2015): 28, http://www.cops.usdoj.gov/pdf/taskforce/TaskForce_FinalReport.pdf (all accessed 19 May 2016).

14. McShane, *Down the Asphalt*, 161–63; Scharff, *Taking the Wheel*, 25–26, 36–50; Rae, *The American Automobile*, 12–15; Michael Brian Schiffer, *Taking Charge: The Electric Automobile in America* (Washington, D.C.: Smithsonian Institution Press, 1994), 135–39; Clarke, *Driving Women*, 18; Georgine Clarsen, "The 'Dainty Female Toe' and the 'Brawny Male Arm': Conceptions of Bodies and Power in Automobile Technology," *Australian Feminist Studies* 15 (32) (2000): 159; Mom, *The Electric Vehicle*; National Museum of American History, "America on the Move," http://amhistory.si.edu/onthemove/themes/story_74_3.html (accessed 18 May 2016).

15. Rae, *The American Automobile*, 17–32; Flink, *The Automobile Age*, 22–33; Seiler, *Republic of Drivers*, 36; Margaret Walsh, "Gender and the Automobile in the United States," http://www.autolife.umd.umich.edu/Gender/Walsh/G_Overview.htm (accessed 3 March 2016); "More Automobiles Than Telephones," *J. Walter Thompson News Bulletin*, July 1924, 15, 20–21; Pamela Laird, " 'The Car Without a Single Weakness': Early Automobile Advertising," *Technology and Culture* 37(4) (1996): 797; Gartman, *Auto Opium*, 53–54, 56; Jennifer Scanlon, *Inarticulate Longings: The Ladies' Home Journal, Gender, and the Promises of Consumer Culture* (New York: Routledge, 1995), 197–98; Chevrolet ad, *LHJ*, April 1990, 64–65; Chevrolet ad, *BHG*1988, Lightner 2, HCD; Toyota ad, 2000, IAP; James D. Norris, *Advertising and the Transformation of American Society, 1865–1920* (Westport, Conn.: Greenwood Press, 1990), 148–50, 153, 167; Stanley Lebergott, *Pursuing Happiness: American Consumers in the Twentieth Century* (Princeton, N.J.: Princeton University Press, 1993), 130.

16. "Bathtub" in Joseph Interrante, "The Road to Autotopia: The Automobile and the Spatial Transformation of American Culture," in *The Automobile and American Culture*, ed. David L. Lewis and Laurence Goldstein (Ann Arbor: University of Michigan Press, 1983), 89; Seiler, *Republic of Drivers*, 55–56; Fuels Institute, *Driver Demographics: The American Population's Effect on Vehicle Travel and Fuel Demand* (2014): 13, https://www.fuelsinstitute.org/ResearchArticles/DriverDemographics.pdf (accessed 3 March 2016).

17. "Where Women Motorists Excel Mere Men," *LD*, 4 December 1920, 73; "How Many People Can Buy Motor Cars," *Automotive Manufacturer*, September 1921, 26; Frank Hobbs and Nicole Stoops, "Sex Ratio by Region: 1900 to 2000," *Demographic Trends in the 20th Century*, https://www.census.gov/prod/2002pubs/censr-4.pdf (accessed 18 May 2016); Walsh, *At Home at the Wheel?*; Department of Commerce, *Fourteenth Census of the United States Taken in the Year 1920*, Volume 2, Chapter 2: Sex Distribution (Washington, D.C.: Government Printing Office, 1922), 101–41; Joan Lowy, "More Women Drivers on U.S. Roads Now," *USA Today*, 12 November 2012 (http://www.usatoday.com/story/money/cars/2012/11/12/women-drivers-men-licenses-roads/1700185/) (accessed 3 March 2016); U.S. Department of Transportation, "Licensed Drivers," https://www.fhwa.dot.gov/ohim/onh00/onh2p4.htm (accessed 3 March 2016); McShane, *Down the Asphalt*, 149–51, 162.

18. Scharff, *Taking the Wheel*, 61; David Cullen, "Women Drivers!" *Fleet Owner*, September 2002; Doron Levin, "Hey Guys, Are You Man Enough to Drive a Chick Car?" *Bloomberg News* 18 April 2006, http://www.sddt.com/news/article.cfm?SourceCode=20060418faa&_t=Hey+guys+are+you+man+enough+to+drive+a+chick+car-.VqWevrArKi4; "The Goddess in the Car—And Out," *Harper's Weekly*, 12 February 1910, 30; "Four Little Maids from School," *FT* 4(4) (1910), 116; "Lady Tourists!—Why Not?" *FT* 6 (November 1912), 78; McShane, *Down the Asphalt*, 157; Kathleen Franz, *Tinkering: Consumers Reinvent the Early Automobile* (Philadelphia: University of Pennsylvania Press, 2005), 44; Herbert Ladd Towle, "The Woman at the Wheel," *SCR*, February 1915.

Of course, not all enthusiasts wanted women to drive. The editor of *Motor* magazine proclaimed in 1927 that "every time a woman learns to drive . . . it is a threat at yesterday's order of things" (Scharff, *Taking the Wheel*, 117).

19. Overland ad, *LHJ*, July 1916, 46; Marguerite Mooers Marshall, "'Lady of the Limousine' and 'Maid of the Motor' Are Queens of Auto Show," *Evening World* (New York), 9 January 1917, Final Edition, 10; "How Women Have Guided the Designing of Closed Cars," *Durant's Standard*, November 1922, 4–5, AAC; Bruce Ashby, "Are the Makers of Automotive Accessories on the Horns of a Sales Dilemma?" *J. Walter Thompson News Bulletin*, February 1927, 1–5, *JWT*, Box MN5; Fisher ad, *LHJ*, January 1932, 42–43; "Cars 'Dressed Up' for Bid to Women," *NYT*, 5 September 1937; Ginger Dawson, "Welcomes Women on Wheels," *American Motorist*, December 1969, 29; Ford ad, *LHJ*, January 1990, 161; Beth Kraig, "Women at the Wheel," PhD diss., University of Washington, 1987, 26–28; Flink, *The Automobile Age*, 162–63; Clarsen, "The 'Dainty Female Toe' and the 'Brawny Male Arm'."

Virginia Scharff counted more than 5,000 such accessories for the Model T alone in a Sears, Roebuck catalog in the early 1920s (*Taking the Wheel*, 122–24).

20. Michael L. Berger, "Women Drivers! The Emergence of Folklore and Stereotypic Opinions Concerning Feminine Automotive Behavior," *Women's Studies International Forum* 9(3) (1986): 258; Scharff, *Taking the Wheel*, 20–22, 28–29, 31; Clarke, *Driving Women*, 4.

Joyce Carol Oates captured the normative pattern of male drivers and female passengers: "Of course he drove the car when they were together" (narrative voice in *Childwold*, 501, cited in Marie T. Farr, "Freedom and Control: Automobiles in American Women's Fiction of the 70s and 80s," *Journal of Popular Culture* [Fall 1995]: 168).

21. For further thoughts, see Bennett, who argued that a "patriarchal equilibrium" simultaneously enabled the continuities of patriarchal power to persist and blinded observers to it. Clarke, *Driving Women*, 7, 16; Sylvia Walby, *Theorizing Patriarchy* (Cambridge, Mass.: Blackwell, 1991); Judith M. Bennett, *History Matters: Patriarchy and the Challenge of Feminism* (Philadelphia: University of Pennsylvania Press, 2006), 54–81. For more recent automotive histories that offer little attention to women, see, for example, Mark S. Foster, *A Nation on Wheels: The Automobile Culture in America Since 1945* (Belmont, Calif.: Wadsworth, 2003); Tom McCarthy, *Auto Mania: Cars, Consumer, and the Environment* (New Haven, Conn.: Yale University Press, 2007); and Steve Parissien, *The Life of the Automobile: The Complete History of the Motor Car* (New York: Thomas Dunne Books, 2014).

Chapter 1

1. Hiram Percy Maxim, "Learning to Drive a Motor Carriage," *The Horseless Age: A Monthly Journal Devoted to Motor Interests* 3(1) (April 1898): 5–6.

2. *Woman's Home Companion* cited in Dorothy Dignam, "We Hopped from Bike to Automobile," *FN*, 18(2) (1938): 37, BFR; Virginia Scharff, *Taking the Wheel: Women and the Coming of the Motor Age* (Albuquerque: University of New Mexico Press, 1992), 42.

3. "Woman Teacher Talks Confidence," *NYT*, 12 April 1914, XX8.

4. Virginia Scharff, "Putting Wheels on Women's Sphere," in *Technology and Women's Voices: Keeping in Touch*, ed. Cheris Kramarae (New York: Routledge, 1988), 140–43; Missouri study and Mary Neth, quoted in Susan Matt, *Keeping Up with the Joneses: Envy in American Consumer Society, 1890–1930* (Philadelphia: University of Pennsylvania Press, 2003), 111–13, 121.

5. "Generous Response Accorded AAA Women Drivers Instruction Course," *AM*, November 1929, 2. There were exceptions, of course. The Young Men's Christian Association (YMCA) of New York City established an Automobile School in 1903 and taught "More than 25,000 Men and Women." The YMCA maintained that its course for women was "identical with that given men, except that it is carefully planned to relieve them of the lifting of heavy parts" (brochure, 1924, BFR).

6. *Ford News* highlighted the driving school's Annual Field Day in 1930, 10(11), 122, BFR; "Drive Miles Standing Still" photo and caption, May 1939, J. Stirling Getchell, Inc., HBS; "'Cars' in Movie-Simulated Traffic Used in Schools to Teach Driving," *NYT*, 25 February 1953, 29; William Carr, "Education and the Motor Age," *Annals of the American Academy of Political and Social Science* (November 1958): 63–72; Stan Luger, *Corporate Power, American Democracy, and the Automobile Industry*, New York: Cambridge University Press, 2000), 58.

7. E. L. Yordan, "Drivers Go to School," *NYT*, 19 September 1937, 193; "Teachers Are Pupils in Drivers' School," *NYT*, 2 April 1946, 24; Arthur Gelb, "Students Don't Cut This Kind of Class," *NYT*, 17 June 1949, 25; June Saylor, "Mademoiselle Motorist," *AM*, March 1957, 30.

On the failings or limitations of driver's education to do more than teach rudimentary skills, see, for example, John Jerome, *The Death of the Automobile: The Fatal Effect of the Golden Era, 1955–1970* (New York: Norton, 1972).

8. General Motors Corporation, *We Drivers: A Series of Brief Discussions on Driving, Dedicated to Safety, Comfort and Pleasure of the Motoring* Public (Detroit: Department of Public Relations, General Motors Corporation, 1936 and 1949); American Automobile Association, *Sportsmanlike Driving Series* (Washington, D.C.: American Automobile Association, 1955); Paul Kearney, *How to Drive Better and Avoid Accidents*, 2nd ed. (New York: Crowell, 1963).

9. Peter Marsh and Peter Collett, *Driving Passion: The Psychology of the Car* (Boston: Faber and Faber, 1986), 160; Richard P. Compton and Patricia Ellison-Potter, *Teen Driver Crashes: A Report to Congress, July 2008*, http://www.nhtsa.gov/DOT/NHTSA/Traffic%20 Injury%20Control/Articles/Associated%20Files/811005.pdf; National Highway Traffic Safety Administration, *Saving Teenage Lives: The Case for Graduated Driver Licensing*

(Washington, D.C., 1998); Robert Lindsey, "Driver Education Criticized Anew," *NYT*, 21 October 1973; "BMV study: Teens Who Take Driver's Ed Class More Likely to Crash," 22 August 2010, http://www.wthr.com/article/bmv-study-teens-who-take-drivers-ed-class-more-likely-to-crash.

10. "'Cars' in Movie-Simulated Traffic Used in Schools to Teach Driving," *NYT*, 25 February 1953, 29; "Girls' School Gets Training Car," *NYT*, 27 October 1959; Allstate ad, *Life*, 22 September 1967; AMC commercial for the Rebel, 1969, https://www.youtube.com/watch?v=-z8TtSoq_Tc; Luger, *Corporate Power*, 58; Betsy Wade, "Back to School for Older Drivers," *NYT*, 3 April 1988.

11. Stuart Elliott, "Allstate Adds Villain, with Car Insurance as Hero," *NYT*, 21 June 2010, B3.

12. "Don't Drive Like This" cartoon, *FN* 1(4) (1920–21): 5; "That's the Last Time I Ride with That Show-off," appeared in April *American Boy* and *Boy's Life*, Acc. 19, Box 148, FMC—Products & Services—Traffic Safety, 1939 T-Y, BFR; "Chuck Grew Up in 3 Seconds Flat!" Acc. 19, Box 148, FMC—Products & Services—Traffic Safety, 1940 C, BFR; "He Learned About Speed on the Bench," Acc. 19, Box 148, FMC—Products & Services—Traffic Safety, 1941 A-H, BFR; "The Empty Desk in Room 42, Acc. 19, Box 149, FMC-Products & Services—Traffic Safety, 1957, BFR; "The Cars Are Safer," *Boys' Life*, February 1960, 31; "How to Earn the Key to Dad's Car," 1966, Acc. 951, Non-Serial Imprints, Box 24, BFR; "Turning Without Signaling Is a Good Way to Meet New People," Acc. 19, Box 149, FMC—Products & Services—Traffic Safety, 1968, BFR.

13. "Good Drivers' League," *FN*, 20(4) (1940): 94, BFR.

14. Historical Archive Corporation, *Classic Drivers Ed Film Library* (Ann Arbor, Mich.: Historical Archive, 2006); Ken Smith, *Mental Hygiene: Classroom Films 1945–1970*, 1st ed. (New York: Blast Books, 1999), 73–82, 125, 140, 158, 173, 182, 225–26.

15. Walter A. Cutter, "Safety by Study," *NYT*, 16 October 1960, A6; David Blanke, *Hell on Wheels: The Promise and Peril of America's Car Culture, 1900–1940* (Lawrence: University Press of Kansas, 2007), 145–52.

16. Anthony Tramondo, "Female Drivers: Less Deadly Than the Male," *NYT*, 27 March 1955, SM26; Juliet Carter, "Mademoiselle Motorist," *AM* (January 1962), 20; Ann Long Wanser, "Mademoiselle Motorist: Teaching Them to Survive," *AM* (September 1971), 26; Hugh Muir, "Women 'Need Longer to Learn to Drive,'" *GU*, 14 February 2005.

17. Jackie Anderson, "Mademoiselle Motorist," *AM* (September 1957), 34; "Driving Schools: How Good, How Fast, How Much?" *GH*, August 1959, 146–47; "Learn to Drive," *AM*, May 1966, 7; "Learn to Drive," *AM*, June 1966, 20; "Who Has More Fun?" *AM*, April 1968, 8; AAA Driving School, *AM*, March 1969, 8. For number of female licensed drivers, see "Women Count as Nearly Half of Total Licensed Drivers," *Vidette Messenger* (Valparaiso, Indiana) 18 October 1973, 8, and Appendix E in Beth Kraig, "Woman at the Wheel: A History of Women and the Automobile in America," PhD diss., University of Washington, 1987, 332; Margaret Walsh, *At Home at the Wheel? The Woman and Her Automobile in the 1950s* (British Library, 2006), https://www.bl.uk/eccles/pdf/baas2006.pdf.

18. Elizabeth Barnes, "Driving School," *NY*, 28 November 1959, 173–80; Karen Rosenberg Caccavo, "Long Island Opinion; Driven to Drive—At Long Last," *NYT*, 23

February 1986, 16; Carol Sanger, "Girls and the Getaway: Cars, Culture, and the Predicament of Gendered Space," *University of Pennsylvania Law Review* 44(2) (December 1995): 725; Amy Collins, *The God of Driving: How I Overcame Fear and Put Myself in the Driver's Seat with the Help of a Good and Mysterious Man* (New York: Simon & Schuster, 2004); Cathy Horyn, "Everyone's Drive to Eat: How Many Arrive in a Bentley?" *NYT*, 29 December 2004. Of course, some women needed lessons because they could not pass the driving test after taking driver's education classes. For a movie short on this subject, see *Driver's Ed* (2005) https://www.youtube.com/watch?v=YMRsVmtGpuk. Ernest Dichter reflected on the psychology of a good driver's education program in his article "A License to Drive or a License to Kill?" published in *Concepts* in 1972 (EDP).

19. Anita Grutzner, "Learning to Be a Good Driver," *NYT*, 9 March 1952, XX18; Dr. Joyce Brothers column, *Anderson Herald* (Indiana), 3 December 1965, 30; David Bahr, "Driver's Ed, Where Driving Is a Blood Sport," *NYT*, 8 September 1996, CY4; Claudia Feldman, "Columnist Katha Pollitt to Speak at Conference," *HOU*, 12 November 2008. Pollitt's story inspired the 2015 movie *Learning to Drive* (m.imdb.com/113062976/). Adam Gopnik explores gendered motivations for driving in "The Driver's Seat" (*NY*, 2 February 2015).

For a consideration of older women, race, and ethnicity in driving, see also Transportation Research Board, *Transportation in an Aging Society: A Decade of Experience* (Conference Proceedings 27) (Bethesda, Md.: 1999): 12–14.

20. Nadine Brozan, "Nondrivers: Resisting the Open Road," *NYT*, 3 August 1987, C18; Katty Kay and Claire Shipman, "The Confidence Gap," *Atlantic*, 14 April 2014. A great deal of Norman Klein's encouraging book, *Drive Without Fear*, centered primarily on alleviating older women's fears (Bloomington, Ind.: 1st Books Library, 2001).

21. "When Friend Wife Rocked the New 'Boat,'" *LD* 64 (13 March 1920): 96–98, cited in Kraig, "Woman at the Wheel," 332; "Teaching the Wife to Drive," *AM*, August 1927, 8-J; Bob Barnes cartoon originally appeared in *American* magazine, reprinted in Lawrence Lariar, *Best Cartoons of the Year 1951* (New York: Crown, 1951); Jackie Anderson, "Mademoiselle Motorist," *AM*, May 1958, 30; "Mademoiselle Motorist: Don't Wreck Your Car and Your Marriage," *AM*, May 1969, 20–21; Mary Neth, *Preserving the Family Farm: Women, Community, and the Foundations of Agribusiness in the Midwest, 1900–1940* (Baltimore: Johns Hopkins University Press, 1995), 252, 325; "I Don't Care What Age You Are, If You Decide You Want to Drive, Do It"; Marilyn Root, *Women at the Wheel: 42 Stories of Freedom, Fanbelts, and the Lure of the Open Road* (Naperville, Ill.: Sourcebooks, 1999), 93–95; Celia Dodd, "Wheel Thing: New Research Reveals Why Some Women Become Wimps in the Driving Seat—and Men Are to Blame," *GU*, 25 May 1999, T6.

This kind of caution about teaching loved ones to drive also extended to teaching young people. A 1964 *NYT* article reported that the New York Department of Motor Vehicles' guide for parents discouraged them from teaching their children, noting, "Most families have complex interrelationships that are only aggravated while the teen-ager is learning to drive" (Barbara Lang, "And Now He (She) Drives," *NYT*, 8 November 1964, SM110). Richard F. Shepard reflects on this teaching relationship in his 1976 article, "On Being Driven to Distraction" (*NYT*, 5 September 1976, 240). Television also explored this tension. See, for example, "Driving Miss D.J.," *Full House*, Season 5, Episode 20, original airdate 25 February 1992.

22. Henry McLemore, "Teaching Wife to Drive Called False Economy," *Kenosha Evening News* (Wisconsin), 21 January 1959; "You Bet Your Life," 5 April 1956, https://www.youtube.com/watch?v=lKW__71BRGM (accessed 23 February 2016).

23. Dr. Joyce Brothers column, *Anderson Herald* (Indiana), 3 December 1965, 30.

24. Ibid.; Michael Kaufman, "Differential Participation: Men, Women and Popular Power," in *Community Power and Grassroots Democracy*, ed. Michael Kaufman and Haroldo Dilla Alfonso (London: Zed Books, and Ottawa: International Development Research Centre, 1997), 153–54, 157.

25. Brothers, 30.

26. Ann Landers column, *Cullman Times Democrat* (Alabama), 15 November 1968, 3; Kaufman, "Differential Participation," 156–57.

27. Richard Winton and Harriet Ryan, "Rihanna Assisting Police in Chris Brown Case," *LAT*, 10 February 2009; *Happy-Go-Lucky*, directed by Mike Leigh (2008); *Driving Miss Daisy*, directed by Bruce Beresford (1989).

28. Beth Bailey, *From Front Porch to Back Seat* (Baltimore: Johns Hopkins University Press, 1989); George Vecsey, "More Women Defy Risks of Hitchhiking," *NYT*, 26 December 1972, 69; "Most Girl Hitchhikers Calculate Perils They Face, *LAT*, 31 July 1977, 2; LaToya Peterson, "The Not-Rape Epidemic," in *Yes Means Yes! Visions of Female Sexual Power and a World Without Rape*, ed. Jaclyn Friedman and Jessica Valenti (Berkeley, Calif.: Seal Press, 2008), 197–98.

29. Behind the Wheel Driving School contract, http://www.btwdrivingschool.com/terms.html; Fearless Driver, Ann's Driving School, San Francisco, http://www.fearlessdriver.com (accessed 18 January 2011); A Woman's Way Driving School, Valley Stream, Long Island, New York, http://tiny.cc/oxpc2x; "Driving Teacher Accused of Sexual Assault," *BG*, 23 January 2003; Tracy Vedder, "State: Driver's Ed Instructor, 74, Took Advantage of Teen Girls," seattlepi.com (Seattle) http://www.seattlepi.com/local/article/State-Driver-s-ed-instructor-74-took-advantage-900037.php; Amanda Milkovits, "Providence Driving Instructor Accused of Sexually Assaulting Student," *Providence Journal* (Rhode Island), 5 February 2014.

30. "Groping Driving Instructor Jailed," 31 October 2005, http://news.bbc.co.uk/2/hi/uk_news/england/manchester/4392658.stm; Matthew Moore, "'Carrot down trousers' driving instructor jailed," 7 December 2007, http://www.telegraph.co.uk/news/uknews/1571772/Carrot-down-trousers-driving-instructor-jailed.html; "'Fake Penis' Sex Attacker Jailed," bbcnews.com, 7 December 2007, http://news.bbc.co.uk/2/hi/uk_news/england/tees/7132628.stm; "Driving Instructor Denies Sexual Assault" (UK) (23 December 2011), http://www.bbc.com/news/uk-england-cumbria-16319731; Benedetta Faedi, "Rape, Blue Jeans, and Judicial Developments in Italy," *Columbia Journal of European Law Online* 13 (2009); "One-Legged Driving Teacher Groped Girls 'as Penalty for Mistakes' and Turned Up Heating to Make Them Strip," *The Mail* (UK) (10 December 2010), http://www.dailymail.co.uk/news/article-1337525/One-legged-driving-instructor-groped-teenage-learner-drivers-making-mistakes.html.

Women commonly sought safety from male assailants by paying for taxis, yet Carol Sanger points to the potential to sexual assaults in those vehicles, including one "driver-rapist" who "testified that sex with passengers was a 'perk' of the job" ("Girls and the

Getaway," 735–36. More recently, the unregulated Uber drivers are exposing this vulnerability for women (WhosDrivingYou.org, http://www.whosdrivingyou.org/rideshare-incidents).

31. Virginia Rinaldo Seitz, *Women, Development, and Communities for Empowerment in Appalachia* (Albany, NY: SUNY Press, 1995), 76–77; Kaufman, "Differential Participation," 153–54, 156–57.

32. Marie T. Farr, "Freedom and Control: Automobiles in American Women's Fiction of the 70s and 80s," *Journal of Popular Culture* (Fall 1995): 160; Margot Mendelson, "The Legal Production of Identities: A Narrative Analysis of Conversations with Battered Undocumented Women," *Berkeley Women's Law Journal* 19(1) (2004): 189–202; Kaufman, "Differential Participation," 153–54, 156–57.

33. Shepard, "On Being Driven"; Richard F. Shepard, "On Long Island," *NYT*, 6 June 1982, L12.

34. Shepard, "On Long Island"; Barbara Ann Porte, "Why They Don't Like to Drive," *NYT*, 25 July 1982, L118; Claudia Feldman, "Columnist Katha Pollitt to Speak at Conference, *HOU*, 12 November 2008; Clay McShane, *Down the Asphalt Path: The Automobile and the American City* (New York: Columbia University Press, 1994), 155.

35. "Women, 18 to 35, Lead Men Rivals in Auto-Driving Test, A.A.A. Finds," *NYT*, 19 July 1952, 17; William Geise, "Takes the Wheel," *Kiplinger's Personal Finance*, May 1994, 103–5; Po Bronson and Ashley Merryman, *Nurtureshock: New Thinking About Children*, 1st ed. (New York: Twelve, 2009), 158; Earl Babbie, *The Practice of Social Research*, 12th ed. (Belmont, Calif.: Wadsworth Cengage Learning, 2007), 365; Chris Woodyard, "One in Five Motorists Would Now Fail DMV Written Test," *USA Today*, 6 September 2010; Hugh Muir, "Women 'Need Longer to Learn to Drive,'" *GU*, 14 February 2005.

36. *Second Annual Report of the Commissioner of Motor Vehicles to the Legislature—Session of 1908* (Trenton, N.J.: MacCrellish & Quigley, n.d.), 7–8; *Seventh Annual Report of the Commissioner of Motor Vehicles to the Legislature of the State of New Jersey for the Year One Thousand Nine Hundred and Twelve* (Union Hill, N.J.: Dispatch Printing Company, n.d.), 1; *Eleventh Annual Report of the Commissioner of Motor Vehicles to the Legislature of the State of New Jersey for the Year One Thousand Nine Hundred and Sixteen* (Trenton, N.J.: MacCrellish & Quigley, 1917), 11; "Less Than Half Car Drivers of County Buy License First Year," *Kentucky New Era*, 17 July 1935, 1; David G. Wittels, "License to Kill," *SEP*, 16 August 1947, 15–17, 121–23; Verlyn Klinkenborg, "To Drive or Not to Drive: That Was Never the Question," *NYT*, 21 January 2008; Virginia Scharff, "Putting Wheels on Women's Sphere," 140. "In 1900, the City Engineer of Chicago complained that many women were not bothering to get licenses" (Scharff, *Taking the Wheeel*, 37). See also Scharff, *Taking the Wheel*, 23, for women in New Jersey, and 25, for first licensed American woman.

37. *Report of the Commissioner of Motor Vehicles to the Legislature of the State of New Jersey for the Year Ending December 31st, 1906* (Trenton, N.J.: John L. Murphy Publishing Co., 1907), 18–22; Commissioner of Motor Vehicles, *Official 1911 Motorist's Manual for New Jersey* (New York: Manual Pub. Co., 1911); "Confer on Tests for Auto Drivers," *NYT*, 25 May 1919, 9; "How Old Must You Be to Drive Legally," *GH*, October 1956, 50; "Driver Licensing . . . A Major Problem of Nonconformity," c. 1975, 1–12, AAA; National Committee on Uniform Traffic Laws and Ordinances, "Driver Licensing Laws Annotated,

1973" (Charlottesville, Va.: Michie Company, 1973), 163–69; McShane, *Down the Asphalt*, 149–50n.260; U.S. Department of Transportation, National Highway Traffic Safety Administration, "Driver Licensing Laws Annotated, 1980," in Northwestern Transportation Library, Northwestern University, Evanston, Illinois.

38. "Color Aids Police," *Reading Eagle* (Penn.), 21 August 1966, 3; "States Put Pictures of Drivers on Licenses," *Milwaukee Journal* (Wisc.), 14 September 1967, 1; Robert E. Miller, "Photo Driver Licenses Popular with Ohioans," *Youngstown Vindicator* (Ohio), 6 February 1974, 16; "Senate Okays Photos on Drivers Licenses," *Telegraph Herald* (Iowa), 11 March 1976, 10; "Bureaucratic Reflex to Proposed License," *Lodi News-Sentinel* (Calif.), 24 April 1984; Nancy Price, "Smile! Driver's License Photos Are Going Digital," *Lawrence Journal-World* (Kansas), 19 April 1994; Iver Peterson, "Lawmakers Backing Plans on Terrorism and Licenses," *NYT*, 4 October 2001; Matthew L. Wald, "A Smarter License: What Can It Tell," *NYT*, 27 October 2004; "A Look Back at the Evolution of Drivers' Licenses in Utah," *Deseret News* (Utah), 5 December 2010.

39. "Auto Women," *BDG*, 28 September 1903, 6.

40. David G. Wittels, "License to Kill," *SEP*, 16 August 1947, 15–17, 121–23; "Drivers' Ages," *NYT*, 9 November 1952, X17; Better Vision Institute ad, *Life*, 18 November 1966, 120.

41. Kermit Hall and David Scott Clark, *The Oxford Companion to American Law* (New York: Oxford University Press, 2002), 288; Clarke, *Driving Women*, 167; Carl Watner, " Drivers Licenses and Vehicle Registration in Historical Perspective," in *National Identification Systems: Essays in Opposition*, ed. Carl Watner and Wendy McElroy (Jefferson, N.C.: McFarland and Company, 2004), 101–15; Simonson Garfinkel, "Nobody Fucks with the DMV," *Wired* (2)2 (February 2004), http://archive.wired.com/wired/archive/2.02/dmv.html?topic=&topic_set=; Social Security Legislative Bulletin, 7 January 2005, Section 7214, https://www.ssa.gov/legislation/legis_bulletin_010705.html.

42. "Auto Women," *BDG*, 28 September 1903, 6; "If You Would Like," *ALE*, 23 February 1934; "Ladies' Day," *NYT*, 30 March 1947; June Rightor, "Mademoiselle Motorist," *AM*, May 1955, 32.

Oscar Wilde, for example, in his 1893 play *A Woman of No Importance*, wrote, "One should never trust a woman who tells one her real age. A woman who would tell one that, would tell one anything." See, The Official Website of Oscar Wilde, http://www.cmgww.com/historic/wilde/. Susan Sontag explores women's aging in her essay, "The Double Standard of Aging," in *On the Contrary: Essays by Men and Women*, ed. Robin Rainbolt and Janet Fleetwood (Albany: State University of New York Press, 1984), 99–12.

43. License images, IAP.

44. "A Married Woman's Name," *Freeport Journal Standard* (Illinois) 1 August 1923; "Woman Attorney Asks for Change of Name," *Berkeley Daily Gazette* 6 September 1929; Amy Vanderbilt, "Safety and Manners," *Cedar Rapids Gazette* (Iowa), 2 September 1956; Lori Ginzberg, *Elizabeth Cady Stanton: An American Life* (New York: Hill and Wang, 2010), 17.

45. "Maiden Name Barred for a Driver's License," *NYT*, 30 September 1971; "Justices Rule Against Ladies," *Beaver County Times* (Penn.), 14 December 1976, A10; "Name Suit Filed Again for Driver's License," *Gadsden Times* (Alabama), 29 June 1977, 3; Susan

Moller Okin, *Women in Western Political Thought* (Princeton, N.J.: Princeton University Press, 1979), 250–51. Copy of Wild license, IAP.

For a sample of lawsuits used in this analysis, please see, for example, *Baumann v. Baumann*, 250 N.Y. 382, 165 N.E. 819 (1929); In Re Kayloff 9 F.Supp. 176 (1934), District Court, S. D. New York, 11 December 1934; *Forbush v. Wallace* 341 F.Supp. 217 (1971), United States District Court, M. D. Alabama, N. D., 28 September 1971; *Dunn v. Palermo*, 522 S.W.2d 679 (1975), Supreme Court of Tennessee, 7 April 1975; *Whitlow v. Hodges* 539 F.2d 582 (1976), United States Court of Appeals, Sixth Circuit, Argued 30 September 1975; *Traugott v. Petit* 404 A.2d 77 (1979), Supreme Court of Rhode Island, 27 July 1979.

46. Email from Barbara Roos to author, 2 February 2013; *Davis* v. Roos, 326 So. 2d 226 (Fla. Dist. Ct. App. 1976), https://www.courtlistener.com/opinion/1833004/davis-v-roos/; "Law with Women on Names," *Naples Daily News*, 4 February 1976, 2B; photo of Barbara Roos, "special for *Miami Herald*," 5 February 1976, IAP; Maxine Margolis, "When Women Keep Their Names," letter to the editor, *NYT*, 1 September 2013.

47. *Davis v. Roos*, 326 So. 2d 226 (Fla. Dist. Ct. App. 1976), https://www.courtlistener.com/opinion/1833004/davis-v-roos/ (accessed 12 February 2016).

48. "The Name Equality Act of 2007," California, http://www.cdph.ca.gov/certlic/birthdeathmar/Documents/NameEqualityActPamphlet-(1-13).pdf; comments in blog section of MissNowMrs.com regarding post, "Maiden to Middle Name Change," https://www.missnowmrs.com/newlywed-blog/2010/07/19/maiden-to-middle-name-change/; "Maiden Name to Middle Name Change," marriagenamechange.com, http://www.marriagenamechange.com/blog/maiden-name-to-middle-name/; Texas Administrative Code, Title 37, Part 1, Chapter 15, Subchapter L, Rule 15.183, a.1.A, https://texreg.sos.state.tx.us/public/readtac$ext.TacPage?sl=R&app=9&p_dir=&p_rloc=&p_tloc=&p_ploc=&pg=1&p_tac=&ti=37&pt=1&ch=15&rl=183 (accessed 12 February 2016).

49. Erma Bombeck, "Laminated Photos in Wallet May Even Pass for Hitler," *PP*, 27 February 1973, 25. Initially called "These Friends of Mine," the pilot *Ellen* episode appeared 29 March 1994, http://www.imdb.com/title/tt0570046/.

50. "Muslim Woman Cannot Wear Veil in Driver's License Photo," *USA*, 6 June 2003; "Amish Find Struggle with Their Faith, New Concern of National Security," *Southeast Missourian*, 16 August 2003, 10A–11A; "Mennonites Are at Odds With License-Photo Rules," *NYT*, 25 March 2007; Allan Pease, *The Definitive Book of Body Language* (New York: Bantam, 2006), 86–87; Thomas Frank, "Four States Adopt 'No-Smiles' Policy for Driver's Licenses," *USA*, 26 May 2009; Marianne LaFrance, *Why Smile* (New York: Norton, 2013).

51. "Guess What," *FT* (2) (December 1945): 49; "It's Like," *NY*, 30 December 1950, 27; "What's the," *NY*, 3 March 1951, 28; "What Do I Do Now?" (1953) *SEP*, appeared in Kraig, "Woman at the Wheel," 112; "I Hope," *NY*, 16 November 1963, 115; Edgar A. Guest, "Ma and the Auto," in *A Heap o' Livin'* (1916) https://archive.org/stream/heapolivin1916gues#page/22/mode/1up>; Recording of Edgar A. Guest reading "Ma and the Auto, 1921, http://www.loc.gov/jukebox/recordings/detail/id/8277/; musical score of "Ma and the Auto," 1928, http://digital.library.msstate.edu/cdm/ref/collection/SheetMusic/id/7466; illustrated broadside version of the poem, 1931, http://www.ebay.com/itm/1931-brown-bigelow-edward-a-guest-ma-and-the-auto-framed-poem-print-car-meiier-/390

849585888; film version of "Ma and the Auto," c. 1930s, https://www.youtube.com/watch?v=h-FNkWeGANA. With thanks to Stanley Blair for alerting me to the Edgar Guest poem and its popularity.

52. Bob Newhart, *I Shouldn't Even Be Doing This! And Other Things That Strike Me as Funny* (New York: Hyperion, 2006), 61–65, 109–10, 175.

53. "Weird Al" Yankovic, "She Drives Like Crazy," *UHF—Original Motion Picture Soundtrack and Other Stuff* (July 1989); Harry Enfield, "Women, For Pity's Sake Don't Drive," https://www.dailymotion.com/video/x2z6unh_harry-enfield-women-for-pity-s-sake-don-t-drive_fun; *Home Improvement*, Season 6, Episode 130 "Burnin' Love," airdate 8 October 1996.

54. Jeannie Thomas, "Dumb Blondes, Dan Quayle, and Hillary Clinton: Gender, Sexuality, and Stupidity in Jokes," *Journal of American Folklore* 110(437) (1997): 277–313; "What Women Say About Men," (box), *CT*, 26 April 1990, 18.

55. "Lucy Learns to Drive," *I Love Lucy*, airdate 3 January 1955; "Lucy Helps Craig Get a Driver's License," *The Lucy Show*, airdate 17 March 1969. Also the premise of "Margaret Learns to Drive," *Father Knows Best,* airdate 20 November 1957.

56. "Scratch My Car and Die," *The Dick Van Dyke Show*, airdate 25 March 1964.

57. "The Fender Benders," *The Brady Bunch*, airdate 10 March 1972.

58. Edgar A. Guest, "Ma and the Auto," *A Heap o' Livin'* (1916), https://archive.org/stream/heapolivin1916gues#page/22/mode/1up (accessed 14 May 2016); Douglas Malloch, "The Back Seat Driver," *AM*, August 1924. An undated cartoon postcard featured a woman driver telling a male mechanic, "There's an irritating little squeak in the back." As with the depictions of women as backseat drivers, this cartoon also portrayed the woman as oversized and unattractive, while her husband was more diminutive and shamefaced (IAP).

59. "If You Would Like," *ALE*, 23 February 1934; "Percent of Population Licensed to Drive, By Age and Sex for 1951–35, 1970, and 1982," in Appendix E, Kraig, "Woman at the Wheel," 332.

In analyzing women's lives in Toronto, Canada, William Michelson reached a similar conclusion about men's propensity to control the only car in one-car families, even if his wife worked full time and had a similarly long commute in *From Sun to Sun: Daily Obligations and Community Structure in the Lives of Employed Women and Their Families* (Totowa, NJ: Rowman & Allanheld, 1985), 125–33.

European countries have seen smaller percentages of their population drive, with women having even lower rates than men. The United Kingdom had the smallest number of women drivers. See Ilan Salomon, Piet H. L. Bovy, and Jean-Pierre Orefeuil, *A Billion Trips a Day: Tradition and Transition in European Travel Patterns* (New York: Springer, 1993), 96–99.

60. Martin Bunn, "Don't Be a Back-Seat Driver!" *Popular Science Monthly*, October 1927, 69, 182.

61. Daniel "Alain" Brustlein cartoon, *NY*, 27 September 1947, 39.

62. "Woman at the Wheel," *LD*, 29 January 1938, 14; Roy Welday, *Your Automobile and You* (New York: H. Holt, 1938), iii; Kentucky Club ad c. 1953, IAP; Yellow Pages ad, *GH*, April 1956, 176; Al Kaufman cartoon appeared in Lawrence Lariar, *The Best of Best Cartoons* (New York: Crown, 1961); Better Vision Institute ad, *Life*, 1 March 1963, 64.

63. Some researchers learned that what divided the brain experiences of passengers and drivers was much less than what we might imagine and helps to explain, at least in part, the desire to weigh in on driving decisions. In studying cognitive neuroimaging, researchers discovered that the brains of observers mirrored those taking the action. They found that "the brain of the scolding passenger shows the same pattern of activity as that of an irritated driver." According to Dr. Michael G. H. Coles, "It's as if the observers were making the errors themselves" (quoted in Anahad O'Connor, "Passengers Feel the Driver's Anxiety, Too," *NYT*, 27 April 2004, 8).

Chapter 2

1. Ford Motor Company, *The Lady and Her Motor Car* (Detroit: Ford Motor Company, 1911); Rollin Car, "Women!" c. 1924, 1–2, HBS; Margaret Walsh, "Gender and Automobility: Selling Cars to American Women After the Second World War," *Journal of Macromarketing* 31(1): 57–72.

2. "Women Big Factor in the Auto Sales," *Fort Wayne Sentinel*, 11 January 1916, 15; A. J. Baime, "Car Sellers Refine Pitch to Women," *WSJ*, 20 August 2014.

3. Deborah Clarke, *Driving Women: Fiction and Automobile Culture in Twentieth-Century America* (Baltimore: Johns Hopkins University Press, 2007), 7–8, 15.

4. "Hyundai Hires FUSE Agency to Handle First African American Advertising Campaign," 28 October 2014, http://targetmarketnews.com/storyid10291401.htm.

5. Ford Motor Company, *The Woman and the Ford*, 1912, Acc. 951, Box 55, BFR; Cadillac ad, quoted in James D. Norris, *Advertising and the Transformation of American Society, 1865–1920* (Westport, Conn.: Greenwood Press, 1990), 156; Marmon ad, *NG*, June 1923; Marmon ad, 1926, AMW; Rollin Car, "Women!" c. 1924, 1–2, HBS; Rollin ad, 5 July 1924, *LD*, 14.

6. Ibid.; Chrysler ad, *LHJ*, May 1926, 117; Packard ad, *GH*, February 1928; Buick Motor Company, "The First Choice of Women," 1930, no. 72007, HBS; Ford V-8, *FN* 20(1), 1940, 24, BFR; Ford ad series, 1947, Domestic ads, FM4, JWT, HCD.

7. Ibid.; Buick ad, http://automotivemileposts.com/riviera/prod1964riviera.html; Chevrolet, "Pretty Soon Every Other Guy Who Walks into Your Showroom Will Be a Woman," 1986, IAP.

8. E. L. Cord, "Women Will Not Tolerate Mediocrity in Motor Cars," *NYT*, 8 January 1928, 144; Mobiloil ads, *LHJ*, May, June 1930; Chevrolet ad, *RD*, March 1968.

9. Virginia Scharff, *Taking the Wheel: Women and the Coming of the Motor Age* (Albuquerque: University of New Mexico Press, 1992), 84.

10. Dodge Brothers, Inc., "Standard Sales Presentation—The Woman Buyer," 1927, BFR; Joseph Ingraham, "Autos and Makers Criticized in Study of 17,000 Women," *NYT*, 10 April 1958; Julie Tripp, "Sexism in the Showroom," *Oregonian*, 17 August 1992; M. Maynard, "Dealer Group Responds to Showroom Chauvinism" and "A Woman Dealer Explains Showroom Sense: Treat All Equally," *USA*, 1 October 1990, in Ford Motor Company Women's Marketing Committee's *Market Trends: Women in the 90s* 1(3) (Winter 1990): 3–4, Vertical File, BFR; Scharff, *Taking the Wheel*, 126–27; Marilyn Gardner, "For Men Only: Women Buy Cars in an Alien Land," 18 October 1988, *Philadelphia Inquirer*;

Maddy Dychtwald, "Transformers: Women and the Automotive Industry," *Forbes*, 18 May 2010, http://www.forbes.com/2010/05/18/women-auto-industry-influence-forbes-woman-leadership-car-dealers.html; Christina LeBeau, "As Car Dealers, Women Are Scarce but Successful," *NYT*, 21 January 2003.

11. Dodge Brothers, "Standard Sales Presentation"; "Dealer's Supplement," *FN* 9(9) (1 May 1929): 105; "Dealer's Supplement," *FN* 10(7) (1 April 1930): 81; Ingraham, "Autos and Makers Criticized"; Tripp, "Sexism in the Showroom"; Mickey Meece, "Candid Talk for Women (Men Allowed, Too), *NYT*, 24 October 2007, 30; Walsh, "Gender and Automobility," 64.

12. Helene M. Lawson, *Ladies on the Lot: Women, Car Sales, and the Pursuit of the American Dream* (New York: Rowman & Littlefield, 2000); Lincoln ad with Julia Mead on *The Ed Sullivan Show*, 1954, https://www.youtube.com/watch?v=OJnbIlBATLM (accessed 30 July 2016); Hal Butler, "Look for the Woman!" *Ford Crest News* 5(12) (1958): 4–5, Acc. 972, BFR; "Vroom, Baby!," *Time*, 27 October 1980; Shirley Lord, "Women and American Cars: What's Coming in the '80s," *Vogue*, February 1981, 293; AMC/Jeep/Renault, 1983 Bulletin, IAP; Raymond Serafin, "Dealers Hold Key to Sales Success in Segment," "Special Showroom Deals in Different Attitudes," and "Venturing into Sales Structure," *AA* (Special Report: Women and the Auto Market) 15 September 1986, S16, 20; Chevrolet, "Pretty Soon Every Other Guy Who Walks into Your Showroom Will Be a Woman," 1986, GMA; accompanying memo and 1987 Certified Product Specialist Study Guide, 40–44, c. 1986, AAC; Walsh, "Gender and Automobility," 64; Carin Rubenstein, "Women in the Driver's Seat," *Across the Board* (April 1986): 43, in JWT, Marketing Vertical File, Box 8, HCD; Darrell Dawsey, "A New Type of Truck Buyer," 1 February 1989, in Ford Motor Company Women's Marketing Committee's *Market Trends: Women in the 90s* 1(1) (Spring 1990): 1, 3, Vertical File, BFR; BMW 1993 Sales & Marketing Training Guide Brochure (Activity: Women's Market Perceptions), listed on www.ebay.com (accessed 27 July 2012; screen shot IAP); M. Maynard, "Dealer Group Responds to Showroom Chauvinism" and "A Woman Dealer Explains Showroom Sense: Treat All Equally," *USA*, 1 October 1990, in Ford Motor Company Women's Marketing Committee's *Market Trends*, 3–4; Ian Ayres and Peter Siegelman, "Race and Gender Discrimination in Bargaining for a New Car," *American Economic Review* 85(3) (June 1995): 304–21.

13. "Vroom, Baby!" *Time*, 27 October 1980; Shirley Lord, "Women and American Cars: What's Coming in the '80s," *Vogue*, February 1981, 293; AMC/Jeep/Renault, 1983 Bulletin, IAP; Raymond Serafin, "Cadillac and *Vogue* Engineer Stylish Promotion," "Dealers Hold Key to Sales Success in Segment," "Special Showroom Deals in Different Attitudes," and "Venturing into Sales Structure," *AA* (Special Report: Women and the Auto Market) 15 September 1986, S6, 16, 20; Chevrolet, "Pretty Soon Every Other Guy"; Accompanying memo and 1987 Certified Product Specialist Study Guide, 40–44, c. 1986, AAC; Rubenstein, "Women in the Driver's Seat"; Darrell Dawsey, "A New Type of Truck Buyer," 1 February 1989, in Ford Motor Company Women's Marketing Committee's *Market Trends: Women in the 90s* (Spring 1990) 1(1): 1, 3, Vertical File, BFR; BMW 1993 Sales & Marketing Training Guide Brochure (Activity: Women's Market Perceptions), listed on www.ebay.com (accessed 27 July 2012; screen shot IAP); "Wine, Baubles, and Glamour Are Used to Help Lure Female Consumer to Ford's Showrooms," *Marketing News*, 6 August 1982; cartoon, *BHG*, September 1980, 190.

14. Eric Hollreiser, "Women and Cars," *Adweek's Marketing Week*, 10 February 1992; Becky Quick, "Car Salesmen: Still Sexist, Still Stupid," *Fortune*, 27 March 2012; Fara Warner, "New Cadillac Reconnaissance: Woman and African-Americans," *Brandweek* 35(9) (28 February 1994): 1–2; Jean Halliday, "GM Looking to Woo Developing Clout of Females," *Advertising Age* 67(25) (17 June 1996), 39; Clarke, *Driving Women*, 78.

15. Warren Brown, "Sexism in the Showroom: Complaints by Women of Mistreatment Spur Changes by Dealers," *WP*, 12 February 1989; Hollreiser, "Women and Cars"; Gwendolyn Freed, "A Driving Force for Change," 23 June 2003, *Star Tribune* (Minneapolis); Meece, "Candid Talk"; Christina Olenchek, "Web Site Gives Control, Respect to Female Automobile Buyers," *Central Penn Business Journal*, 1 August 2008, 13; Dychtwald, "Transformers"; Baime, "Car Sellers," 20 August 2014. "Ninety-five percent of new car dealerships belonging to the National Automobile Dealers Association are owned by men" (Libby Copeland, "Baby, You Can't Drive My Car," Slate.com, 19 March 2013, http://www.slate.com/articles/double_x/doublex/2013/03/car_ads_for_women_does_the_industry_get_it_all_wrong.single.html.)

16. Copeland, "Baby, You Can't Drive My Car"; "Wine, Baubles, and Glamour Are Used to Help Lure Female Consumers to Ford's Showrooms," *Marketing News* 16(3) (6 August 1982), 1–2; Andi Young, "Selling Cars to Women," *Automotive Age*, October 1982, 14–16; John Holusha, "The Selling of Cars to Women," *NYT*, 21 December 1985, 33; Chevrolet, "Pretty Soon Every Other Guy Who Walks into Your Showroom Will Be a Woman," 1986; "Women Can Get the Credit They Deserve," June 1985, GMA; "The Women's Market," 14 February 1986, 13, GMA; Raymond Serafin, "Cadillac and *Vogue*," S6; Julie Candler, "Women Are the Subject of Promotions," *AA* (Special Report: Women and the Auto Market) 15 September 1986, S6; Raymond Serafin, "Dealers Hold Key," S16; "Women Car Buyers: Advertising and Special Programs," 5–6, 26–27 March 1986, GMA; Oldsmobile WOMAN press release, 27 March 1986, GMA; Rubenstein, "Women in the Driver's Seat"; "Image, Practicality Speak to Women Auto Buyers," *MTW* 10(10) (31 October 1997): 1; Julie Halpert, "Chevy's Ads Evolved with the Changing Role of Women in Society," *AA*, 31 October 2011, 28–30; King of Prussia and Chevrolet Announce Exclusive Marketing Alliance, http://www.theautochannel.com/news/2005/10/31/147035.html; Female Buyer Study, *Road and Travel Magazine*, 2004, cited in "Catering to the Most Buyers: Women," Chicago Auto Trade Association, http://www.cata.info/catering_to_the_most_buyers_women/ (accessed 30 July 2016).

17. Robin Fields, "Hyundai's Unconventional Approach to Women," *LAT*, 8 July 1999; Ruth Mortimer, "Driving Sales to Women," *Brand Strategy*, July 2002, 28; PR Newswire, "Power of the Purse(TM) Takes the Stress Out of Car Buying," 8 September 2005, http://www.prnewswire.com/news-releases/power-of-the-pursetm-takes-the-stress-out-of-car-buying-54786432.html; George Blumberg, "To Sell a Car That Women Love, It Helps if Women Sell It," *NYT*, 26 October 2005.

18. Baime, "Car Sellers."

19. Ford ad, *FT*, May 1914, 350; Chevrolet ad, *NG*, 1923, Lightner 2, JWT; Chevrolet ad, *GH*, November 1923, Lightner 2, JWT; Dodge ad, *Women's Home Companion*, May 1925, Lightner 4, JWT; Plymouth ad, 1931, Lightner 9, JWT; Ruth Schwartz Cowan, *More Work for Mother: The Ironies Of Household Technology From The Open Hearth To The*

Microwave (New York: Basic Books, 1985); Roland Marchand, *Advertising the American Dream* (Berkeley: University of California Press, 1985), 161; Scharff, *Taking the Wheel*, 125; Winton ad, *Pittsburgh Press*, 3 October 1915, 7; Jennifer Berkley, "Women at the Motor Wheel: Gender and Car Culture in the U.S.A., 1920–1930," PhD diss., Claremont Graduate School, 1996, 91; "Autos Likened to Home," *NYT*, 15 November 1936; Buick ad, *NG*, March 1940; Ford ads, March and June 1949, Domestic Advertisements, FM4, JWT; Ford ad, July 1949, J. Walter Thompson, Domestic Advertisements, FM4, JWT; Dodge ad, 1957, AAC; Body by Fisher ad, *Life*, 20 October 1958, 90–91; Body by Fisher ad, *Life*, 13 April 1962, 121; Body by Fisher ad, *Life*, 14 January 1966, 41; James Barron, "Fuzzy Dice Décor: The Car Interior as Living Room," *NYT*, 25 August 1988; Oldsmobile ad, *BHG*, July 2000, z11; John Heitmann, *The Automobile and American Life* (Jefferson, N.C.: McFarland, 2009), 96–98; Carol Sanger, "Girls and the Getaway: Cars, Culture, and the Predicament of Gendered Space," *University of Pennsylvania Law Review* 44(2) (December 1995): 728.

20. Hudson ad, *LHJ*, March 1931, n.p.; Dodge ad, *Holiday*, April 1948, Lightner 4; Ford ad, *Life*, 2 May 1955, 162–63; Buick ad, *Life*, 25 March 1966, 5; "Ways Women Influence Car Design," *Redbook*, c. September 1973, 201.

21. Overland ad, *LHJ*, July 1916, 46; Sesamee ad, c. 1920, AMW; Chevrolet ad, *NYT*, 21 March 1937, 22b; Genie ad, *GH*, September 1958, 212; Frederick C. Russell, "Lifting the Hood," *AM*, March 1961; June Rightor and Barbara Phillips, "Mademoiselle Motorist," *AM*, October 1954, 32; Don Klein, "This Commercial for the Honda: Odyssey's Built-in Vacuum Doesn't Suck," caranddriver.com, 16 October 2013, http://blog.caranddriver.com/honda-commercial-for-the-odysseys-built-in-vacuum-doesnt-suck-the-ad-section/.

22. Oldsmobile ad, *BHG*, July 2000, z11; Dodge ad, *NG*, September 1989; Ford ad, 1992, IAP; "Dog Friendly Travel with the 2013 Ford Escape," lifeanddog.com, December 2012; Clarke, *Driving Women*, 142.

23. Texaco ad, *LHJ*, May 1930; Ford ad, *Gazette & Daily* (York, Pennsylvania), 11 May 1931, 3; Paul de Kruif, "Accidents Don't Happen," *LHJ*, June 1935, 8–9, 52, 54, 56, 58; Loring Schuler, "I Will Drive Safely, *LHJ*, August 1935, 26, and July 1935, 23; "Mother, It's Up to *You!*" *AM*, February 1941, 3, 11; Paul Ingrassia and Gregory A. Patterson, "The American Way of Buying: Is Buying a Car a Choice or a Chore?—Huge Selection Has Its Pluses—and Its Minuses," *WSJ*, 24 October 1989: 1.

24. Ford ad, *Motor Age*, 1 January 1920, 3; Charles L. Sanford, "'Woman's Place' in American Car Culture," in *The Automobile and American Culture*, ed. David L. Lewis and Laurence Goldstein (Ann Arbor: University of Michigan Press, 1983), 147.

25. "Weed Chains—and Expectant Mothers," *Advertising & Selling* 31(7) (29 October 1921): 13, 48; Fisk ad, *Country Life*, May 1929, 119; Weed Tire Chains, *LHJ*, February 1930, 98; Arvin Car Heaters ad, *SEP*, 24 October 1931, 109; Firestone ad, 1936, Acc. 657, Box 11, Parts—Tires—Firestone, 1930–39, BFR; Fisk ad, 1945, IAP; Chevrolet ad, *LHJ*, June 1948.

26. Scharff, *Taking the Wheel*, Claudy cited 41, 128; Clarke, *Driving Women*, 75–78, 82–83; Gordon Motor Crib Co. ad, *GH*, March 1927, 243; Mary Swartz Rose, "The Baby's Automobile Kit," *LHJ*, June 1928, 42; Dorothy Dignam, "Going to Grandma's," *FT*, 1939 19(6), 135, and 1939 19(7), 160; Dorothy Dignam, "Mothers Will Get Behind These New

Models," *FT*, 1940 20(6), 136; Charlotte Montgomery, "When the Children Go Along," *GH*, May 1951,44, 161–62; Welsh Co. ad, *GH*, July 1951, 204; GM ad, *RD*, April 1980, 40–41.

27. Ford ad, *Life*, 28 January 1946; Buick ad, 1958, IAP; Kortney Stringer, "Goodwrench Commercials Getting Serious," *Knight Ridder/Tribune Business News* 24 October 2005, 1.

28. Tennant Pneumatic ad, *The Automobile*, 26 December 1903, 41; Pennyslvania Oilproof Vacuum Cup Tire ad, c. 1910, IAP; Kelly-Springfield ads in *LD*, 11 June 1910, 7 June 1913, 28 April 1917; Goodrich ad, 1914, IAP; Kelly-Springfield ad, *Country Gentleman*, April 1931, 68; Weed Chains ad, *GH*, February 1929; Chevrolet ad, 1937; Goodyear ad, *Life*, 10 July 1939, 10; Fisk ad, 21 May 1945, *Life*, 74; Goodyear ad, *Saturday Review*, 29 July 1961; General Tire ad, *Life*, 18 March 1966, 26; Pirelli ad, 1971, IAP; Kelly Tire ad, *American Magazine*, 1923, 118; Goodyear ads, 1935 and 1937, IAP; Fisk tire ad, 1937, IAP; General Tire ad, November 1937, Acc. 657, Box 11, Parts—Tires, BFR; Goodyear ads, *NG*, 1940; General Tire ads, 1935, 1937, 1950, IAP; Goodyear ads, c. 1935, c. 1940, c. 1956, c. 1960, IAP; Katherine Parkin, "'Bring Them Back Alive!': Fear and the Macabre in U.S. Automobile Tire Advertising," *Advertising & Society Quarterly* 18 (1) April 2017, https://muse.jhu.edu/article/652406.

Challenging many gendered expectations, in 1987 advertisers found that men and women were equally likely (27 percent) to be members of an auto club that would assist them if their car broke down (Research Alert, 15 May 1987, Marketing Vertical File, Box 8, JWT).

29. Fisk ad, 1939, IAP; Ford ad, *Life*, 29 January 1946; Goodyear ad, *Saturday Review*, 29 July 1961; Firestone ad, *Ebony*, July 1962, 54–55; Chrysler ad, *Life*, 15 December 1958, 5; Goodyear ad, *Life*, 21 April 1961, 72–73; Rambler ad, *Life*, 13 April 1962, 95; GM ad, *Life*, 19 August 1966, 33; Ford ad, *Southern Living*, June 1984; Peter Dougherty, "Advertising: Michelin's Broader Approach," *NYT*, 10 January 1985; Goodyear ad, 1996, https://www.youtube.com/watch?v=mGFe07Ro7r0; Morgan & Wright ad, 1904, IAP; Kelly-Springfield ad, *LD*, 11 June 1910; General Tire ads, c. 1940s and 1950s, IAP; Goodyear ad, 1967, IAP; Merchant's Tire Center ad, *AM*, April 1971; Firestone ads, 1972 and 1973, IAP; Parkin, "'Bring Them Back.'"

30. Plymouth ad, *GH*, 29 February 1960, 66; Chrysler ad, 15 September 1972, *Life*, 38; Goldfarb Consultants, "Qualitative Insights on the Women's Market," December 1980, Detroit Office, Ford Research Reports, 1974–88, JWT; "OnStar Provides Peace of Mind to Cadillac Women Drivers," Cadillac press release, July 1996, GMA; Packard brochure, "A Woman's Place . . . ," 1955, AAC, 16; Charlotte Montgomery, "What About Seat Belts?" *GH*, January 1956, 24; Advertising Outlook, *PI*, 4 August 1961, 5; Chrysler ad, *Life*, 15 December 1958, 5; GM ad, *Life*, 19 August 1966, 33; Goodyear ad, *Life*, 21 April 1961, 72–73; Bernadine Morris, "Color and Style Aren't All a Woman Driver Wants," *NYT*, 2 April 1967; "A New Safety Feature," *Ford Newsletter* 15 January 1971, 2, Acc. 1885, Box 1, Newsletters 1970–72, No. 5, BFR; Columbus ad, *Life*, 14 May 1971, 91.

31. Volvo ads, *Playboy*, August 1973, 2, and IAP; Clarke, *Driving Women*, 83–88; "Crash Test Mommy," http://new.volvocars.com/enewsletter/07/summer/p03.html; Jean Kilbourne, *Can't Buy My Love: How Advertising Changes the Way We Think and Feel* (New York: Simon & Schuster, 1999), 79–80.

32. "The Ford Motor Company—and Women," c.1948, Acc. 536, Box 113, Women's Influence, BFR.

33. "Design—Women's Influence," 10 January 1952, Acc. 536, Box 28, 1–2, BFR; Eleanor Kelly, "Some People Like Women Drivers!" *AM*, September 1954, 11–12; Morris, "Color and Style"; "Ways Women Influence Car Design," *Redbook*, c. September 1973, 201; J. Walter Thompson Company, "Personality Profile Project," May 1958, Information Center Records, 23(47), JWT; Clarke, *Driving Women*, 89.

34. Carl Gisler, "Is the Buying Influence of Men Underestimated?" *PI*, 24 September 1948, 38–39, 68; Rainwater, *Workingman's*, 191–92; "96% of Women Say: Any Car You Say," *NYT*, 17 April 1960, A10; Whitey Sawyer, "Female Influence Rates High in Auto Industry," *Evening News* (Newark), 23 July 1964; Carl Bialik, "Who Makes the Call at the Mall, Men or Women?" *WSJ*, 23 April 2011; Ford ad, *Capper's Farmer*, February 1949, DA, FM4, JWT; Chevrolet ad, c. 1989, IAP; Arlie Hochschild, *The Second Shift* (New York: Viking, 1989); Walsh, "Gender and Automobility," 59. For more on the illusion that women dominated consumer spending, see Katherine J. Parkin, *Food Is Love: Food Advertising and Gender Roles in Modern America* (Philadelphia: University of Pennsylvania Press, 2006), 152.

Some observers remained unconvinced by assertions of women's buying power. Repeated by historians and marketing analysts was a supposition that modern women's consumer role was dominant, constituting 80 percent of all purchasing decisions. However, critics have noted that it is "not a credible figure" and there were counter-suggestions all along. Surveys across the century reflected varying rates of gender influence on brand selection. One 1948 study, for example, determined that men influenced the make of the car purchased nearly two-thirds of the time. Some researchers also believed that most working-class women did not participate in choosing the family car in the 1950s. According to sociologist Lee Rainwater, "They usually feel that the automobile is, properly speaking, the husband's department." While these husbands often stranded their wives when they used the car to get to work and although the car often proved to be the family's "unwisest purchase," women still acceded 10 percent of the family's budget to buying a car and took pleasure in their husband's enjoyment of it. A brief notice in the *New York Times* in 1960 suggested that women rarely participated in the purchase of a car, leaving men the power to make the sole decision on 96 percent of car purchases. Building on Rainwater's contention of deference, a 1964 investigation by Chevrolet also challenged women's role when Chevrolet discovered that "while the wife likes to be consulted, she shies away from complete responsibility. Insistence on her choice would, she feels, offend her husband's ego. Besides, she is not confident enough of her judgment to risk the censure certain to be voiced should the purchase later prove to be a disappointment" (Whitey Sawyer, "Wives' Opinions Gain Force in Auto Purchases," *Spokane Daily Chronicle*, 24 July 1964, 28).

35. Ella Howard, "Pink Truck Ads: Second-Wave Feminism and Gendered Marketing," *Journal of Women's History* 22(4) (Winter 2010): 137–61; Jill Avery, "Defending the Markers of Masculinity: Consumer Resistance to Brand Gender-Bending," *International Journal of Research in Marketing* 23 April 2012.

36. "Image, Practicality Speak to Women Auto Buyers," *MTW* 10(10) (31 Oct 1997); "News on Women," *MTW* 18(2) (February 2005), 9.

37. "Homemakers Want Fact, Less Fluff, in Ads," *PI*, 6 October 1961, 15; Lillian Borgeson, "Hunting for a New Auto? Learn the Six Tricks of the Trade-in," *Vogue*, March 1980; Janet Guthrie, "Buying a New Car," *WW*, October 1981, 42; Young, "Selling Cars," 10–11, 14–16; Howard, "Pink Truck Ads," 152; John Holusha, "The Selling of Cars to Women," *NYT*, 21 December 1985, 33; Stuart Elliott, "What Do Chevrolet, Conde Nast and Macy's Have in Common? A Customer Base of Young Women," *NYT*, 1 May 1996; "Women and Wheels: Automakers Learning Better Approaches to Growing Market," *TG*, 7 January 1993, 10C; Gloria Steinem, "Sex, Lies, and Advertising," *Ms.* 8(2) (1997): 18–21; Amy Harmon, "Auto Industry Struggling to Cope with Growing Importance of Women Buyers," *SW*, 26 June 1992, D2; "News on Women," *MTW* 18(2) (February 2005), 9.

38. "Homemakers Want Fact, Less Fluff, in Ads," *PI*, 6 October 1961, 15; Carol Caldwell, "You Haven't Come a Long Way, Baby," *New Times*, 10 June 1977 57, 62, Box 2, JWT-Archives—Rena Bartos Collection, HCD.

39. Ibid.; Goldfarb Consultants, "Qualitative Insights on the Women's Market," December 1980, JWT, Detroit Office, Goldfarb Consultants, Ford Research Reports, 1974–89, JWT; Young, "Selling Cars," 10–11, 14–16; Mediamark Research, Inc., "Who's Doing the Buying?" Mediamark Research Product Report, Spring 1990, summary IAP.

40. Meece, "Candid Talk."

41. Chevrolet ad, 23 August 1924, 41; "Automobile Saturation?" *News Bulletin*, July 1926, 26; GM ad, *Gazette & Daily* (York, Pennsylvania), 11 April 1928, 11, Baden 1, JWT; GM ad, *American*, April 1929, 121; Charles Coolidge Parlin, *The Passenger Car Industry* (Philadelphia: Curtis Publishing, 1932), 21–22; Marchand, *Advertising the American Dream*, 161; Scharff, *Taking the Wheel*, 115–17, 170.

42. Chevrolet ad, *LD*, 20 October 1928, 33; Charles E. Gallagher, "Companionate Motoring," *AM*, October 1929, 23, 45; Chevrolet ad, *American Magazine*, April 1930; Chevrolet ad, *LHJ*, n.d., IAP; Cotton Seiler, *Republic of Drivers: A Cultural History of Automobility in America* (Chicago: University of Chicago Press, 2008), 60. Susan Matt describes this emphasis on efficiency and the yearning for success for men in *Keeping Up with the Joneses: Envy in American Consumer Society, 1890–1930* (Philadelphia: University of Pennsylvania Press, 2003), 93–94.

43. Ford ad, *SEP*, 24 June 1950, Baden, Small 1, JWT; letter from Woodrow Wirsig, *Women's Home Companion* to Charles LaCroix, Ford Motor Company, 9 July 1953, Acc. 762, Box 3, B. R. Donaldson-1953, "W," BFR; Ford ad, 1953, Baden, Small 21, JWT; Ford ad, *Holiday*, June 1954, Lightner 5, JWT; Guy Henle, "The Two Car Family," *Woman's Home Companion*, June 1955, 62–63, 76; Ford ad, *Life*, 6 February 1956; Rainwater, *Workingman's*, 154; Packard ad, n.d.; Chevrolet ads, *GH*, February, April, July, September 1956, 25; DeSoto ad, *Holiday*, March 1957; Ford ad, 1957, Lightner 5, JWT.

44. Rambler ad, 1955, AAC; Ford ad, c. 1956, http://www.archive.org/details/TwoFordFreed; AMC ad, *GH*, May 1958, 20; "The Young Marrieds," *Progressive Grocer*, June 1966, Box 21, JWT, Marketing Vertical File, HCD; General Motors, "Wouldn't It Be Nice to Have an Escape Machine?" August 1969, AAC; Tom McCarthy, *Auto Mania: Cars, Consumers, and the Environment* (New Haven, Conn.: Yale University Press, 2007), 148–49; Jeremy Packer, *Mobility Without Mayhem: Safety, Cars, and Citizenship* (Durham, N.C.: Duke University Press, 2008), 33–39; David Gartman, *Auto Opium: A Social History of American Automobile Design* (New York: Routledge, 1995), 185; Ellen J. Gerl and Craig

L. Davis, "Selling Detroit on Women: Woman's Day and Auto Advertising, 1964–1982," *Journalism History* 38(4) (Winter 2013): 210.

45. Chevrolet ad, *Life*, 12 March 1955, 171; Chevrolet ad, *Life*, 17 March 1961, 30; Chevrolet ad, *Life*, 18 April 1965, 62; American Motors Rambler brochure, "Why Every Woman Should Have a Car of Her Own (And How She Can Do It!), 1955, AAC. As early as 1929, Buick featured an ad with a woman signing paperwork with the dealer instructing her where to sign. The ad promoted the dealer's "good name" and assured the reader that used cars were a good investment and value (*SEP*, 14 September 1929, 76); Chevrolet ad, *Life*, 23 March 1967, 80; Barbara Holliday, "Does Your Wife Drive?" *FT* 60(4) (April 1967): 24–27; GMA ad, *Life*, 30 August 1968, 63; Chevrolet ad, *Life*, 28 March 1968, 84.

46. Chandler Six ad, *NG*, 1922, Lightner 2, JWT; Chevrolet ad, *NG*, 1923, Lightner 2, JWT; Ford ad, *McCall's*, December 1928; Essex ad, *The Country Gentleman*, May 1930; Chevrolet ad, *LD*, 17 February 1934; Ford ad, *Time*, 16 June 1947; Ford ad, *Time*, 1 September 1947; Buick ad, 1958, in Tony Swan, *Retro Ride: Advertising Art of the American Automobile*, 1st ed. (Portland, Ore.: Collectors Press, 2002); Mercury ad, 1967, IAP; Chevrolet ad, 1970, Lightner 3, JWT; Chris Lezotte, "The Evolution of the 'Chick Car' Or: What Came First, the Chick or the Car?" *Journal of Popular Culture* 45(3) (2012): 519–21; Judy Vaknin, *Driving It Home: 100 Years of Car Advertising* (London: Middlesex University Press, 2008), 45–46.

47. Marmon ad, 1926, AMW; Scharff, *Taking the Wheel*, 129.

48. Jeep ad, February 1966, Lightner 7, JWT; Jeep commercial in Rubenstein, "Women in the Driver's Seat," 40; Cindy Donatelli, "Driving the Suburbs: Minivans, Gender, and Family Values," *Material History Review* 54 (Fall 2001): 91; Clarke, *Driving Women*, 19–21.

49. Ernest Dichter, "The Motivation of Car Buying," n.d., Hagley; Dichter, quoted in Rubenstein, "Women in the Driver's Seat."

50. Cover art, *Life*, 13 January 1927; Chrysler ad, *LHJ*, April 1930, 103; Buick ads, *LHJ*, February 1931, January 1932, and May 1932; Plymouth ad, *LHJ*, March and April 1932; Chevrolet ad, 9 January 1939, 31; Chrysler ad, *LHJ*, 1940, IAP; Chrysler ad, *Collier's*, 6 April 1940, 55; De Soto press release and accompanying photo, c. 1940, HBS; Oldsmobile, 20 January 1941, 6; Plymouth ad, *LHJ*, (no month) 1958, 22; Scharff, *Taking the Wheel*, 115.

In a similar vein, historian Virginia Scharff (*Taking the Wheel*) found that "Delco and Cadillac initially ignored gender in promoting the electric starter" (62). Moreover, she notes that the self-starter was not standard on the Model T into the 1920s (63).

51. Oldsmobile ad, *Life*, 9 January 1960, 8; Hudson, *Life*, 27 February 1950, 15; Chevrolet ad, *Life*, 30 March 1950, 52; Chevrolet ad, *PM*, April 1960, 79.

52. Ford ad, *Life*, 17 February 1967, 117; Ford ad, *Life*, 22 December 1967, 99; GM ad, 1969, IAP; Volkswagen ad, *News and Courier* (Charleston, South Carolina), 9 April 1973, 3B; Goodyear ad, *Life*, 10 December 1965, 107; Dodge ad, 1977, Lightner 4, JWT; Chevrolet ad, 1998, Lightner 3, JWT; Mustang ad in Ford Motors, *Ford Mustang: Forty Years of Fun* (2004), 53; Shirley Lord, "Women and American Cars: What's Coming in the '80s," *Vogue*, February 1981, 292–93, 314. A 1986 Oldsmobile Market Research Study (0314186), "Characteristics of the Next New Car," found that while 50 percent of women considered automatic transmission a "Must have," so did more than 40 percent of men.

The percentage of men and women who considered a manual transmission a "Must have" was tied at 30 percent (General Motors Media Archive, 1986).

53. Ford ad, 1986, Lightner 6, JWT; Ford ad, *PM*, January 1987, 10 (three-page ad insert); Chicago Automobile Show, *The Automobile*, 3 February 1910; "Women Discriminating Autoists," *Evening World* (New York), 12 January 1922, 12; Willys ad, *Collier's*, 24 January 1931; Buick ad, *Life*, 18 April 1960, 16; Corvair ad, *Life*, 3 April 1964, 47; Julie Halpert, "Chevy's Ads Evolved with the Changing Role of Women in Society," *AA*, 31 October 2011, 28–30.

54. La Comtesse and Le Comte cars, http://www.imperialclub.com/Yr/1954/specs.htm—equipment; Patrick R. Foster, *The Metropolitan Story* (Milford, Conn.: Old Milford Press, 1996); Nash letter re jewelry, 3 May 1954, http://www.metropolitan-library.com/Nash_Jewelry.jpg; Jim Motavalli; "From 1955, a Car Just for Women (But the Color Is All Wrong!)," 26 April 2002; Tim Brooks, "Nash Metropolitan, the First Car for Women," *The National* (Abu Dhabi), 23 December 2011.

55. "Dodge's LaFemme Is First Automobile with a Gender—It's Female," *PM*, January 1955, 133; www.dodgelafemme.com; Edward Malone, "Chrysler's 'Most Beautiful Engineer': Lucille J. Pieti in the Pillory of Fame," *Technical Communication Quarterly* 19(2) (2010): 169.

56. Martin Smith and Patrick Kiger, *Oops: 20 Life Lessons from the Fiascoes That Shaped America* (New York: Collins, 2006), 84–93.

57. "Oldsmobile 'Chanteuse' Is Product of Feminine Design," press release, 4 June 1947; "Oldsmobile 'Mona Lisa' Features Brilliant Tangerine Motif," press release, 4 June 1947; "Oldsmobile 'Chanteuse,' 'Mona Lisa' Are Feminine Inspired," press release, 25 May 1957; "Carousel" by Peggy Sauer, 1958 Oldsmobile, n.d,, all GMA.

58. DeSoto ad, *Holiday*, March 1957; Lark brochure, 1962, 07-S2704, AAA; Georgine Clarsen, "The 'Dainty Female Toe' and the 'Brawny Male Arm': Conceptions of Bodies and Power in Automobile Technology," *Australian Feminist Studies* 15(32) (2000): 155–59.

59. Ford Motor Company, "Home Is Everywhere You Are: Ford and Maytag Equip Minivan with Washer/Dryer, Microwave and Vacuum," http://www.drivingenthusiast.net/sec-ford/FMC-concepts-prototypes-showcars/windstar-solutions/default.htm; Pete Bigelow, "Honda Odyssey's New Onboard Vacuum Surprisingly Easy to Use," autoblog.com, 28 March 2013, http://www.autoblog.com/2013/03/28/honda-odyssey-vacuum-cleaner-minivan-new-york/; Alex Zolbert, "Honda's Pitch: She's Pretty in Pink," CNN, http://edition.cnn.com/2012/11/27/business/japan-cars-females. In the early twenty-first century, Mazda considered designing its 626 for women, but it "never got off the drawing board" (Motavalli, "From 1955").

60. Andrea Heiman, "Beyond Thinking Pink: Cars Have Long Reflected Men's Needs. But Now Designers Have Women in Mind," *LAT*, 2 June 1992; Amy Harmon, "Auto Industry Struggling to Cope with Growing Importance of Women Buyers," *SW*, 26 June 1992, D2; "Cadillac Meets Women's Needs for Comfort, Convenience and Control," Cadillac press release, July 1996, GMA; Smith and Kiger, *Oops*, 91; Jamie LaReau, "How to Make Big SUVs More Female Friendly," 4 September 2006, http://europe.autonews.com/article/20060904/ANE/60901086-ixzz2W9JkHRCF; "Ford Using Pregnancy Simulator in Design Process," *Road and Travel*, http://www.roadandtravel.com/newsworthy/newsand

views03/fordpregnancysuit.htm; Paul Eisenstein, "Honda Introduces Car Designed Just for Women," today.com, 26 October 2012, http://www.today.com/money/honda-introduces-car-designed-just-women-1C6709945; "Increasing Economic Clout and Independence Boost Women's Power as Major Force in Automotive Market," Cadillac press release, July 1996, GMA; Clarke, *Driving Women*, 89.

61. Goldfarb Consultants, "Qualitative Insights on the Women's Market," December 1980, Detroit Office, Ford Research Reports, 1974–88, Appendix, 4, 10, JWT; Jeff Bennett, "Are You Tough Enough for Chrysler's 'Man Van'?" http://blogs.wsj.com/drivers-seat/2011/02/09/are-you-tough-enough-for-chrysler%E2%80%99s-man-van%E2%80%99/; Simpsons Canyonero, http://simpsons.wikia.com/wiki/Canyonero and http://simpsons.wikia.com/wiki/Marge_Simpson_in:_"Screaming_Yellow_Honkers".

62. Jennifer S. Goddard, *On the Road: The Savvy Girl's Guide to Cars* (Girl Scouts of USA, 2006), 16; Volvo press release, "Your Concept Car—by Women for Modern People; Bootie Cosgrove-Mather, "A Volvo by Women, for Women," 5 December 2007; cbsnews.com; Tatiana Butovitsch Temm, "If You Meet the Expectations of Women, You Exceed the Expectations of Men" in *Gendered Innovations in Science and Engineering* (Stanford, Calif.: Stanford University Press, 2008).

63. Jordan ad, *SEP*, June 1923; Sally H. Clarke, *Trust and Power: Consumers, the Modern Corporation, and the Making of the United States Automobile Market* (New York: Cambridge University Press, 2007), 175–77; Juliann Sivulka, *Soap, Sex, and Cigarettes*, 1st edition (Belmont, Calif.: Wadsworth, 1998), 175–77; Peter Marsh and Peter Collett, *Driving Passion: The Psychology of the Car* (Boston: Faber and Faber, 1989), 53; Clarke, *Driving Women*, 25–26; Vaknin, *Driving It Home*, 28–30.

Chapter 3

1. Virginia Scharff, *Taking the Wheel: Women and the Coming of the Motor Age* (Albuquerque: University of New Mexico Press, 1992), 67–88 (suffrage), 89–109 (World War I).

2. A'Lelia Bundles, *On Her Own Ground: The Life and Times of Madam C. J. Walker* (New York: Scribner, 2002).

3. "Women Drivers Increase," *NYT*, 23 June 1912, x14; Mrs. A. Sherman Hitchcock, "Woman at the Motor Wheel," *American Homes and Gardens*, April 1913, vi–viii; Scharff, *Taking the Wheel*, 26–33, 173; Michael Berger, "Women Drivers: How a Stereotype Kept Distaff Drivers in Their Place," *Road and Track* (May 1985): 56–60; Michael Berger, "Women Drivers! The Emergence of Folklore and Stereotypic Opinions Concerning Feminine Automotive Behavior," *Women's Studies International Forum* 9(3) (1986): 257–63; Deborah Clarke, *Driving Women: Fiction and Automobile Culture in Twentieth-Century America* (Baltimore: Johns Hopkins University Press, 2007), 14.

4. "Women at the Wheel," *NYT*, 4 September 1915, 6; AHA "A Woman as Her Own Chauffeur," *NYT*, 8 September 1915; F. C. Lockd, "Women at the Wheel," *NYT*, 12 September 1915; S. E. Armstrong, "Accidents from Women Drivers," *NYT*, 21 September 1915, 10; "A Coroner Speaks in Haste," *NYT*, 11 October 1915, 8; James T. Sullivan, "Women Drivers Are Careful," *NYT*, 13 February 1916, 48; "Many Unsuited to Drive Motor Cars," *NYT*, 16 October 1916, xx4; Berger, "Women Drivers!" 261–62; Margo Scholanger, "Women Behind the Wheel: Gender and Transportation Law, 1860–1930,"

in *Feminist Legal History: Essays on Women and Law*, ed. Tracey Thomas and Tracey Jean Boisseau (New York: New York University Press, 2011).

5. "Women Unfit to Drive Cars, Says Court as He Fines One," *NYT*, 11 April 1925, 15; Michael Kaufman, "Differential Participation: Men, Women and Popular Power," in *Community Power and Grassroots Democracy*, ed. Michael Kaufman and Haroldo Dilla Alfonso (London: Zed Books, 1997), 153–54, 157.

6. Edna Purdy Walsh, "Giving the Woman Driver the Double-O," *Motor Life*, March 1924; "How to Pick Women Who Can Drive Cars," *LD*, April 1924, 58–62; "Stout Women Best Drivers Declares Motorist Instructor," *BDG*, 7 December 1924, 61; Kaufman, "Differential Participation," 153–54. See also Epilogue for discussion of social patina afforded men.

7. "Can a Woman Drive a Car?" *LD*, 4 July 1924, 56–57; "More Men Than Women in Accidents," *FN*, May 1925, 3; F. A. Moss, "Are You a Better Driver Than Your Wife?" *AM*, August 1925, 16–17, 36, 38, 46; "Who's the Better Driver, You or Mrs.?" *BDG*, 18 December 1925.

8. Paul W. Kearney, "Women Are Good Drivers," *Esquire* 5(3) (March 1936): 92–93, 130, 133; "Public Would Rather Ride in Auto Driven by Man," *PP*, 16 July 1939; "Women Drivers," *NYT*, 23 July 1939.

9. Margaret Wilkinson, "How Good Are Women Drivers?" *BDG*, 2 December 1925, 11; "Women Prove to Be Good Auto Drivers," *BDG*, 19 February 1926, 9; women driver compilations: https://www.youtube.com/watch?v=4wT7zM8XgXQ and https://www.youtube.com/watch?v=OrI3GjiS2Sk; Joanne Gilbert, *Performing Marginality: Humor, Gender, and Cultural Critique* (Detroit: Wayne State University Press, 2004), 8–9; Mahadev L. Apte, *Humor and Laughter: An Anthropological Approach* (Ithaca, N.Y.: Cornell University Press, 1985), 18, 72; Alfred Habegger quoted in Nancy Walker, "Humor and Gender Roses: The 'Funny' Feminism of the Post–World War II Suburbs," *American Quarterly* 37(1) (Special Issue: American Humor) (Spring 1985): 101; "Women at the Wheel," *LD*, 29 January 1938, 14; "The Car Belongs to Mother," *LHJ*, November 1939; "What Do the Women of America Think About Automobile Driving?" *LHJ*, December 1939, 12; "Woman Driver: A Myth Exploded," *NYT*, 4 November 1951, 190; E. B. White, "Notes and Comment," *NY*, 4 April 1931, 15; Mark J. Price, "Local History: Darned Women Drivers! 1946 Battle of the Sexes Aimed to Prove Who Was Safer Behind Wheel," *Beacon Journal* (Akron, Ohio), 28 August 2016.

10. Price, "Local History."

11. "Woman Driver Signals a 'Civil Rights' Protest," *NYT*, 1 February 1952, 10; "Mademoiselle Motorist," *AM*, June 1957, 30.

12. Texaco ad, *LHJ*, June 1930; Ethyl ad, *Collier's*, 19 October 1946, 7; Volvo ad, *Daytona Beach Morning Journal*, 17 January 1974; Mobil ad, *LHJ*, November 1930; American Automobile Association 1925 study states women more stable, in James Flink, *The Automobile Age* (Cambridge, Mass.: MIT Press, 2001), 163.

13. "How to Run Out of Gas" ad, *LHJ*, May 1932, 1936; American Tourister ad, *Life*, 12 December 1969, 79.

14. "Strictly Objective Tale About a Woman Driver," *NYT*, 24 February 1954, 27. This same "joke" appeared in Paul Woods's *Modern Handbook of Humor* (New York: McGraw-Hill, 1967), 358.

15. Volkswagen ad, 14 August 1964, *Life*, 15. Cotton Seiler suggests, paralleling the contention of humor, that this aggressive tendency grew more "pronounced during moments in which American masculinity was construed as threatened or enervated" in *Republic of Drivers: A Cultural History of Automobility in America* (Chicago: University of Chicago Press, 2008), 85.

16. *National Automobile Chamber of Commerce*, Facts & Figures of the Automobile Industry (New York, 1930), 78–79; "Women Drivers," *Scientific American*, July 1937, 35; "Women More Skilled Than Men in Driving," *NYT*, 27 November 1938, 34; "Men Versus Women at the Wheel," *LD*, 26 December 1941, 34; "Auto Club Praises Female Driver; Finds Married Women Excel Single," *NYT*, 3 October 1951, 35; Lesley Hazelton, *Everything Women Always Wanted to Know About Cars* (New York: Doubleday, 1995), 135–37; "Are Female Drivers Safer? An Application of the Decomposition Method," *Epidemiology* 9(40) (July 1998): 379; Seiler, *Republic of Drivers*, 85–86.

17. "Transport: Men v. Women," *Time*, 23 August 1937; "Why Women Are Like That," *AM*, January 1943; "Study Says Women Drivers Top Men on Safety Record," *Milwaukee Journal*, 20 May 1946; Helen Bryant, "The Female Is Less Deadly Than the Male," *NYT*, 9 February 1947, SM22; "Women Better Drivers," *Olean Times Herald* (New York), 21 September 1949, 7; "Women Drive Better," *SD*, 35(3) (March 1954): inside cover; Alice Marble, "Plea: 'Don't Be a Woman, Driver,'" *NYT*, 30 October 1955, SM25; Jackie Karlson, "Mademoiselle Motorist," *AM*, May 1959, 18; "Women Drivers," *NYT*, 5 May 1963, 192; "Men Better Drivers Than Women?" *SD*, October 1956, 33; Clay McShane, *Down the Asphalt Path: The Automobile and the American City* (New York: Columbia University Press, 1994), 158–59.

18. Bryant, "The Female Is Less Deadly"; Margo Fischer, "So You Think Women Can't Drive!" *SEP*, September 1951, 34, 142–44; "Ladies From Now on Take the Term of 'Woman Driver' As a Compliment," *Florence Morning News* (South Carolina), 8 July 1951; no author, "Mademoiselle Motorist," *AM*, September 1953, 3, 4; "Facts Disprove Man's Superiority Behind the Wheel," *Altoona Mirror* (Pa.), 20 February 1955; Margaret Walker, "Mademoiselle Motorist," *AM*, April 1968, 10; Bonnie Remsberg, "Woman Behind the Wheel," *Redbook*, September 1973, 43–44; Leslie Milk, "He Drives Me Crazy," *Washingtonian*, March 2005.

19. Matthew L. Wald, "Walking? Beware the Male Driver," *NYT*, 9 April 1999, F1; *The Office*, Season 1, Episode 2, 2005, https://www.youtube.com/watch?v=9aVUoy9r0CM; "Freakonomics Blog: Why You'd Rather Ride with a Woman Than a Man," *NYT*, 17 March 2010, http://freakonomics.com/2010/03/17/why-youd-rather-ride-with-a-woman-than-a-man/; Scharff, *Taking the Wheel*, 172–73; "Fox & Friends Explores 'Gender Myths' Like Equal Pay," Title IX, http://www.huffingtonpost.com/2013/08/08/fox-friends-gender-myth-title-ix_n_3726285.html; Rachel McRady, "Golden Globes 2016," USmagazine.com (10 January 2016), http://www.usmagazine.com/celebrity-news/news/golden-globes-2016-ricky-gervais-controversial-jokes-from-monologue-w161237.

20. *Whiskey Tango Foxtrot* (Paramount Pictures 2016); *Zootopia* (Disney 2016).

21. Leon Brody, "Who's Driving . . . You or Your Emotions," *This Week*, 4 March 1940; Alan Finder, "Ward Stumbles into Women-Drivers Issue," *NYT*, 18 September 1987, B1; Anneli Rufus, America's Worst Drivers: The States, Gender, with the Most

Accidents, http://www.thedailybeast.com/articles/2011/12/31/america-s-worst-drivers-the-states-genders-with-the-most-accidents.html; Jim Edwards, "Yes, Talking on a Hands-Free Cellphone While Driving Is as Bad as Driving Drunk," http://www.businessinsider.com/talking-on-a-hands-free-cellphone-is-as-bad-as-driving-drunk-2013-8.

22. Saginaw ads: *GH*, January 1955, 26; *GH*, May 1955, 26; *GH*, June 1955, 26; *GH*, September 1955, 24; *GH*, January 1956, 24; *GH*, March 1956, 24. Ford ad, *Time*, 31 August 1953.

23. Lark ad, *Life*, 19 January 1959, 42; Chrysler ad, *Life*, 9 February 1959, 103; Chevrolet ad, *Life*, 22 February 1960, 91; Studebaker ad, *Life*, 29 January 1965, 74.

24. Lizabeth Cohen, *A Consumers' Republic: The Politics of Mass Consumption in Postwar America* (New York: Knopf, 2003), 278; Studebaker ad, *Life*, 21 March 1938, 1; Studebaker ad, *Life*, 13 June 1949, 46; Studebaker ad, *Life*, 6 June 1955, 1; Chevrolet ad, *Ebony*, February 1962, 17; Ford ad, *Life*, 27 September 1968, 2; *SEP*, 1 April 1950, cover; "Gertrude!" *SEP*, 1952.

25. Pinto ad, *Life*, 25 September 1970, 2; Volkswagen ad, *Life*, 9 July 1971, 7; Chevelle ad, *Life*, 21 January 1972, 12; Volvo ad, 1973, IAP; Toyota ad, *Texas Monthly*, April 1984, 171.

26. Ethyl ads, 1929, Lightner collection, Box 3, HCD; Ethyl ads, *World's Work*, 1929; Ethyl cartoon, L. H. "Dude" Larsen, 1949; 1950s commercial for Ethyl, https://www.youtube.com/watch?v=mkTxI0o9Hfw. Another campaign in 1932 instructed women that Ethyl would make everything better, like "what vanilla adds to cake" or what "vitamins are to food" (see *LHJ*, May and June).

27. Texaco ad, *SEP*, 1927; Texaco ad, 1929, IAP; Venus motor oil ad, 1929, IAP; Flying A Service calendar, 1940, IAP; Texaco ad, *SEP*, 1947; Quaker State ad, 1967, IAP; Danica Patrick is new spokesperson, noted in "Peak Launches Motor Oil Brand with IndyCar Series," 6 November 2007, http://www.enginebuildermag.com/2007/11/peak-launches-motor-oil-brand-with-indycar-series-indianapolis-500-partnerships/; Peter J. Boyer, "Changing Lanes," *NY*, 31 May 2010, 52–61; Clarke, *Driving Women*, 187.

28. Union Oil Company ad, 1933, IAP; Gulf ad, 1957, IAP; Gulf ad, *Life*, 2 November 1959, 99.

29. Citgo ad, *Barron's National Business and Financial Weekly*, 18 May 1970, 20; Ginger Dawson, "Mademoiselle Motorist: Muses on Mink-Trimmed Mechanics," *AM*, March 1979; Susan V. Spellman, "All the Comforts of Home: The Domestication of the Service Station Industry, 1920–1940," *Journal of Popular Culture* 37(3) (2004): 463–77; Jim Draeger and Mark Speltz, *Fill 'er Up: The Glory Days of Wisconsin Gas Stations* (Madison: Wisconsin Historical Press, 2008), 1–27, 88, 120, 156.

30. Ibid.; Robert C. Daniels, Wor*ld War II in Mid-America: Experiences From Rural Mid-America During the Second World War* (Bloomington, Ind.: AuthorHouse, 2012), 56; Moran Filling Station promotions in Michael Karl Witzel, *Gas Station Memories* (Oseola, Wisc.: Motorbooks International, 1994), 15.

31. Texaco ads: *Life*, 25 April 1938, 64–65; *Life*, 13 May 1940, 86–87; *Life*, 22 July 1940, 55; *LHJ*, July 1941, 119; *GH*, July 1951, 195; *Life*, 18 July 1955, 5; *SEP*, 8 June 1957; *Life*, 2 June 1958, 96–97. In the 1960s and 1970s, Texaco promoted a "Customer Service

Patrol," https://archive.org/details/dmbb32014, https://archive.org/details/dmbb13408, and https://archive.org/details/dmbb13409.

32. Union 76 ad, 1959, IAP; Gulf ad, 1965, IAP; Gulf ad, *Holiday*, July 1966, 20; Gulf ad, *Holiday*, July 1967; "Highway Hostesses Give Aid to Traveling Public," *News-Palladium* (Benton Harbor, Michigan), 8 August 1940, 5; William Kaszynski, *The American Highway: The History and Culture of Roads in the United States* (Jefferson, N.C.: McFarland and Company, 2000), 73; Draeger, *Fill'er Up*, 27.

33. Rita Pyrillis, "'Why Should We Be Public's Toilet?' Asks Gas Station Owners, Downey Restroom Requirement Fuels Debate," *LAT*, 17 July 1986, 5; Beth Ann Krier, "The Restroom Wars: Should Gas Stations Be Required to Provide Facilities for Travelers?" *LAT*, 9 September 1987, 1.

34. Spellman, *All the Comforts*, 466, 474.

35. MacMillan ad, *SEP*, 27 September 1947; Cartoons, *NPN*, July 1970, 103, and September 1970, 133; Irvin Molotsky, "In the Suburbs, It's the Women Who Wait," *NYT*, 22 June 1979, A16.

36. Charles Coolidge Parlin, *The Passenger Car Industry* (Philadelphia: Curtis, 1932), 95; Texaco ad, c. 1960s, https://archive.org/details/dmbb10001.

37. MacMillan ad, *SEP*, 27 September 1947; Cartoons, *NPN*, July 1970, 103, and September 1970, 133; Molotsky, "In the Suburbs."

38. Texaco ad, c. 1970s removed from youtube.com; Shell ad, 1987, https://www.youtube.com/watch?v=dycHksbYwPY.

39. Don Klein, "Audi's 'The Station' TDI Diesel Commercial Is Almost Perfect," 1 November 2013, *Car and Driver*, http://blog.caranddriver.com/audis-the-station-tdi-diesel-commercial-is-almost-perfect-the-ad-section/.

40. Shell Oil, "Alice in Motorland: The Woman Behind the Wheel" brochure, 1944, AES; "Businessmen Probe the Feminine Approach," *PI*, 24 November 1961, 5.

41. Shell Oil, "Travel a la Car," 1949, and "Are Women Necessary?" 1950, AES.

42. Mid-century Rand McNally cartoon ad, n.d., IAP; Union 76 commercial, https://www.youtube.com/watch?v=R6AjTFs1BU8.

43. Draeger and Speltz, *Fill 'er Up*, 120; Paul Robinson cartoon, 1930, "All His Customers Were Women. . . ," in Beth Kraig, "Women at the Wheel," PhD diss., University of Washington, 1987), 37; Spellman, "All the Comforts," 474; Witzel, *Gas Station*, 29; Texaco ad for Libby glassware, 1960s/1970s, https://archive.org/details/dmbb23101; AC/GM ads, *NPN*, September and October 1970; David Landis, "Gas-Station Giveaways Return to Pump Up Sales," *USA*, 24 May 1988.

44. Carol Sanger, "Girls and the Getaway: Cars, Culture, and the Predicament of Gendered Space," *University of Pennsylvania Law Review* 44(2) (December 1995): 707.

45. AAA timeline and history, http://newsroom.aaa.com/about-aaa/aaa-timeline/1902-1909/ (accessed 13 May 2016); AAA ad, *AAA Travel*, April 1933; AAA, *Handbook of Advertising for AAA Clubs*, c. 1934; AAA ad, *AAA Travel*, March 1939; Richard Lauterbach, "Three Million Rescues a Year," *AAA Travel*, 1949; AAA Club of Missouri ad, April 1973; *The Best of AAA Line Art*, 2nd ed., 1976; AAA ad, *AAA World*, July/August 1988; AAA ad, *AAA World*, January/February 1992.

46. Ibid.

47. Jackie Karlson, "Mademoiselle Motorist," *AM,* September 1958, 28; Margaret Walker, "Mademoiselle Motorist," *AM,* October 1964, 15; Margaret Walker, "Mademoiselle Motorist," *AM,* February 1968, 20; AAA ad and Stephanie Faul, "Driving Safely After Dark," *AAA World,* January/February 1989.

48. "Nor Sleet, Nor Hail, Nor Gloom of Night," *AM,* December 1968, 6; "Supernumber Goes National," *AAA World,* July/August 1982, 14; Joseph Younger, "A Traveler's Guide for Summer Breakdowns," *AAA World,* July/August 1987, 10–11; MemberShop ad, *AAA World,* May/June 1988.

49. "A Device for Connecting Automobile Telephone Sets with Line Wires," *Telephony: The American Telephone Journal,* 24 September 1910, 357–58; "The Auto Phone," *FT,* 1910, 3(7): 4–5; *FT,* 1910, 3(23): 6.

50. National ad, *Life,* 8 April 1966, 109; Jay Koblenz, "Calling All Cars: Hooking Up to Cellular Phones," *Black Enterprise,* November 1984, 96–97; Frank Vizard, "Phones on a Roll," *PM,* January 1986, 94–96; GE ad, *AAA World,* July/August 1986, 16; SOS Phone ad, *Kiplinger's Personal Finance,* August 1998, 162; "Seniors Phone Home," *Seniors Phone Home,* January 1999, 10

51. Chevrolet ad, *NYT,* 13 February 1924, 12; GTE ad, *Tampa Bay Magazine,* January/February 1988, 84; Cellular One ad, *AAA World,* March/April 1988, 2h; Motorola ad, *Ukiah Daily Journal* (California), 29 March 1989, 2; Centel ad, 1989, https://www.youtube.com/watch?v=ptbJZ9HBw2k&feature=player_embedded; Radio Shack ad, 1990, https://www.youtube.com/watch?v=694TX2lQ7Uo&feature=related; Hazelton, *Everything Women Always Wanted to Know About Cars,* 157; Matt Richtel, "Driven to Distraction: Promoting the Car Phone, Despite Risks," *NYT,* 7 December 2009, A1, A21; "Playing It Safe," *Texas Monthly,* November 1991, 149; "Women Respond to Crime Fears by Curtailing Their Shopping," *MTW,* 10(12) (31 December 1997). See interactive timeline in Richtel's "Driven to Distraction" for early cell-phone advertising history.

52. Charles L. Sanford, "'Woman's Place' in American Car Culture," in *The Automobile and American Culture,* ed. David L. Lewis and Laurence Goldstein (Ann Arbor: University of Michigan Press, 1983), 147–48; Goodyear ads, *Life*: 24 April, 22 May, 21 August, 4 December 1964, and 18 March 1966; *NY,* 28 May 1966, 72–73.

53. Libby Copeland, "The Car Industry's Lame Attempts to Entice Women," March 2013, http://www.slate.com/articles/double_x/doublex/2013/03/car_ads_for_women_does_the_industry_get_it_all_wrong.single.html; Bernice Fitz-Gibbon, "Going Steady with Studie," 1964, http://www.raylinrestoration.com/Stuff/GSWS/GSWS.htm.

54. Goodyear ads in *Life*: 26 June 1964; 18 December 1964; 18 March 1966, 92–93; 29 July 1966; Susan Brownmiller, *Against Our Will: Men, Women, and Rape* (New York: Ballantine, 1993).

55. Goodyear Polyglas commercial, https://www.youtube.com/watch?v=Y9k2CUZJDp0.

56. Goodyear ad, 15 March 1953, 80–81; Goodyear ad, *Life,* 17 February 1958, 66–67; B. F. Goodrich ad, *Life,* 15 September 1961, 61; AAA Chicago Motor Club ad, 1969, IAP.

57. Shirley Lord, "Women and American Cars: What's Coming in the '80s," *Vogue* 171 (February 1981), 314; Andrea Heiman, "Beyond Thinking Pink," *LAT,* 2 June 1992.

58. Ford ad, *Money*, June 1994; Cadillac ad, *Southern Living*, June 1993; Cadillac, "Cadillac Meets Women's Needs for Comfort, Convenience and Control," July 1996, GMA; Ford, "As Roles of Women Change, Ford Recognizes Their Societal Status," 2010, http://www.ford-trucks.com/articles/as-roles-of-women-change-ford-recognizes-their-societal-status-ndash-and-their-unique-purchasing-punch/.

59. Lee Lorenz cartoon, *NY*, 20 March 1965, 83; Peter Arno cartoon, *NY*, 17 July 1965, 32; "Many Women Value Driving as Time Alone," *About Marketing to Women* 11(5) (31 May 1998): 5.

60. "Women Are Concerned About Personal Safety When Driving," *About Marketing to Women* 8(13) (31 October 1995): 4; Hazelton, *Everything Women Always Wanted to Know About Cars*, 161; "OnStar by GM: Safety Is No. 1 Concern for Women at the Wheel," *RT* (1 March 2006).

61. Rachel L. Miller, "All By Myself; A Girl's Guide to the Open Road," *RT* (15 August 2003); Jessica Howell, "Parking Lot Predators," *RT* (2006), http://www.roadandtravel.com/safetyandsecurity/2006/parkinglotsafety.htm; Courtney Caldwell, "Taking a Road Trip? Safety Tips for Women Traveling Alone," *RT* (2012), http://www.roadandtravel.com/traveladvice/2012/travelling-alone-safety-tips.html and "Traveling Alone: What Women Need to Know Before They Go!" *RT* (15 May 2012). *Road & Travel* targeted middle-aged women, http://www.roadandtravel.com/company/marketing/mission.html.

62. Nicholas Pileggi, "How to Stay Out of Trouble," *NYM*, 8 February 1982, 24; Linda Fairstein, "Read This Before You Drive Alone," *Cosmopolitan*, April 2010; Linda Fairstein, "How Serial Rapists Target Their Victims," *Cosmopolitan*, October 2010; Linda Fairstein, *The Five Most Dangerous Places for Women* (Kindle edition) (Open Road Media, 2007). The Fairstein articles included advertising blurbs for her most recent crime thrillers, a gross exploitation and revealing sleight of hand.

63. Hazelton, *Everything Women Always Wanted to Know About Cars*, 154–56; *Eyewitness Travel: Boston* (London: Dorling Kindersley, 2001), 185; Cheryl Jensen, "Be Street Smart! How to Stay Safe on the Road," *RT* (15 June 2001); *The Rough Guide to Florida* (Google ebook): 11 October 2012 (accessed 12 February 2014); "Sexual Assault/Rape Prevention: In Your car," Muscogee County Sheriff's Office, http://www.columbusga.org/sheriff/assault.htm; "Personal Safety Tips: Safety in Your Vehicle," Fort Worth Police, http://www.fortworthpd.com/safety/personal-safety-tips.aspx.

64. Ibid.; *Designing Women*, airdate 8 May 1989, http://www.designingwomenonline.com/Episodes/Summaries/063.php; *The Sopranos*, airdate 18 March 2001, http://sopranosautopsy.com/season-3-2/employee-of-the-month-3-04/.

65. "House of Cars: Innovation and the Parking Garage," National Building Museum, Washington, D.C. (exhibit ran 17 October 2009–11 July 2010), brochure.

66. "First Motor Emporium in Boston," *Horseless Age* 4(7) (17 May 1899): 6; U.S. Department of Justice, "Sex Offenses and Offenders," Bureau of Justice Statistics, February 1997, 3, http://bjs.gov/content/pub/pdf/SOO.PDF; Bureau of Justice Statistics, "Criminal Victimization in the United States," 1996–2007, Table 63, http://www.bjs.gov/; Rape, Abuse, and Incest National Network, https://rainn.org/get-information/statistics/sexual-assault-offenders; Jim Gibbons, "Parking Lots," Technical Paper 6, Nonpoint Education for Municipal Officials, 1999, 1; Buck Simpers, "Making Safety a Priority in Parking

Garages," *PT*, November 2003; Melissa Bean Sterzick, "Why Women Fear the Parking Structure," *PT*, October 2007; Randy Atlas, "Fear of Parking," *PT*, March 2008; "Woman Reports Rape At L.I. Mall Garage," *NYT*, 16 December 1994; "Man arrested for Vanderbilt Campus Sexual Assault," 13 February 2012, http://www.wsmv.com/story/16917977/police-make-arrest-in-vanderbilt; "House of Cars brochure; Isaiah Mouw and Ben Bronsink, "Gritty Crime and the Parking Garage," June 2011, *PT*; Nasutsa M. Mabwa, Hotel La Salle and underground garages, "Parking, " encyclopedia.chicago history.org, http://www.encyclopedia.chicagohistory.org/pages/959.html; Malini Basu, "Woman with Flat Tire Sexually Assaulted by Fake Cop," KHOU.com (Houston, Texas), 16 October 2013, http://www.khou.com/story/news/local/2014/07/23/12185894/; AP News Report, "Police Officer Indicted on Rape Charge," 19 December 1992, http://www.apnewsarchive.com/1992/Police-Officer-Indicted-On-Rape-Charge/id-92f0030ae4eb324ddb208e1fabcafab3; "Lights-Out Policy for Parking Lots Worries Students," *NYT*, 19 August 1990; Matt Ford, "What Caused the Great Crime Decline in the U.S.?" *Atlantic* 15 April 2016.

Thank you to Marie Mele Thomas for her guidance in interpreting this phenomenon, especially in tracking down more statistics and grappling with the numbers.

67. "For Women on the Move," *NYM*, 12 March 1984, 13A; Ann Brown, "Amenities for Women Travelers," *Black Enterprise*, December 1992, 155; "Women Respond to Crime Fears by Curtailing Their Shopping," *MTW* 10(12) (31 December 1997); CBS News/AP, "Marriott Reverses on Blaming Rape Victim, 27 August 2009, http://www.cbsnews.com/news/marriott-reverses-on-blaming-rape-victim/; Monica Potts, "Stamford Marriott Claims Woman Was Negligent in Her Own Rape," http://www.stamfordadvocate.com/news/article/Stamford-Marriott-claims-woman-was-negligent-in-6314.php.

68. "How to Identify Undercover Officers When Pulled Over," *RT* (2006), http://www.roadandtravel.com/safetyandsecurity/2006/identifyanofficer.htm; Basu, "Woman with Flat Tire."

69. Thomas Barker, "An Empirical Study of Police Deviance Other Than Corruption," *Journal of Police Science and Administration* 6(3) 1978, 267–71; Cara E. Rabe-Hemp and Jeremy Braithwaite, "An Exploration of Recidivism and the Officer Shuffle in Police Sexual Violence," *Police Quarterly*, 16(2) (June 2013): 129, 143.

A New Jersey teenager brought charges in federal court, recounting that she endured kissing, hugging and fondling in Schauder's squad car, in "secluded, wooded locations" (Cheryl Armstrong, "Girl Says Cop Groomed Her for Sex," *CN*, 2 November 2009, http://www.courthousenews.com/2009/11/02/Girl_Says_Cop_Groomed_Her_for_Sex.htm.

70. Diane Suchetka, "'Bimbo Hunting': Abusing the Badge," *Charlotte Observer* (North Carolina): 15 February 1988, 1B; "Mary M. v. City of Los Angeles," morelaw.com, https://www.morelaw.com/verdicts/case.asp?n = B022761.&s = CA&d = 47179; Peter B. Kraska and Victor E. Kappeler, "To Serve and Pursue: Exploring Police Sexual Violence Against Women," *Justice Quarterly* 12(1) (March 1995): 93–94; Lauren Sher, "Cop Issues Speeding Ticket, Asks Driver for a Date and She Sues Him," ABC News Blogs, 5 January 2012, https://gma.yahoo.com/blogs/abc-blogs/cop-issues-speeding-ticket-asks-driver-date-she-002427538.html.

71. Samuel Walker and Dawn Irlbeck, *Driving While Female: A National Problem in Police Misconduct* (Omaha: University of Nebraska: Police Professionalism Initiative,

2002); Samuel Walker and Dawn Irlbeck, *Police Sexual Abuse of Teenage Girls: A 2003 Update on "Driving While Female"* (Omaha: University of Nebraska: Police Professionalism Initiative, June 2003).

72. Danielle McGurrin and Victor E. Kappeler, "Media Accounts of Police Sexual Violence: Rotten Apples or State-Supported Violence?" in *Policing and Misconduct*, ed. Kim Michelle Lersch (Upper Saddle River, N.J.: Prentice Hall, 2002): 121–42; Josh White, "Ex-Trooper Sentenced for Soliciting Sex—Former Standout Officer Apologizes," *WP*, 20 September 2002; Greg Moran, "City to Pay Cop's Victim $795K," *U-T San Diego*, 27 September 2013. Of course, women did not even need to be traveling in a car, as the police forced women into their squad cars to assault them. See, for example, Joel Rubin's article on a 2013 alleged kidnapping and assault against a Los Angeles woman by two officers, "Woman Who Fell from Police Car Alleges Sexual Assault by Officer," *LAT*, 12 January 2014.

73. S. G. Walker and D. Irlbeck, *Driving While Female: A National Problem in Police Misconduct* (Omaha: University of Nebraska: Police Professionalism Initiative, 2002). CNN reported on the study in a segment titled "Study Says Police Harassment of Women Is Widespread," 14 June 2002, http://transcripts.cnn.com/transcripts/0206/14/lt.29.html.

For an example of the breadth and depth of the effects of profiling drivers, see David A. Harris's American Civil Liberties Union report, "Driving While Black: Racial Profiling on Our Nation's Highways," 7 June 1999.

74. Claudia Puig, "Simi Police to Review Policy on Scouts in Wake of Sex Charges," *LAT*, 6 April 1987; Jonathan Kaminsky, "The Boy Scouts' Police Problem," City Pages .com, Minneapolis, Minnesota, 30 December 2011, http://www.citypages.com/news/the-boy-scouts-police-problem-67539 96.

75. Kraska and Kappeler, "To Serve and Pursue," 89–91, 99–101; Christina Cauterucci, "Baltimore Police Blamed Victims for Sex Assaults, Exploited Sex Workers, According to DOJ," 10 August 2016, http://www.slate.com/blogs/xx_factor/2016/08/10/baltimore_police_blamed_victims_for_sexual_assaults_traded_immunity_for.html; Jack Bouboushian, "They Serve, Protect, and Humiliate You," *CN*, 3 February 2014, http://www.courthousenews.com/2014/02/03/65038.htm. In 2012, the libertarian Cato Institute began operating the policemisconduct.net chronicle of media reports of police misconduct, which was first started by a private researcher in 2009. David Packman maintained in 2009 that sexual misconduct by police ranked as either the first or second offense reported each month (see, for example, David Packman, "The Police Brutality Nobody Talks About—Officer-Involved Sexual Misconduct," Cato Institute, 5 November 2009, http://www.policemisconduct.net/the-police-brutality-nobody-talks-about-officer-involved-sexual-misconduct/); Deborah Hastings, "Texas State Troopers Caught on Camera Probing Women's Privates Aren't Isolated Incidents: Lawyers," *New York Daily News*, 2 August 2013.

76. Rabe-Hemp and Braithwaite, "An Exploration," 131, 142.

77. Ralph Ellis and Marlena Baldacci, "Cop Denies Sexually Assaulting Woman After Traffic Stop," CNN.com, 25 November 2013, http://www.cnn.com/2013/11/25/justice/san-antonio-officer-sex-assault/; telephone interview with Lou Reiter, Public Agency Training Council, 31 January 2014, notes IAP; Mark D. Wilson and J. Almendarez, "SAPD Accused of Rape," *Houston Chronicle*, 23 November 2013.

78. "Failure to Yield Charge Dropped Against Woman Who Drove to Well-Lit Area in Traffic Stop," thenewspaper.com, 6 June 2008, http://thenewspaper.com/news/24/2412.asp; Wes Johnson, "Department Doesn't Fault Woman for Delayed Stop," 7 June 2008, available online at http://www.1branson.com/forum/t35875.html, http://www.news-leader.com/apps/pbcs... = 2008806070373, copy IAP; "Police Misconduct Danger to Women," 25 June 2008, News-Leader.com (Springfield, Missouri), available online at http://behindthebluewall.blogspot.com/2008/06/driving-while-female.html,http://www.news-leader.com/apps/pbcs.dl...6/OPINIONS, copy IAP.

79. Shelby Schwartz and Brian Ward, "Memorandum to Prof. Katherine Franke," 2 November 2008, Re: Police Sexual Misconduct Policies and Training Research, http://blogs.law.columbia.edu/genderandsexualitylawblog/files/2008/11/police-coercive-sexual-conduct.pdf; Lou Reiter, "Handling Sexual Misconduct by Public Safety Officers Is a Job for Us, Not the Courts," Public Agency Training Council, http://www.patc.com/weeklyarticles/job-for-us.shtml.

80. McGurrin and Kappeler, "Media Accounts," 126–27, 132–34; "Officer Accused in Rape of Car Passenger," *NYT*, 9 October 2000; Matthew Spina, "When a Protector Becomes a Predator," BuffaloNews.com, http://projects.buffalonews.com/abusing-the-law/index.html (accessed 20 September 2016).

81. Allen Powell III, "Jefferson Parish Deputy Booked with Traffic-Stop Rape, Fired, *Times-Picayune* (La.), 5 November 2009, http://www.nola.com/crime/index.ssf/2009/11/jefferson_parish_deputy_booked.html; Eliott C. McLaughlin et al., "Oklahoma City Cop Convicted of Rape Sentenced to 263 Years in Prison," 22 January 2016, http://www.cnn.com/2016/01/21/us/oklahoma-city-officer-daniel-holtzclaw-rape-sentencing/; Cauterucci, "Baltimore Police."

82. Dick Hogan, "Cedar Rapids Police Officer Sued Over Stop," 27 November 2001; Steve Gravelle, "More Complaints of Sexual Harassment Are Made Against C.R. Police Officer," 8 December 2001; Steve Gravelle, "C.R. Officer Being Sued for Harassment Loses Job," 3 January 2002, TG. All articles found referenced in law-firm summary of successful cases: http://www.eiowalaw.com/wp-content/uploads/2015/04/Ralstonv-Harrelson.pdf; "Ex-Trooper Sexual Abuse Case: Alabama High Court Rules That Supervisors Remain on the Hook," AL.com, 15 March 2010, http://blog.al.com/live/2010/03/ex-trooper_sexual_abuse_case_a.html; Keegan Kyle, "Crooked Cops Go to Prison," Voice of San Diego, 2 February 2012, http://www.voiceofsandiego.org/2012/02/10/crooked-cops-go-to-prison/; Catherine Green, "City Still Feeling the Fallout from Arevalos Scandal," Voice of San Diego, 27 September 2013, http://www.voiceofsandiego.org/2012/02/10/crooked-cops-go-to-prison/.

83. Ibid.; telephone interview with Lou Reiter, notes IAP; Zoë Carpenter, "The Police Violence We Aren't Talking About," *Nation* 27 August 2014, http://www.thenation.com/article/police-violence-we-arent-talking-about/.

84. McShane, *Down the Asphalt*, 157; Scharff, *Taking the Wheel*; "Persistent Myth: It's at Least 2,100 Years Old," *San Antonio Light* (Texas), 20 March 1949; "Chariot Parking Trouble," *Huronite and the Daily Plainsman* (South Dakota), 5 May 1949; Association of Casualty and Surrey Companies, 1963, "Look, Lady!" brochure, IAP. The brochure was promoted in articles around the country: *Schenectady Gazette* (N.Y.), 9 July 1963; *Albuquerque Tribune* (N.M.), 20 July 1963; *Findlay Republican-Courier* (Ohio), 15 October

1963. For a rare example of the correct telling of Cato the Elder's role, see William Duiker and Jackson Spielvogel's textbook *World History*, vol. 1 (Boston: Cengage Learning, 2012), 7th ed., 162. Several accounts, including the two articles cited above, struggled with the dates, often attributing the laws prohibiting women's behavior to 205 BCE.

85. R. Joy Littlewood, *A Commentary on Ovid's Fasti*, Book 6, 181. Livy associated the two-wheeled carriage, known as a *carpentum*, with "moral laxity" in women. Livy also told the story of Tullia Minor who ran over her father, King Servius's mutilated body strewn in the street, with her carpentum. Matthew Dillon and Lynda Garland, *Ancient Rome: From the Early Republic to the Assassination of Julius Caesar* (New York: Routledge, 2005), 386; Susan Bell, *Women: From the Greeks to the French Revolution* (Stanford, Calif.: Stanford University Press, 1973), 38–40; Marilyn Bailey Ogilvia, *Women in Science: Antiquity Through the Nineteenth Century: A Biographical Dictionary with Annotated Bibliography* (Cambridge, Mass.: MIT Press, 1990), 5; Dillon and Garland, *Ancient Rome*, 385; Steven Green, *Ovid, Fasti*, 2004, 284; Mary Lefkowitz and Maureen Fant, *Women's Life in Greece and Rome: A Source Book in Translation*, 2nd ed. (Baltimore: Johns Hopkins University Press, 1992).

Chapter 4

1. Michael L. Berger, "Women Drivers! The Emergence of Folklore and Stereotypic Opinions Concerning Feminine Automotive Behavior," *Women's Studies International Forum* 9(3) (1986): 258–60; Virginia Scharff, *Taking the Wheel: Women and the Coming of the Motor Age* (Albuquerque: University of New Mexico Press, 1992), 100–102; Clay McShane, *Down the Asphalt Path: The Automobile and the American City* (New York: Columbia University Press, 1994), 153.

2. *Leslie's Illustrated Weekly Newspaper*, 6 January 1916, cover, AMW; *Motor*, November 1923, cover; Julie Wosk, *Women and the Machine: Representations from the Spinning Wheel to the Electronic Age* (Baltimore: Johns Hopkins University Press, 2001), 144–45, plate 27; Scharff, *Taking the Wheel*, 26–27, 29, 37; "Chicago Warns Women Automobilists," *Horseless Age* 12 September 1900, 24.

3. Dorothy Levitt, *The Woman and the Car: A Chatty Little Handbook for All Women Who Motor or Who Want to Motor* (Oxford, UK: Old House Books, 2014), 28–29, 31–40.

4. Ibid., 31–40, 87; Patricia Marks, *Bicycles, Bangs, and Bloomers: The New Woman in the Popular Press* (Lexington: University of Kentucky Press, 1990).

5. Priscilla Hovey Wright, *The Car Belongs to Mother* (Boston: Houghton Mifflin, 1939), 52–58.

6. Thanking men: Dorothy Jackson, *What Every Woman Should Know . . . About Her Car*, 1st ed. (Radnor, Pa.: Chilton Book Co., 1974), vii; Mary Jackson, *The Greaseless Guide to Car Care Confidence: Take the Terror Out of Talking to Your Mechanic* (New York: John Muir Publications, 1989), viii; Bridget Kachur, *Every Woman's Quick & Easy Car Care: A Worry-Free Guide to Car Troubles, Trials, & Travels* (North Adams, Mass.: Storey Books, 2002), v; Erika Stadler, *In the Driver's Seat: A Girl's Guide to Her First Car* (San Francisco: Zest Books, 2009), 127.

Thanking women: Denise McCluggage, *Are You a "Woman Driver"?* (New York: Grosset & Dunlap, 1966), ii; Lyn St. James, *Lyn St. James's Car Owner's Manual for*

Women Harmondsworth, England: Penguin Books, 1984), v; Lisa Chapman, *The Savvy Woman's Guide to Cars* (New York: Bantam, 1995), v.

7. McCluggage, *Are You*, back cover of hardback edition; Jackson, *The Greaseless*, vii; Patty De Roulf, *A Woman and Her Car* (Indianapolis: Bobbs-Merrill, 1974), 118; Ren Volpe, *The Lady Mechanic's Total Car Care for the Clueless* (New York: St. Martin's Griffin, 1998); Courtney Hansen, *The Garage Girl's Guide to Everything You Need to Know About Your Car* (Nashville: Cumberland House, 2007).

8. Carmel Reingold, *A Woman's Guide to the Care and Feeding of an Automobile* (New York: Stein & Day, 1973), 15; Jackson, *What Every*, 2; St. James, *Lyn St. James's*, 77; Jackson, *The Greaseless*, vii–viii; Mary Jackson, *Car Smarts: An Easy-to-Use Guide to Understanding Your Car & Communicating with Your Mechanic* (Santa Fe, N.M.: John Muir Publications, 1998), v–vi.

A 4 November 1950 *New Yorker* cartoon had a woman explaining to the service man, "It went 'grrzlackity, grrzlackity, grrzlackity, *honk*' " (47). Five years later, two women sat in the car while it was being repaired, and the one exclaimed, "I looked under the hood once. I couldn't drive again for a month" (*NY*, 1 October 1955, 39).

9. McCluggage, *Are You?*

10. Ibid.; Jackson, *What Every*; "Winter Car Care for Sisters," *Ebony* 60(1) (November 2004): 120, 122.

11. Deborah Clarke, *Driving Women: Fiction and Automobile Culture in Twentieth-Century America* (Baltimore: Johns Hopkins University Press, 2007), 115.

12. Charlotte Montgomery, *Handbook for the Woman Driver* (New York: Vanguard Press, 1955).

13. Julie Candler, *Woman at the Wheel* (New York: Paperback Library, 1967), cover, 7–8; Ellen Gerl and Craig Davis, "Selling Detroit on Women: *Woman's Day* and Auto Advertising, 1964–82," *Journalism History* (Winter 2013): 209–20.

In an interview, Candler affirmed that car advertisers told advertising sales representatives that they did not want to advertise in *Woman's Day* because they were able to reach female consumers through their products' sponsorship of football (26 September 2011 email to author).

14. Texaco ad, *GH*, July 1951, 195; "The Woman and Her Car" and Body by Fisher ad, *GH*, November 1951, 46–47; "The Woman and Her Car" and Saginaw ad, *GH*, May 1956, 24; Julie Candler, "Woman at the Wheel," *Woman's Day*, 1965–83.

15. Car ads in *Vogue*: 15 September 1962, 18–21; 1 January 1963, 9; February 1976, 45–50, 152–57; January 1980, 30; February 1980, 149, 206–7; March 1980, 268; September 1982, 322–23, 404, 406; and *Glamour*, January 1980, 54, 60, 21.

16. Elizabeth Hemmerdinger, "Demystifying Your Car," *Ms*, July 1972, 36–38.

17. Zelia Zigler, *Alice in Motorland: The Woman Behind the Wheel* (Shell Oil Co., 1944), 1–13.

18. Ibid.

19. Studs Terkel, *"The Good War": An Oral History of World War Two* (New York: Pantheon Books, 1984), 19.

20. Ibid., Zigler, *Alice in Motorland*, 1–13; Maureen Honey, *Creating Rosie the Riveter: Class, Gender, and Propaganda During World War II* (Amherst: University of Massachusetts Press, 1984), 123.

21. Champion Spark Plug Company, *Car Talk in a Woman's Language: The Inside Story About Your Car and Its Engine, Written by Women Expressly for Women!* (Toledo, Ohio: Champion Spark Plug Co., 1956), 2.

22. *A Woman's Guide to Car Care* (Harbor Service Stations, 1967); Jiffy Lube, "Men Not Necessarily More Car-Care Savvy Than Women," c. 2006, https://www.jiffylube.com/news-and-press/men-not-necessarily-more-car-care-savvy-than-women.

23. Goodyear Tire and Rubber Company, *Tire Talk for Women* (Akron, Ohio: Goodyear, 1968).

24. Charlotte Montgomery, *Car Talk for Women Drivers* (Tulsa, OK: Cities Service Oil Co., 1971).

25. "Knows About Motors," *BG*, 5 May 1912, 53; "Oldest Auto School," *BG*, 9 March 1913, 71; Burr C. Cook, "Women as Auto Mechanics," *Illustrated World* 22 (1916): 503–4; "Says Women Take Good Care of Car," *LAT*, 13 July 1919, V16; Clarke, *Driving Women*, 18.

26. "When Women Take to Motoring," *BDG*, 6 March 1910, 70; Harry A. Tarantous (associate editor of *Motor)*, "Selecting an Automobile," *GH*, May 1917, 140–42; Harry A. Tarantous, "Driving an Automobile," *GH*, June 1917, 128–30; Maggie Walsh, *At Home at the Wheel? The Woman and Her Automobile in the 1950s* (London: British Library, 2006), 1.

27. De Roulf, *A Woman and Her Car*, 355.

28. "Engines Damaged on American Liner," *NYT*, 13 September 1915, 3.

29. "Training Women for Auto War Work," *NYT*, 29 April 1917, 79; Fred H. Caley, "Cleveland's School of Motorology," *AM*, March 1918, 23.

30. This contrasts with the emphasis on femininity for World War II with Maureen Honey's *Creating Rosie* and Melissa A. McEuen's *Making War, Making Women: Femininity and Duty on the American Home Front, 1941–1945* (Athens: University of Georgia Press, 2011).

31. Ibid.; "Mobilization of American Women," *MA*, 10 May 1917, 40–41; "The Ladies—God Bless 'em!" *AM*, November 1917, 20; J. G. Childs, "The Motor Corps of the National League for Women's Service, *National Service* 3 (February–March 1918), 360–64; "Women in Red Cross Motor Service," *AM*, August 1918, 12.

32. "Woman's Work in the World War," *MA*, 26 April 1917, 32–33; "State Registration Plans Completed," *NYT*, 8 June 1917, 3; "U.S. Women," *MA*, 9 August 1917, 33; "Proving Their Case by Driving," *MA*, 16 August 1917, 36; "Women and the World War," *MA*, 23 August 1917, 35; "Women as Solution of Service Problem," *MA*, 15 August 1918, 17; "Women Prove Efficient Mechanics: Service Manager Says He May Never Go Back to Men for Same Work," *MA*, 22 August 1917, 24–25; John Walker Harrington, "Women Show Skill as Auto Drivers, *NYT*, 2 February 1919, 92; Byron Farwell, *Over There: The United States in the Great War, 1917–1918* (New York: Norton, 1999), 29; Scharff, *Taking the Wheel*, 89–109.

33. Scharff, *Taking the Wheel*, 89, 100–102.

34. Girl Scouts of the United States of America, *Scouting for Girls, Official Handbook of the Girl Scouts*, 1st ed. (New York: The Girls Scouts Inc., 1920), 523; Scharff, *Taking the Wheel*, 108–9; "Automobiling," Girl Scout Badges—White Felt, http://vintagegirlscout.com/.

35. "Women Study Defense," *NYT*, 20 October 1940, 20; "American Designed Canteen for British," *NYT*, 12 January 1941, D4; "400 Toledo Women to Start Motor Defense Corps Course," *TB*, 11 June 1941; Jane Cochran, "Women Warned Not to Squander Energies on Programs of Little Use to Defense," *St. Petersburg Times*, 5 July 1941; "Women Get Auto Repair Advice Today," *HC*, 17 September 1941, 20; "City Trains 50,000 for Defense Jobs," *NYT*, 13 October 1941, 19.

36. "Call for Volunteers Issued by Women's Ambulance Corps," *Eugene Register-Guard*, 10 December 1941; "Facts Every Woman Motorist Should Know," *AM*, January 1943, 11; "'Clubmobile' Program AAA Model Course," *AM*, April 1943, 10; "Motor Pool Welcomes New WAAC Mechanics," *Signal Corps Message* (Fort Monmouth, NJ), 28 May 1943, 1, 6; "Just Like Training Children," *FT* 1(6) (11 June 1943): 12; cover, *LHJ*, March 1943; "Anita Brenner, 'Occupation: Housewife'—No Amateur Job," *NYT*, 13 June 1943, SM16; Kay Swift and Chappell and Co., *Fighting on the Home Front Wins: The National War Song of the American Housewife* (New York : Chappell & Co., 1943), 1–5; "Auto Mechanics on Scarce List, Survey Shows," *Miami News*, 25 August 1943, 11A; "Auto Repair Course Offered at School," *Berkeley Daily Gazette*, 11 January 1944; Exide Automobile Batteries ad, *Life*, 21 February 1944, 128; gas station ad, *SEP*, 29 April 1944, described in Honey, *Creating Rosie*, 128.

So central did car care become to the homemaker's arsenal that as late as 1971 home economics extension courses trained women leaders so that they could teach the "Powder Puff Mechanics" course to their respective membership ("28 Women Take Course in Mechanics," *Gettysburg Times*, 7 April 1971).

37. "Navy Wife Learns Man's Work While Husband Learns to Cook and Such," *FT*, 14 May 1943, 3, BFR; Honey, *Creating Rosie*, 98.

38. "The Mechanic Is a Lady," *FT* 2 (August 1945), 44–46, BFR.

39. "Are Most Garage Men Honest?" *Your Car*, May 1925, 13–15, 95; Bert Pierce, "Automobiles: Upkeep: Women Encouraged to Learn Mechanics of Cars as an Added Safety Measure," *NYT*, 26 December 1954, X23; Eddie Abbott, "Don't Tell Me Women Are Helpless!" *SEP*, 26 February 1955, 32–33, 118–19; "Citgo Show 'n Tell! Majors Aim Efforts at Women Drivers," *NPN* (July 1970): 71; "Woman Represents Mobil: She's No Token When She Boosts Consumer," *BG*, 14 May 1972, 78A; John Jakle, *Motoring: The Highway Experience in America* (Athens: University of Georgia Press, 2008), 98–99.

40. Gene Nora Jessen, *Powder Puff Derby of 1929* (Naperville, Ill.: Sourcebook, 2002), 66; "Powder Puff Derby: Ladies Stage a Real Show on Their Big Day at Pimlico," *Cumberland Evening Times* (Maryland), 6 May 1941, 18); George W. Herald, "Sounds Like Fun, Girls!" *HC*, 5 February 1952, 7; "Women with Wrenches," *HC*, 3 April 1955, SM2; "WOW's Set to Spot Things in Education, Church, Music," *BAA*, 14 March 1972; Nancy Baltad, "Male Stronghold Invaded: GM Car Care Clinic Fascinates and Mystifies 100 Club Women," *LAT*, 3 January 1974, CS6; "Don't Panic!" *Palm Beach Post* (Florida), 3 February 1974, D21; "Women on Wheels," *TB*, 21 April 1974, D9; Susan Vaughn, "Women Enjoy Auto Repair," *HC*, 23 March 1975, 7A.

For significance of dirt, place, and pollution, see Mary Douglas, *Purity and Danger: An Analysis of Concepts of Pollution and Taboo* (New York: Routledge, 2002), and Kathleen M. Brown, *Foul Bodies: Cleanliness in Early America* (New Haven, Conn.: Yale University Press, 2009).

41. Ibid.; Merrill Folson, "Westchester Attendance Tripled," *NYT*, 14 October 1957, 22; Carol Liston, "Woman's Place Is in the Garage?" *BG*, 9 March 1967, 3; Vin L. Rossitto, "Female Grease Monkeys Are Now in Training," *HC*, 12 March 1967, 9C; James F. Donohue, "Powder Puff Mechanics Learning About Cars," *FLS*, 29 March 1967; Doris Faber, "Women vs. Mechanics: The Language Barrier," *NYT*, 5 April 1964, A7; "Mechanics' Know-How Acquired by Women in Weekly Y Classes," *LAT*, 24 October 1965, OC14; Bonnie Joe Ayers, "Basic Maintenance for Ladies," *AM*, August 1969, 6; "Women Learn Delicate Details of Auto Body," *Evening Independent* (Florida), 7 April 1970; Dorothy Kincaid, "Women Study Cars," *Milwaukee Sentinel*, 9 September 1975, 4; Mobil "Observations," *Chicago Daily Tribune*, 11 June 1978; Ladies' Car Care Clinic ad, *Kokomo Tribune* (Indiana), 19 March 2000; Luis Perez, "Car Clinic Helps Women Learn Basics of Auto Care," *St. Petersburg Times* (Florida), 21 September 2008; "Ladies Night in the Lube Bay," Sinclair Oil Corporation (n.d., c. 1960s, IAP); womenatthewheel.net.

42. Ibid.; Dorothy Kincaid, "Women Study Cars," *Milwaukee Sentinel*, 9 September 1975, 4.

43. Wertz quoted in Sylvia Porter, "New Group Is Guardian for Women Drivers," *Modesto Bee* (Calif.), 31 July 1964; Margaret Dana, "Women Take New Look at Safety of Auto Tires," *PP*, 19 March 1967; Sally Wright Brown, "'Powder Puff' Mechanics Tune Up," *SM*, 20 November 1971.

44. Ibid.; "Survey Shows: Women Hard-Bargainers with Auto Repair Men," *FLS*, 11 January 1964; C. H. Claudy, "The Woman and Her Car," *Country Life in America* 23 (January 1913): 42 in Beth Kraig, "Women at the Wheel," PhD diss., University of Washington, 1987, 144.

45. Duncan Osborn, "Yuma Girls Invade Auto Mechanics Class," *Yuma Daily Sun* (Arizona), 1 July 1968, 16; Will Dennis ad, *TB*, 20 May 1973; Susan Vaughn, "Women Enjoy Auto Repair," *HC* 23 March 1975, 7A; Irvin Molotsky, "Auto Mechanics School: For Women on the Road to Self-Sufficiency," *NYT*, 12 November 1977, FS22.

46. "Car Course for Ladies Is Now Statewide," *Midwest Motorist*, June 1971; "Powder Puff Mechanics Class Slated," *Times Daily* (Alabama), 21 February 1972; "WOW's Set to Spot Things in Education, Church, Music," *BAA*, 14 March 1972; Edward Lechtzin, "Gals Make Tracks in Auto Industry, *Ludington Daily News* (Michigan), 27 April 1973, 3; Nancy Baltad, "Male Stronghold Invaded: GM Car Care Clinic Fascinates and Mystifies 100 Club Women," *LAT*, 3 January 1974, CS6; Kincaid, "Women Study Cars," 4; "Women Learn Car Care," *Bangor Daily News* (Maine), 13 January 1978; John Perduyn, "Car Care Clinic Proposal (27 April 1987)," Box 42, GTR.

47. Abbott, "Don't Tell," 118–19; Baltad, "Male Stronghold Invaded"; Maureen Gallagher, "Women Improve 'Motor Skills' in YWCA-Sponsored Course," *HC* 19 March 1977, 27.

48. "Women Fix Cars, Change Gears," *SM*, 3 October 1976; John Perduyn, "Car Care Clinic Proposal (27 April 1987)," Box 42, GTR.

49. Janice Mall, "Feminine Flair for Auto Repair," *LAT*, 12 June 1977, J18; John Eaton, "Car-Care Classes Aimed at Women," *DP*, 19 April 1977, D3; "Repair Shops Changing Views on Female Customers," *HC*, 20 September 1981, L10; email interview with Ren Volpe, 11 April 2011, IAP; Chicago Auto Presents Its First Free Car Care Seminar for Men!" Boomer Kennedy, Box 4, Folders 1, 3, and 5, AES.

50. John R. White, "Lazzaro Takes the Mystery—and the Mister-y—Out of Auto Maintenance," *BG*, 30 July 1994, 37; Jane Ganahl, "Newest Category of Grease Monkeys: Over-40 Wonder Women," *SFC*, 13 July 2003, E2.

51. Peter Scott, "Woman Race Driver Helps Cure 'Autophobia' in Girls; Clinic Stresses Car Care Isn't Just a Guy Thing," *Atlanta Constitution*, 30 April 2001, B5.

52. "What Every Woman (and Man) Should Know About Cars," *Ebony*, May 2001, 132, 134; *My Cousin Vinny* (1992), http://www.imdb.com/title/tt0104952/.

53. Earle Eldridge, "More Women Tackle Own Car Repairs: Getting Savvy Under Hood Saves Them Time, Money," *USA Today*, 20 March 2002, B3; Melissa Preddy, "Women Should Study Car Repair 101," *Detroit News*, 10 December 2009, E1; www.greatbearauto.com (accessed 29 September 2010, now defunct); www.rockymountainautoclinic.com (accessed October 22, 2010, now defunct). It took time for repair shops to concede their indulgence and assertion of their hypermasculinity, and some never did. There were exceptions. In 1958, the *Reading Eagle* reported that one company had a "babysitting service for mothers who want to watch the repair work" ("Garages Tone Up for Lady Drivers," 30 March 1958). Reflecting on the closing of her father's garage in 1980, Patricia Du Brul noted that she once complained to him that the pinup girl calendars adorning the walls of his office were "sexist and therefore offensive to women, his answer was that an auto-repair shop would be incomplete without such a calendar or two" ("Chalk Up Another One for 'Progress,'" *NYT*, 7 December 1980, NJ47).

54. "Training Offered to Women as Car Mechanics' Aides," *HC*, 21 June 1943, 5; John R. White, "Ladies Night at the Garage; One Company Offers Basic Car Care Instruction to Women Only," *BG*, 7 November 1982, 1; Borg, *Auto Mechanics*; Lois Scharf, *To Work and to Wed: Female Employment, Feminism, and the Great Depression* (Westport, Conn.: Greenwood Press, 1980).

55. "This Year Choose a Car That Won't Require Repair Men," Hudson ad, *AM*, March 1916, 4.

56. Amy Bix, "Creating 'Chicks Who Fix': Women, Tool Knowledge, and Home Repair, 1920–2007," *Women's Studies Quarterly* 37(1) (June 3, 2009): 6, 9; Scharff, *Taking the Wheel*, 93–94; Lucy Adlington, *Great War Fashion: Tales from the History Wardrobe* (Stroud, England: History Press, 2013).

57. Marie Coolidge Rask, "Why I'm a Workwoman," *BDG*, 28 February 1915, 59; Georgine Clarsen, *Eat My Dust: Early Women Motorists* (Baltimore: Johns Hopkins University Press, 2008), 71–72; Wosk, *Women and the Machine*, 125–27.

58. Harry Clifford Brokaw, *Putnam's Automobile Handbook: The Care and Management of the Modern Motor-Car* (New York: G. P. Putnam, 1918), 303–7.

59. Ibid.; "Pretty Women, in Trousers, Now Hold Jobs on Gasoline Row," *LAT*, 12 August 1917, V18; "Odd Items from Everywhere," *BDG*, 13 April 1918, 14; "Garage for Women Only and with Only Women Machinists," *BG*, 21 August 1921, 47; "Girl Mechanic Knows Autos from Wheel to Hood," *Bridgeport Telegram* (Conn.), 13 January 1922, 26; Bertram Reinitz, "Tire Repairing a Woman's Job," *NYT*, 14 April 1929, I44.

60. "Topless Attendants!" cartoon, *NPN*, February 1970, 125; "A Dallas Station Has an Attendant in 'Hot Pants,'" *NPN* June 1971, 32.

61. "By George," *Miami News*, 30 October 1964; "Dear George," *News Journal* (Mansfield, Ohio), 16 September 1967, 14; Charles B. Camp, "The Owners of Clinics

That Diagnose Car Ills Have Some Headaches," *WSJ*, 17 October 1968; *Playboy*, April 1969, 178; Maggie Patterson, "Auto Firm 'Shifts' to Women," *PP*, 11 December 1970; Cornell Fowler, "Topless Mechanics Hired at Des Moines Auto Repair," *Mohave Daily Miner*, 5 October 1986; Carol Sanger, "Girls and the Getaway: Cars, Culture, and the Predicament of Gendered Space," *University of Pennsylvania Law Review* 44(2) (December 1995): 709.

62. Barbara Cloud, "Woman Invades World of the Grease Monkey," *PP*, 29 August 1964; "Auto Repair Tips Given to Women," *Spokesman-Review* (Wash.), 25 May 1968; "Her First Love Is Automatic Transmission," *Gadsden Times* (Maryland), 3 July 1968; "A Pennsylvania Grandma Gets Under the Hood," *Time*, 1996; Gina Cortez, "Senior Women Love Work as Mechanics," *TP*, 20 March 1997, 1A1.

63. " 'Sister Fixit' Finds God Under Hood," *RE*, 12 March 1977; "Nuns Learn Automobile Mechanics," *Spokane Daily Chronicle*, 9 August 1979.

64. See, for example, "Kitchens' Repair," *Owosso Argus-Press* (Mich.), 12 January 1963; "Wife Learns Auto Repair," *RE*, 1 December 1963; Diane White, "Ever Consider a Career as Auto Expert, Girls?" *BG*, 1 November 1966, 29; Essie Norwood, "Betty Edmonds, 'Girl Mechanic,' Maintains Her Femininity," *Daily Times-News* (North Carolina), 17 October 1970, 2; "Racer's Wife Is a Top Flight Mechanic," *Winchester Evening Star* (Virginia), 16 May 1972, 11; Thomas Nord, "Mechanic Doing Her Part to Repair Sexism Problem," *Detroit News*, 7 June 1995, D9; Bruce R. Posten, "Taking a New Turn," *RE*, 21 October 1998; Jane Ganahl, "Newest Category of Grease Monkeys: Over-40 Wonder Women," *SFC*, 13 July 2003, E2.

65. "Lori and Valerie Working at Wrenchwomen, 1978," *Eye to Eye: Portraits of Lesbians* in *Queerly Visible 1971–1991: The Work of JEB (Joan E. Biren)*; Chicago auto advertisements 1984–86, Boomer Kennedy, Box 4, Folder 1, AES; Leslie Smith and Toni White, "Feminist Community from 1969–1979," *Off Our Backs*, 28 February 1980 (10)2, 13; "Hot Female Mechanics," *Curve*, March 2009.

66. "Garage for Women Only and with Only Women Machinists," *BG*, 21 August 1921, 47. For a literary example, see Rebecca Solnit, "Men Explain Things to Men: Facts Didn't Get in Their Way," http://www.tomdispatch.com/post/174918/ (accessed 5 February 2016).

67. Donna Scheibe, "Today's Women Even Do Their Own Brake Jobs," *LAT*, 29 February 1976, A1; Chicago auto advertisement, *The Tab*, 16 July 1985, 17, Boomer Kennedy, Box 4, Folder 1, AES.

68. "Women" classified ad, *TB*, 23 October 1949; "Auto 'Damage Doctors,' " *Lewiston Daily Sun*, 8 August 1952; Jackie Karlson, "Mademoiselle Motorist," *AM*, November 1958, 26; "Pretty Mechanic," *Oakland Tribune*, 20 May 1971, 26; Lillian Borgeson, "Woman Mechanic: New Auto Ally," *Vogue*, June 1980, 88, 90; email interview with Ren Volpe, 11 April 2011, IAP; Borg, *Auto Mechanics*, 116–18; Household Data Annual Averages, Bureau of Labor Statistics, Department of Labor, 2014, http://www.bls.gov/cps/cpsaat11.htm.

69. McShane, *Down the Asphalt*, 160; "She Is a Machinist," *MA*, 19 July 1917, 34; Scharff, *Taking the Wheel*, 27–29; "Has Nice Chassis, Too: Texas Lass Earns Living Renovating Auto Engines," *LAT*, 25 January 1955, B1; "Monkey Wrench Proves Enough for

Teen Girl Mechanic," *San Antonio Light*, 2 October 1955, 30; "Lady Mechanic Taught by Pop," *Sarasota Herald-Tribune*, 22 November 1979; Nancy Tillman Romalov, "Mobile Heroines: Early Twentieth-Century Girls' Automobile Series," *Journal of Popular Culture* (Spring 1995): 235.

70. Joseph C. Ingraham, "Autos and Makers Criticized in Study of 17,000 Women," *NYT*, 10 April 1958, 31; Borgeson, "Woman Mechanic," 88, 90; Susan Perry, "Ex-Secretary Unlocked Secrets Under the Hood and Never Looked Back," *LAT*, 5 December 1985, 2; Bob Ross, "Women Unite at Car Repair Shop," *TP*, 19 August 1995, Money, C1; Joan Boram, "Looking for Ms. Goodwrench," *Nation's Business* 84(10) (October 1996): 14; Jeanne Wright, "More Women Are Beginning to Take Peek Under the Hood," *LAT*, 23 February 2000, G1; Marci Alboher Nusbaum, "Breaking into More Male Strongholds," *NYT*, 13 November 2003, C8; Stephanie Cline, "Colorado Springs Woman Owns Women-Friendly Auto Shop," *Colorado Springs Business Journal*, 22 October 2004; Cynthia Needham, "Woman Makes Mark as a Mechanic," *Providence Journal*, 30 September 2007.

71. White, "Ever Consider," 29; "Her First Love Is Automatic Transmission," *Gadsen Times* (Alabama), 3 July 1968; "Top-Dollar Job: Auto Mechanics," *WW*, August 1979, 57; Boram, "Looking for Ms. Goodwrench," 14; Caroline Louise Cole, "Good Mechanics Are Hard to Find; Just Don't Call Her Mr. Goodwrench," *BG*, 1 August 1999; Natalie Neff, "Manly Hands," *Autoweek* 60 (11) (7 June 2010): 11.

This observation brings to mind one of the conclusions made a hundred years earlier about women's generally smaller hands and their skills with regard to the typewriter (Margery W. Davies, *Woman's Place Is at the Typewriter* (Philadelphia: Temple University Press, 1984). Indeed, a male manager at the De Luxe Automobile Co., Oldsmobile distributor in St. Louis, Missouri, contended that "the women's fingers appear to be more adaptable than those of men and they put on fenders, etc., more quickly and with less damage to the parts than men" ("Women as Solution of Service Problem," *MA*, 15 August 1918, 17). Eighty years later, another male manager again argued, "With the computers and complexity of cars today, it's more a question of brains now than brawn. And if anything, her small hands give her a big advantage getting into tight spaces" (Cole, "Good Mechanics").

72. "And They Drive More Cars Every Year," *FN* 8(19) (15 August 1928): 179; "Women Appreciate Our COURTEOUS SERVICE" ad, *FN* 10(14) (15 July 1930): 165; Charles Parlin and Curtis Publishing Company, *The Passenger Car Industry* (Philadelphia, 1932), 97–98; "Women on Wheels," *AM*, September 1961, 10, 12.

73. "Garagemen Praise Feminine Drivers," *HC*, 14 November 1963, 25; White, "Ever Consider," 29; "Female Mechanic Can Take Kidding," *Daily News* (Kentucky), 28 February 1972; Denise Smith Amos, "Car Repair Is Women's Work at Lace-n-Armor, *St. Louis Post-Dispatch*, 3 July 1995, Business Plus, 3; Joshua Macht, "An Electronic Field Day," *Inc. Technology* 17(9) 1995(2): 88; Cole, "Good Mechanics"; Vanessa Parks, "Car Repair with a Differential Women's Touch at Marlborough Shop," *BG*, 12 September 1999, 1; Jim Lovel, "Car Shop Chain for Women Rolls into Area," *Atlanta Business Chronicle* 24(48) (3 May 2002): A3; Vauhini Vara, "Auto Shops Go Upscale, Repair Chain Touts Amenities," *DP*, 5 August 2002, C01; Bonnie Tsui, "Reinventing the Wheel," *O, The Oprah Magazine*, November 2010.

74. Laura Mulvey, "Visual Pleasure and Narrative Cinema," *Screen* (1975) 16 (3): 6–18; Maggie Wykes and Barrie Gunter, *The Media and Body Image: If Looks Could Kill* (Thousand Oaks, Calif.: SAGE Publications, 2005).

75. Chevrolet ad, *Life*, 9 January 1970, 85; *The Bikini Carwash* (1992), http://www.imdb.com/title/tt0103812/; "Bikini Carwash Owner Pursuing City License," *Daily Herald* (Illinois), 4 January 1995, 143; "Bikini Car Wash to Open," *Aiken Standard* (South Carolina), 25 March 1992, 17; Barry Janoff, "A Course on Carnal Knowledge," *Brandweek* 47(16) (17 April 2006): 56; Eagle One commercial, Cheerleaders vs. Nuns, https://www.youtube.com/watch?v=rD-GrQyM3Lw.

76. Nathan Lee, "New 'Transformers,' Same Old Mechanics," 24 June 2009, http://www.npr.org/templates/story/story.php?storyId=105753147; *Heat Lightning*, 1934, http://www.imdb.com/title/tt0025228/; *Urban Cowboy*, 1980, http://www.imdb.com/title/tt0081696/; *My Cousin Vinny*, 1992, http://www.imdb.com/title/tt0104952/; Wrench Wench at http://tvtropes.org/pmwiki/pmwiki.php/Main/WrenchWench (all accessed 20 September 2016).

77. "Lubri-Kate" postcard, Denver: Williamson-Haffner Co., 1906, and "Yes—I know" postcard, illustrated by Irby, n.d., AMW.

78. Gillette Elvgren, *Gil Elvgren: All His Glamorous American Pin-Ups* (New York: Taschen, 2008), 197, 221; postcards of mechanic mailed to Boomer Kennedy, 1984, and topless mechanic, 1983, Boomer Kennedy, Box 4, Folders 1, 3, and 5, AES; Bananarama,1983 video, "Cruel Summer," https://www.youtube.com/watch?v=9ePIZugahFc; Beyoncé, 2010 video, "Why Don't You Love Me?" https://www.youtube.com/watch?v=QczgvUDskk0; Rihanna, 2009, "Shut Up and Drive," https://www.youtube.com/watch?v=up7pvPqNkuU.

79. Jaime Hernandez, *Maggie the Mechanic (Love and Rockets)* (Seattle, Wash.: Fantagraphics Books, 2007); Jim Meddick, "Monty," 29 September 2004 and 19 February 2006; Robb Armstrong, "Jumpstart," 15–20 November 2004 (both accessed at www.comics.com.

80. See for example, *The Buckets*, 13 July 2001 and 22 April 2006. See also, *Arlo and Janis*, 3 January 2000, www.comics.com.

81. Glenn Harlan Reynolds, "In Age of High-Tech, Are Americans Losing Touch with DIY Skills?" 10 September 2007, *PM*, http://www.popularmechanics.com/home/how-to/a2104/4221637/.

82. Citgo ads in *Life*: 23 April 1971; 30 April 1971; 14 May 1971, 26; Citgo ad, *NPN*, August 1971, 116–17; Clarke, *Driving Women*, 193.

83. "How to Take Care of Your Husband's Baby" ad, *Life*, 18 June 1971, 57; "The Better Small Car," *PM*, January 1971, back cover.

84. "Caring About Your GM Car Keeps Mr. Goodwrench in Business" ad, Lightner collection, HCD; Mr. Goodwrench ads appeared in *WW* (February–July 1981) and *PM* (March, April, May 1981); "How to Choose a Repair Shop," *AAA World* (November/December 1988), cover, 11–13; Jiffy Lube ad campaign, 2005, https://www.jiffylube.com/news-and-press/new-jiffy-lube-television-ads-emphasize-service-depth-and-expertise; "Men Not Necessarily More Car-Care Savvy Than Women," Jiffy Lube survey, 2006, https://www.jiffylube.com/news-and-press/men-not-necessarily-more-car-care-savvy-than-women.

85. June Saylor, "Mademoiselle Motorist," *AM*, December 1955, 30; Kraig, *Woman at the Wheel*, 164.

86. "In 10 Minutes" ad, *AAA World*, July–August 1989, AAA; "Come to Jiffy Lube Now" ad, c. 1980s, AAA; Jiffy Lube ad, 2012, IAP.

87. Sally H. Clarke, *Trust and Power: Consumers, The Modern Corporation, and the Making of the United States Automobile Market* (New York: Cambridge University Press, 2007); Ford ad, *Life*, 28 October 1966, 2; Keith Wheeler, "And When Love Comes in It Takes the Auto for a Spin," *Life*, 11 January 1968, 30–31; Volvo ad, *Life*, 13 March 1970, 5; "Ford Enters Pinto into Small-Car Race; Accents Easy Maintenance," *NPN*, October 1970, 59; "What Marketers Are Learning from New Generation Car-Care Centers," *NPN*, December 1970, 52–57; Carin Rubenstein, "Women in the Driver's Seat," *Across the Board* 23 (April 1986): 40–45; Toyota ad, *WW*, February 1987, 27; Volvo ad, *WW*, October 1987, 38; OnStar, https://www.onstar.com/us/en/home.html.

88. Ann Long Wanswer, "Mademoiselle Motorist and the Mechanics of Medicine," *AM*, February 1971, 26; "The GM Continuous Protection Plan" ad, *WW*, March 1979, 46; "Announcing a First . . . Car Repairs Guaranteed for Life" ad, *WW*, June 1983, 55; "Let Us Repair Your Car Today" ad, *WW*, November 1983, 53.

Chapter 5

1. Oldsmobile, 1970, IAP; Cadillac commercial, 1996, http://www.youtube.com/watch?v=rRNWnKNHWLQ (accessed 4 May 2014); John Richardson, "Newt Gingrich: The Indispensable Republican," *ESQ*, September 2010, http://www.esquire.com/features/newt-gingrich-0910-8 (accessed 30 April 2014); Victoria de Grazia and Ellen Furlough, eds., *The Sex of Things: Gender and Consumption in Historical Perspective* (Berkeley: University of California Press, 1996); Mary Louis Roberts, "Gender, Consumption, and Commodity Culture," *American Historical Review* 103(3) (1998): 817–44; Penny Tinkler and Cheryl Krasnick Warsh, "Feminine Modernity in Interwar Britain and North America: Corsets, Cars, and Cigarettes," *Journal of Women's History* 20(3): 113–43; Ford ad, 1956, http://www.allclassicads.com/ford-vintage-ads-1950.html (accessed 1 June 2014); Chrysler ad, 1963, IAP; Barbara Stern and Michael Solomon, "'Have You Kissed Your Professor Today?': Bumper Stickers and Consumer Self Statements," *Advances in Consumer Research* 19 (1992): 169–73; Russell W. Belk, "Possessions and the Extended Self," *Journal of Consumer Research* (September 1988): 139–68; Blaine Brownell, "A Symbol of Modernity: Attitudes Toward the Automobile in Southern Cities in the 1920s," *American Quarterly* (March 1972): 21–24; Cotton Seiler, *Republic of Drivers: A Cultural History of Automobility in America* (Chicago: University of Chicago Press, 2008); Peter Marsh and Peter Collett, *Driving Passion: The Psychology of the Car* (Boston: Faber and Faber, 1986), 62–64, 79.

2. Pankaj Aggarwal and Ann L. McGill, "Is That Car Smiling at Me? Schema Congruity as a Basis for Evaluating Anthropomorphized Products," *Journal of Consumer Research* 34 (December 2007): 468–79; Jacob A. Benfield, William J. Szlemko, and Paul A. Bell, "Driver Personality and Anthropomorphic Attributions of Vehicle Personality Relate to Reported Aggressive Driving Tendencies," *Personality and Individual Differences* 42 (2007): 247–58; Nicholas Epley, Adam Waytz, and John T. Cacioppo, "On Seeing Human:

A Three-Factor Theory of Anthropomorphism," *Psychological Review* 114(4) (2007): 864–86; Stewart Guthrie, *Faces in the Clouds: A New Theory of Religion* (New York: Oxford University Press, 1995), 39–40. Early scholars also associated the human proclivity to animate goods and experiences with George W. Gilmore offering global examples ranging from rainbows to yams (*Animism or Thought Currents of Primitive Peoples* [Boston: Marshall Jones Company, 1919], 61–93.)

3. Ibid.; Guthrie, *Faces in the Clouds*, 134; Pamela Hollie, "Advertising; Encore Ads Go a Step Further," *NYT*, 31 August 1984; 1985 Renault Encore ad, https://www.youtube.com/watch?v=_Qf3HVGbg9E (accessed 23 February 2016).

4. Jonathan Welsh, "Automobiles: Why Cars Got Angry," *WSJ*, 10 March 2006; Guthrie, *Faces in the Clouds*, 60.

5. Aggarwal and McGill, "Is That Car Smiling," 468–79.

6. "Conundrum," *Madison Daily Herald* (Indiana), 21 March 1917, 2; "Model T Facts," 5 August 2012, https://media.ford.com/content/fordmedia/fna/us/en/news/2013/08/05/model-t-facts.html (accessed 30 April 2014); Elizabeth Popularity, http://www.ourbabynamer.com/Elizabeth-name-popularity.html (accessed 30 April 2014); Deborah Clarke, *Driving Women: Fiction and Automobile Culture in Twentieth-Century America* (Baltimore: Johns Hopkins University Press, 2007), 39, 74; Virginia Scharff, *Taking the Wheel: Women and the Coming of the Motor Age* (Albuquerque: University of New Mexico Press, 1992), 113; Jill Avery, "Defending the Markers of Masculinity: Consumer Resistance to Brand Gender-Bending," *International Journal of Research in Marketing* (December 2012): 322–36.

7. Scharff, *Taking the Wheel*, 53; "To Lizzie in France," *Ogden Examiner* (Utah), 23 June 1918, 11; Walter Prichard Eaton, "The Passing of Eliza," *AM*, January 1928, 22–24; Valvoline ad, *Life*, 28 February 1944; Rocky R. Miracle, *Mrs. Cordie's Soldier Son: A World War II Saga* (College Station: Texas A&M University Press, 2008), 51; G503 Military Vehicle Message Forums, http://g503.com/forums/viewtopic.php?f=10&t=184189 (accessed 30 April 2014); Marilyn Monroe Union Oil commercial, 1950, http://www.youtube.com/watch?v=FyS_86_XbLg; Barbara Holliday, "Does Your Wife Drive?" *FT* (April 1967): 25; Marsh and Collett, *Driving Passion*, 12–13; Jennifer Parchesky, "Women in the Driver's Seat: The Auto-Erotics of Early Women's Films," *Film History* (2006): 178; Kay Armatage, *The Girl from God's Country: Nell Shipman and the Silent Cinema* (Toronto: University of Toronto Press, 2003), 132; Benfield et al., "Driver Personality," 249, 251; Lesley Hazelton, *Everything Women Always Wanted to Know About Cars* (New York: Doubleday, 1995), 26; Marilyn Root, *Women at the Wheel: 42 Stories of Freedom, Fanbelts and the Lure of the Open Road* (Naperville, Ill.: Sourcebooks, 1999), 93–95; Janet Ruth Falon, "Christening a Companion: What Shall We Name the Volvo?" *NYT*, 27 September 2002; "Nationwide Insurance Finds Nearly One-Fourth of Car Owners Name Their Four-Wheeled 'Baby,'" http://www.nationwide.com/about-us/093013-jtn-baby.jsp (accessed 30 April 2014); DMEautomotive, "Baby, Want to Name My Car?" http://www.dmeautomotive.com/announcements/baby-want-to-name-my-car-younger-and-female-car-owners-most-likely-to-name-their-vehicles-nicknames-#.U2E4Y_ldWSo (accessed 30 April 2014); Clifford Krauss, "America Is Hitting the Road Again," *NYT*, 3 June 2016.

8. George Worthington, "Electric Vehicles—1911 Models," *Electrical Review and Western Electrician*, 11 February 1911, 303; "The Kind of Car a Man Wants," *Electric*

Vehicles, June 1916, 173–74; Scharff, *Taking the Wheel*, 55; Clarke, *Driving Women*, 46; Mercury ad, *Pittsburgh Post-Gazette*, 3 May 1955; *The Love Bug*, 1968, http://www.imdb.com/title/tt0064603/, and KITT from *Knight Rider*, 1982–86, http://www.imdb.com/title/tt0083437/ (accessed 17 May 2014); *Turbo Teen*, https://www.youtube.com/watch?v=j18e_ID-DpA; "Brad" commercial for Liberty Mutual (2014), https://www.youtube.com/watch?v=t6_M9bXYy2s; Karal Ann Marling, "America's Love Affair with the Automobile in the Television Age," *Design Quarterly* 46 Autoeroticism (1989): 7; Briscoe ad, *Milwaukee Sentinel*, 8 September 1916; Cougar ad, *Wellsville Daily Reporter* (New York), 12 January 1967; Oldsmobile ad, *Holiday*, December 1967; Mercury ad, 1966 and Volkswagen ad, 1965, IAP; Mercury ad, *Indiana Evening Gazette* (Pennsylvania), 17 November 1966; Marsh, *Driving Passion*, 60–61; Daniel Miller, "Driven Societies," in *Car Cultures*, ed. Daniel Miller (New York: Berg, 2001), 2–3; GTO, quoted in Marsh, *Driving Passion*, 183; Welsh, "Automobiles"; Mark S. Foster, *A Nation on Wheels: The Automobile Culture in America Since 1945* (Belmont, Calif.: Wadsworth, 2003), 75–77.

Sidonie Smith maintained, "In the imagination, the automobile itself is bisexual. Men often imagine their cars as female; they are possessions. But they also imagine them as prosthetic extensions of the sexual organ. They are in this sense, possessed of phallic power" (*Moving Lives: Twentieth-Century Women's Travel Writing* [Minneapolis: University of Minnesota Press, 2001], 183). Grant McCracken concurs that for some men the car is often a reflection of themselves, noting that they "don't see any difference between themselves and the car. You spit on the car, you spit on them" (*Culture and Consumption II: Markets, Meaning, and Brand Management* [Bloomington: Indiana University Press, 2005], 11–12).

Some postwar ads also drew on phallic imagery of cars and rockets. David L. Lewis, "Sex and the Automobile: From Rumble Seats to Rockin' Vans," in *The Automobile and American Culture*, ed. David L. Lewis and Laurence Goldstein (Ann Arbor: University of Michigan Press, 1980), 127; Oldsmobile ads in *Life*: 20 February 1950, 20; 17 April 1950, 21; 22 May 1950, 28; 3 September 1951.

9. Chevy ad, 1997, IAP; Anthony Young, *Camaro* (Osceola, Wis.: Motorbooks International, 2000), 75, 145; Gillian Frank, "Discophobia: Anti-Gay Prejudice and the 1979 Backlash Against Disco," *Journal of the History of Sexuality* 16 (2) (May 2007): 276–306; Alice Echols, *Hot Stuff: Disco and the Remaking of American Culture* (New York: Norton, 2010), 215.

10. "The Model (T) Family," *FT* 5(9) July 1912; Quips in *FT*, September and October 1913; Francis Picabia in http://sauer-thompson.com/conversations/archives/002742.html (accessed 1 June 2014) and Smith, *Moving Lives*, 173. Artist Mel Ramos later painted a naked woman alongside an AC Delco sparkplug (1964) http://collections.si.edu/search/results.htm?q=record_ID:hmsg _66.4178 (accessed 3 August 2014).

11. Charles Coolidge Parlin, *Passenger Car Industry*, 1932, 90; Saab ad, *Life*, 21 April 1967; Chevy ad, *WW*, November 1983, 108, and *RD*, October 1980, 280–81; Geo commercial, 1980s, http://www.youtube.com/watch?v=kXLLGC0l-R8 (accessed 1 June 2014); Smith, *Moving Lives*, 182; Emily Bobrow, "Sex and Advertising: Retail Therapy," *Economist*, 17 December 2011; Daniel Horowitz, *The Anxieties of Affluence: Critiques of American Consumer Culture, 1939–1979* (Amherst: University of Massachusetts Press, 2005),

53; Franz Kreuzer, Gerd Prechtl, and Christoph Steiner, eds., *A Tiger in the Tank: Ernest Dichter, An Austrian Advertising Guru*, trans. Lars Hennig (Riverside, Calif.: Ariadne Press, 2007), 71.

12. Ford ad, *FN*, 21(8) (1941): 224; William Faulkner, *Intruder in the Dust* (New York: Vintage, 1991 (1948)), 233–34; Lincoln-Continental, Acc. 1007, Box 1, Reason for Discontinuation, BFR; Volkswagen ad, *WW*, May 1979, 38; Toyota ad, *BHG*, August 2000, 205.

Some have speculated that the Ford Edsel's front grille appeared to look like a vagina and that this similarity strongly contributed to its failure, considered the biggest in automotive corporate history (Stephen Bayley, *Sex, Drink, and Fast Cars* [New York: Pantheon, 1986], 19–22).

13. Cars decorated with flowers found in *The Automobile*, 1904; *Labor Day Parade*, 1904, http://vimeo.com/63255357; http://www.tennessee.gov/tsla/exhibits/suffrage/images/33865.jpg; Chevy ad, 1972 and American Hatch Corp, 1977, http://justacarguy.blogspot.com/2010/01/stupid-decals-hard-to-believe-first-set.html; Gijs Mom, *The Electric Vehicle: Technology and Expectations in the Automobile Age* (Baltimore: Johns Hopkins University Press, 2012), 59; Clarke, *Driving Women*, 23; Zan Dubin, "Coast to Coast in a Gender Bender," *LAT*, 7 June 1985; Meg Cox, "Either That Car Is a 1967 Porsche or the Quickest Doily on Wheels, *WSJ*, 18 April 1985; Phyllis Yes, Portia-Porsche, http://allcarcentral.com/Porsche_911_1960s.html#.WHFCd7YrLuQ; Peter Valdes-Dapena, "Dodge's New Tough-Guy Color: Furious Fuchsia," cnn.com, 8 February 2010, http://money.cnn.com/2010/02/08/autos/dodge_challenger_furious_fuschia/; Jeanne Moos, "Batting Your Car Lashes," cnn.com, https://youtu.be/G0O6OrDbayI (all accessed 9 August 2014).

License plates ultimately proved to be gender neutral; adding personalized plates did not feminize the car (Irvin Molotsky, "The License Plates That Spell VANITY," *NYT*, 27 January 1980).

14. Jonathan Welsh, "What Men Want: A Volkswagen Beetle?" *WSJ* 19 September 2011; Paul Eisenstein, "VW Looking to Lure Americans with Its Latest Beetle Makeover," 16 August 2011, http://www.nbcnews.com/id/44162314/ns/business-the_driver_seat/t/vw-looking-lure-americans-its-latest-beetle-makeover/#.U5hdgPldWa8 (accessed 11 June 2014) and "First Drive: 2012 Volkswagen Beetle," 15 July 2011, http://www.thedetroitbureau.com/2011/07/first-drive-2012-volkswagen-beetle/ (accessed 17 May 2014); Phil Patton, "2012 Volkswagen Beetle: A Bug with a Rampaging Y Chromosone," *NYT*, 18 April 2011, and "To Be Cute as a Bug Isn't Enough Anymore," *NYT*, 20 January 2012; Avery, "Defending the Markers of Masculinity"; Scharff, *Taking the Wheel*, 131; Chris Lezotte, "The Evolution of the 'Chick Car' Or: What Came First, the Chick or the Car?" *Journal of Popular Culture* 45(3) (2012): 524–26.

A gay college student discovered the association some made between homosexuality and the new Beetle when a vandal spray painted her car, festooned with a rainbow sticker, with "fag" and "u r gay," and made a documentary in 2009 called *Fagbug*, http://www.imdb.com/title/tt1320378/ (accessed 21 May 2014). Analysts believe appeals to women existed in both the new and reformed Beetles with the standard inclusion of dual illuminated vanity mirrors (Ruth Mortimer, "Driving Sales to Women," *Brand Strategy*, July 2002, 28;

http://autos.aol.com/cars-Volkswagen-New+Beetle-2002/equipment/ and http://autos.aol.com/cars-Volkswagen-Beetle-2014/equipment/ (accessed 8 August 2014).

15. Sarah Mower, "Prada Review," *Vogue*, http://www.vogue.com/fashion-week-review/863139/prada-spring-2012/; GM, "Fashion and Cars: The Matching of Soles and Souls," 16 July 2012, http://media.gm.com/media/us/en/gm/news.detail.html/content/Pages/news/us/en/2012/Jul/0713_chevy_shoe.html; Andrea Silvuni biography, http://www.mobilitytech.it/relatori-2011-1.php-id=53.htm (all accessed 17 May 2014).

16. Scharff, *Taking the Wheel*, 42–43; James D. Norris, *Advertising and the Transformation of American Society, 1865–1920* (Westport, Conn: Greenwood Press, 1990), 150, 155; Ryland P. Madison, "The Lady and the Electric," *CLA*, 15 July 1912, 36; electric car ads and Ryland P. Madison and Harold Whiting Slauson, "The Meaning of HP," *CLA*, May 1913, 100–108; Michael L. Berger, "Women Drivers! The Emergence of Folklore and Stereotypic Opinions Concerning Feminine Automotive Behavior," *Women's Studies International Forum* 9(3) (1986): 261; Borland ad and Ryland P. Madison and C. H. Claudy, "Building Character with a Motor Car," *CLA*, August 1913, 80–84. Scharff indicates it was fellow columnist C. H. Claudy who was the author of "The Lady and the Electric" quotation.

17. Some historians' conclusions appear predicated on the analysis of a photograph taken of cars assembled in Detroit about 1914, in which thirty-two of the thirty-five cars parked at the Detroit Athletic Club are determined to be electrics. Mom argues that this is a narrow piece of evidence and questions its central role in perpetuating an expectation. Even in 1923, Scharff cites evidence that across ten states, only 5 percent of women had registered as car owners. Mom, *The Electric Vehicle*, 31–32, 105–7, 119, 221, 276–81; Scharff, *Taking the Wheel*, 37, 117; Michael Brian Schiffer, *Taking Charge: The Electric Automobile in America* (Washington, D.C.: Smithsonian Institution Press, 1994), 135–39; "Women Drivers Increase," *Los Angeles Herald*, 19 September 1909; "Women Motorists," *AM*, April 1938, 18.

18. Carin Rubenstein, "Women in the Driver Seat," *Across the Board*, April 1986, 44, MVF, Box 8 of 24, JWT; *Who Killed the Electric Car?* 2006, http://www.whokilledtheelectriccar.com/ (accessed 17 May 2014).

19. Bill Britt, "Audi Seeks to Broaden Customer Base with A2," *Automotive News* (11 October 1999): 32L; *The Other Guys*, 2010, http://www.imdb.com/title/tt1386588/; *No Strings Attached*, 2011, http://www.imdb.com/title/tt1411238/; *The Dilemma*, 2011, http://www.imdb.com/title/tt1578275/; Fisker Karma Plug-in Hybrid, 2010, https://www.youtube.com/watch?v=mo5YOZ2saZk (all accessed 8 August 2014). Comic Jeff Dunham used the expectation that his blue Prius was gay as a staple of his skits. See, for example, https://www.youtube.com/watch?v=scHApkp8AjI (accessed 8 January 2017).

20. Judy Wajcman, "The Built Environment: Women's Place, Gendered Space," in *Women, Science, and Technology*, ed. Mary Wyer et al. (New York: Routledge, 2001), 194–208; Walt Munson, "Scram! Postcard," 1941, IAP; Smith, *Moving Lives*, 186–89; Scharff, *Taking the Wheel*, 139–41; Carol Sanger, "Girls and the Getaway: Cars, Culture, and the Predicament of Gendered Space," *University of Pennsylvania Law Review* 44(2) (December 1995): 732–34; Peter Ling, "Sex and the Automobile in the Jazz Age," *History Today* 39(11) (November 1989), 23; Clarke, *Driving Women*, 132.

21. Chrissie Hynde, "Thumbelina" (1984), http://www.allmusic.com/song/thumbelina-mt0032075633/lyrics; Jon Pareles, "Chrissie Hynde Makes Peace with the Past," *NYT*, 22 January 1984; Tracy Chapman, "Fast Car" (1988), http://www.azlyrics.com/lyrics/tracychapman/fastcar.html; Melissa Etheridge, "You Can Sleep While I Drive" (1990), http://www.azlyrics.com/lyrics/melissaetheridge/youcansleepwhileidrive.html (all accessed 7 August 2014); Beth Kraig, "Women at the Wheel: A History of Women and the Automobile in America," PhD diss., University of Washington, 1987), 279–80; Katherine Parkin, "The Key to the Universe: Springsteen, Masculinity, and the Car," in *Bruce Springsteen and the American Soul* ed. David Garrett Izzo (Jefferson, N.C.: McFarland, 2011), 136–41; Scharff, *Taking the Wheel*, 167; Sanger, "Girls and the Getaway," 710; Chris Lezotte, "Born to Take the Highway: Women, the Automobile, and Rock 'n' Roll," *Journal of American Culture* 36(3) (2013): 169–70.

22. "The Queen as a Mechanic," https://www.youtube.com/watch?v=R2grMaRttws (accessed 15 June 2014); Bea Arthur Secret Past as a Truck-Driving Marine, 10 December 2010, http://jezebel.com/5711367/bea-arthurs-secret-past-as-a-truck-driving-marine (accessed 1 June 2014).

23. Chevy ad, 1983, IAP; GMC ad, 1985, IAP; *LAT* op-ed referenced in Alex Williams, "Gay by Design, or a Lifestyle Choice?" *NYT*, 12 April 2007.

24. Karen Stabiner, "Tapping the Homosexual Market," *NYT*, 2 May 1982.

25. Toyota ad, 1993, IAP; Michael Wilke, "Sponsors Ponder 'Ellen' Plotline," *AA*, 7 October 1996; Dana Canedy, "As the Main Character in *Ellen* Comes Out, Some Companies See an Opportunity; Others Steer Clear," *NYT*, 30 April 1997; Stuart Elliott, "Advertising," *NYT*, 30 June 1997; B. Ruby Rich, "Riding in the Car with Girls," *Advocate*, 30 April 2002, 49; C. J. Prince, "Designated Driver," *The Advocate*, 18 March 2003; Williams, "Gay by Design." Alex Mayyasi, "How Subarus Came to Be Seen as Cars for Lesbians," *Atlantic*, 22 June 2016.

26. Cindy Donatelli, "Driving the Suburbs: Minivans, Gender, and Family Values," *Material History Review* 54 (Fall 2001): 92.

27. *My Mother the Car*, Season 1, Episode 29, aired 29 March 1966, https://www.youtube.com/watch?v=yE9C1fQ—LQ (accessed 5 January 2016); Clarke, *Driving Women*, 73–74.

28. Mobil Oil ad, 1941, http://graphic-design.tjs-labs.com/show-picture?id=1167602083 (accessed 8 January 2017); Ann Long Wanser, "Mademoiselle Motorist and the Mechanics of Medicine," *AM*, February 1971, 26; Herbert Hadad, "Man's Relationship with New Cars Is More Than Skin Deep," *NYT*, 17 May 1987; Nationwide commercial, https://www.youtube.com/watch?v=GCCnUCahkv8 (accessed 25 January 2016).

29. Dodge's LaFemme Is First Automobile with a Gender—It's Female," *PM*, January 1954, 133; Chrysler ad, *Life*, 21 January 1957; Pontiac ad, *Life*, 1 June 1959; Marsh and Collett, *Driving Passion*, 17; Beth Bailey, *From Front Porch to Back Seat: Courtship in Twentieth-Century America* (Baltimore: Johns Hopkins University Press, 1989), 70; Chevy ads, *NY*, 28 March 1964, and *Life*, 29 May 1964, 43; Toyota ad, 1969, IAP; Lezotte, "The Evolution," 516; Bernard Schoenbaum cartoon, *NY*, 29 July 1991.

30. Chuck Berry, "Maybellene" (1955), http://www.azlyrics.com/lyrics/chuckberry/maybellene.html; Bruce Springsteen, "Pink Cadillac" (1984), http://www.metrolyrics

.com/pink-cadillac-lyrics-bruce-springsteen.html; Aretha Franklin, "Freeway of Love" (1985), http://www.metrolyrics.com/freeway-of-love-lyrics-aretha-franklin.html; Lezotte, "Born to Take," 161–76; McCracken, *Culture and Consumption II*, 77. For a list of a hundred songs about cars, see http://coolrain44.wordpress.com/2009/07/19/songs-about -cars-driving/ (all accessed 3 August 2014). See also Warren Belasco, "Motivatin' with Chuck Berry and Frederick Jackson Turner," in *The Automobile and American Culture*, ed. David L. Lewis and Laurence Goldstein (Ann Arbor: University of Michigan Press, 1980), 262–79; Gerald Silk, *Automobile and Culture* (New York: Harry N. Abrams, 1984), 153.

31. Wilson Pickett, "Mustang Sally" (1966), http://www.songfacts.com/detail.php ?id = 5798; Prince, "Little Red Corvette" (1983), http://www.metrolyrics.com/little-red -corvette-lyrics-prince.html ; Clay McShane, *Down the Asphalt Path: The Automobile and the American City* (New York: Columbia University Press, 1994), 161.

32. Scharff, *Taking the Wheel*, 166; Strickland Gillian, "The Motor Philanderer to His Newest Flame," *AM*, January 1930, 29; E. B. White, "Farewell, My Lovely!" *NY*, May 16, 1936; Valvoline ad, *Time*, 16 February 1942.

33. Dow Chemical, "A Car Is a Woman," Public Service Announcement movie, 1958, http://www.youtube.com/watch?v = E0QR-ij8EV8 (accessed 4 May 2014); *Gettysburg Times*, 5 August 1958.

34. Austin Healy (1960), Lotus (1961), Chrysler (1966), Ford (1966), AMC (1968), BMW (1970) all IAP; Keith Wheeler, "And When Love Comes in It Takes the Auto for a Spin," *Life*, 11 January 1963, 30–31; H. F. Moorhouse, *Driving Ambitions: An Analysis of the American Hot Rod Enthusiasm* (Manchester, England: Manchester University Press, 1991), 178; Karal Ann Marling, "America's Love Affair with the Automobile in the Television Age," *Design Quarterly* No. 146, Autoeroticism (1989): 5–20; Queen, "I'm in Love with My Car" (1975), http://www.azlyrics.com/lyrics/queen/iminlovewithmycar.html (accessed 3 August 2014); Stephen King, *Christine*, http://stephenking.wikia.com/wiki/ Christine_(car) (accessed 30 April 2014); Jean Kilbourne, *Can't Buy My Love: How Advertising Changes the Way We Think and Feel* (New York: Simon & Schuster, 1999), 95–107; Stephen Bayley, *Sex, Drink, and Fast Cars* (New York: Pantheon, 1986), 25–30; Clarke, *Driving Women*, 74.

35. Erma Bombeck, "A Wife Is Only a Wife, But a Man's Car Is Sacred," *Daytona Beach Morning Journal*, 4 July 1971; Pontiac ad, 1979, IAP; "Drivers Admit to Expressing Love for Their Vehicles," 2008, http://news.jiffylube.com/article/drivers-admit-to-ex pressing-love-for-their-vehicles.aspx (accessed 7 May 2014); Honda ad, 1986, and Firestone flier, 2013, both IAP; Edward Koren cartoon, *NY*, 14 November 1988; Marshall Schuon, "My Love Is Like a Red, Red Roadster," *NYT*, 10 July 1994; Shania Twain, "That Don't Impress Me Much," http://www.youtube.com/watch?v = mqFLXayD6e8&fea ture = kp, and Taylor Swift, "Picture to Burn," (accessed 4 May 2014); Kilbourne, *Can't Buy My Love*, 77–78.

36. Buick ad, *WW*, February 1979, 45; Jaguar ad, 2003, IAP.

37. "Man Wants to Marry His Car, Clerks Says No," 6 March 1999, http://amarillo .com/stories/030699/usn_mancar.shtml (accessed 4 May 2014).

38. Oldsmobile, 1970, IAP; Cadillac commercial, 1996, http://www.youtube.com/ watch?v = rRNWnKNHWLQ (accessed 4 May 2014); Richardson, "Newt Gingrich."

39. *Fast Times at Ridgemont High,* 1982, http://www.imdb.com/title/tt0083929/synopsis and http://sanfernandovalleyblog.blogspot.com/2013/05/filming-locations-fast-times-at.html; Chevrolet ad, 1987, IAP; *Mystic Pizza* clip, 1988, https://www.youtube.com/watch?v=ikqDLmNc678; *Waiting to Exhale,* http://www.youtube.com/watch?v=ZGwV4mrOCJo, and "Detroit Woman Copies 'Waiting to Exhale' Scene, Sets Boyfriend's Car on Fire," *Jet,* 19 February 1996, 25; "Target Women: Carl's Jr." https://www.youtube.com/watch?v=feW7E9h7AdM; Carrie Underwood, "Before He Cheats," http://www.youtube.com/watch?v=WaSy8yy-mr8, and Jazmine Sullivan, "Bust Your Windows," http://www.youtube.com/watch?v=mOzdfaEPaR0; "Have You Ever Vandalized Someone's Car?" poll, 2013, http://www.971zht.com/articles/971-zht-text-topics-440396/have-you-ever-vandalized-someones-car-11199874/. Carrie Underwood also uses a Cadillac to kill a cheating husband and boyfriend in "Two Black Cadillacs," https://www.youtube.com/watch?v=oVEBZLrjpw4 (all accessed 19 August 2014); Ben Keeshin, "The Demolished Cars of Beyoncé's 'Lemonade,'" https://www.yahoo.com/autos/demolished-cars-beyonc-lemonade-160000185.html (accessed 1 May 2016).

40. "Conundrum," *Madison Daily Herald* (Indiana), 21 March 1916, 2; Velie Six Known as Woman's Car," *BDG,* 4 March 1917, 83; Auburn ad, *LAT,* 20 April 1924, 15; Franklin ad, *VF,* June 1929.

41. E. E. Cummings, "XIX," in *Drive, They Said: Poems About Americans and Their Cars,* ed. Kurt Brown (Minneapolis: Milkweed Editions, 1994), 235–36; Lewis H. Miller Jr., "Sex on Wheels: A Reading of 'she being Brand/ -new,'" *Spring* 6 (1997): 55–69, http://faculty.gvsu.edu/websterm/cummings/Miller6.htm; Silk, *Automobile and Culture,* 154.

42. Simoniz ads, *Life,* 31 May 1937, 57; *Life,* 26 July 1937, 93; *Life,* 12 June 1939, 34; postcard images, c. 1930s and 1944, IAP; Tinkler and Warsh, "Feminine Modernity," 122–27; Sinclair ad, *Life,* 2 May 1949, 115; Rally ad, 1969, IAP; Laura L. Behling, "Fisher's Bodies: Automobile Advertisements and the Framing of Modern American Female Identity," *Centennial Review* (Fall 1997): 515–28; *Big Business Girl* (1931) in Julie Berebitsky, *Sex and the Office: A History of Gender, Power, and Desire* (New Haven, Conn.: Yale University Press, 2012), 127; Fisher ad, *Life,* 9 November 1962; Sanger, "Girls and the Getaway," 707; Marsh and Collett, *Driving Passion,* 192–97; Clarke, *Driving Women,* 7.

43. Simonz ads, *Life,* 31 May 1937, 57; *Life,* 26 July 1937, 93; *Life,* 12 June 1939, 34; postcard images, c. 1930s and 1944, IAP; Tinkler and Warsh, "Feminine Modernity," 122–27; Sinclair ad, *Life,* 2 May 1949, 115; Rally ad, 1969, IAP.

44. McCracken, *Culture and Consumption II,* 12; "Sex and Advertising: Retail Therapy," *The Economist,* 17 December 2011; Ernest Dichter, *Getting Motivated* (New York: Pergamon Press, 1979), 40–41; Corvair ad, *Life,* 29 May 1964, 43; Fiat ads, 1965 and 1966, Cadillac ad (1999), all IAP. Brooke Shields starred in a 2009 ad for Ford, "First Love," talking about her early, long-standing love for a red Mustang. The actor and the language purposefully allude to her pre-pubescent sexual role in *Pretty Baby* and her fourteen-year-old, nearly nude acting in *The Blue Lagoon* (see http://www.adforum.com/creative-work/ad/player/48611/sxi:6889759sxi:6889759 and http://www.imdb.com/name/nm0000222/bio?ref_=nm_ov_bio_sm).

45. Mort Sahl, "Charmed by the Snake," *Playboy,* 1 January 1970, 141; Subaru ad, *Playboy,* 1973; Kreuzer et al., *A Tiger in the Tank,* 60–61, 119.

Howard notes that in ads found in *Playboy* magazine "Men's relationships to cars were occasionally equated with human ones," citing the example of one that read, " 'Like all honeymoons, the first few months of new car ownership are generally a period of adjustment.' The new bride was rendered a machine, to be driven by a skilled operator" (Ella Howard, "Pink Truck Ads: Second-Wave Feminism and Gendered Marketing," *Journal of Women's History* 22 [4] [2010]: 148–49).

46. Dodge ad, *Holiday*, December 1962; Ford ad, *Mademoiselle*, July 1971; Lincoln ad, 4 October 1976, ABC commercial, https://www.youtube.com/watch?v=cYmYDvAkwQE (accessed 21 August 2014); Carol Caldwell, "You Haven't Come a Long Way, Baby," *New Times,* 10 June 1977, 57, Rena Bartos Papers, Box 2, 97–202, JWT; Ford ad, *Southern Living*, May 1987; Cavalier ad, 1988, IAP.

47. Dodge press releases, 168, AAC; Pontiac promotional materials and press releases, 1983, AAC; Larry Sussman, "Pontiac Fires Up Its Image," *Milwaukee Journal*, 22 November 1982.

48. Toyota ad, 1970, IAP; Honda ad, *WW*, August 1987, 2–3.

49. Hyundai ad, 1996, IAP; Nissan commercial, 2011, https://www.youtube.com/watch?v=ojHbKN3oTvA (accessed 25 January 2016). Popular culture encouraged this type of association. See, for example, *Gone in 60 Seconds*, which used feminine pronouns, "explicitly gendered by the female names they are given," and referred to as people: "Always a sucker for a redhead" (Cristina Stasia, "Butch-Femme Interrupted: Angelina Jolie, Bisexuality, and the New Butch Femme" in *Bisexuality and Transgenderism: InterSEXions of the Others*, ed. Jonathan Alexander and Karen Yescavage [New York: Routledge, 2012], 194); "The Truth—and Translation—Behind the Fiat 500 Super Bowl Ad" http://www.walksofitaly.com/blog/current-events/fiat-500-usa-superbowl-ad-translation-italy (accessed 15 June 2014). Also, see sexual power of cars in 2008 and 2009 Cadillac CTS commercials, featuring Kate Walsh. She asked, "When you turn your car on, does it return the favor?" https://www.youtube.com/watch?v=jkEw1rsBUak&feature=kp and https://www.youtube.com/watch?v=4o6LD-M3ZD4 (accessed 25 January 2016).

50. Anthony Cortese, *Provocateur: Images of Women and Minorities in Advertising* (New York: Rowman and Littlefield, 2007), 60–61; Libby Copeland, "Baby, You Can't Drive My Car," Slate, http://www.slate.com/articles/double_x/doublex/2013/03/car_ads_for_women_does_the_industry_get_it_all_wrong.single.html; Lexus commercial, http://www.youtube.com/watch?v=S0rSz8r-m58; Scion commercial, http://vimeo.com/39784788; Mercedes commercial, https://www.youtube.com/watch?v=eqBGabTKajE; Rihanna, "Shut Up and Drive," 2007, http://www.azlyrics.com/lyrics/rihanna/shutupanddrive.html and http://www.youtube.com/watch?v=up7pvPqNkuU&feature=kp (all accessed 18 May 2014); *Dreamworlds 3* (Media Education Foundation, 2007).

51. Tinkler and Warsh, "Feminine Modernity," 127; Jonathon Ramsey, "Erotic Auto Window Sticker Stirs Freedom of Speech Debate," 8 November 2011, http://www.autoblog.com/2011/11/08/erotic-auto-window-sticker-stirs-freedom-of-speech-debate-w-pol/; Four doors sticker, http://www.amazon.com/doors-whores-sticker-drifting-racing/dp/B00ATGHS46 and full-figured sticker, http://www.amazon.com/Beautiful-Women-Window-Laptop-Sticker/dp/B00FFCNGPY (all accessed 29 May 2014).

52. The identity of the car in *My Strange Addiction* is male, and while Smith's "primary" commitment is to a female car named Vanilla, he is not limited to "her" or

"female" cars in general. TLC, "My Strange Addiction: My Car Is My Lover," 2012, http://www.tlc.com/tv-shows/my-strange-addiction/videos/my-car-is-my-lover/; Barcroft TV, "Man Has Slept with Over 1,000 Cars," 2013, http://www.youtube.com/watch?v=OrLMLFE5Eec; Ron Dicker, "Hyundai Dealer's 'Erection' Ad Gives Viewers a Hard Sell," *Huffington Post*, 30 October 2013, http://www.huffingtonpost.com/2013/10/30/hyundai-erection-ad_n_4178444.html; Shoe comic, "Auto-eroticism," 22 September 2007, https://cidutest.files.wordpress.com/2007/09/shoe-auto.gif (all accessed 8 January 2017); Rubenstein, "Women in the Driver Seat," 45; Clarke, *Driving Women*, 132.

53. "Aim to Restrict Petting Autos," *NYT*, 19 February 1926; "Motorized Petting a Menace," *NYT*, 7 June 1929; Seiler, *Republic of Drivers*, 56–58; Paula Fass, *The Damned and the Beautiful: American Youth in the 1920s* (New York: Oxford University Press, 1979): 47, 102n.197, 218; Scharff, *Taking the Wheel*, 138–39; Brownell, "A Symbol," 36–39; Lewis, "Sex and the Automobile," 709–11; Jordan ad, *NYT*, 4 May 1924, 7; David Langum, *Crossing Over the Line: Legislating Morality and the Mann Act* (Chicago: University of Chicago Press, 2007), 130–31; Peter Ling, "Sex and the Automobile in the Jazz Age," *History Today*, 18–24; Marsh and Collett, *Driving Passion*, 187–92.

54. Bailey, *From Front Porch*, 19, 86; James Flink, *The Automobile Age* (Cambridge, Mass.: MIT Press, 2001), 158–62; Jonathan Gathorne-Hardy, *Kinsey*, PBS documentary, http://www.pbs.org/wgbh/amex/kinsey/filmmore/pt.html (accessed 29 May 2014); William Bowdern, *Problems of Courtship and Marriage* (St. Louis: Queen's Work, 1939), 20–21; Sanger, "Girls and the Getaway," 730; Scharff, *Taking the Wheel*, 103, 107, 171; Clarke, *Driving Women*, 28.

55. "Automobiles: What They Mean to Americans," *CT*, 1953; Ruth Imler, "#1 Dating Menace: The Automobile," *LHJ*, November 1955, 54; Pontiac ad (1961), Chevy ad (1962), and AMC ad (1977), all IAP; Flink, *The Automobile Age*, 159–62.

56. "What Are the Odds?" *Ames Daily Tribune* (Iowa), 12 December 1962, 7; Flink, *The Automobile Age*, 162; "Falling in Love," *Jet*, 10 January 1974, 47; Devon J. Hensel, Julie Newcamp, Jeren Miles, and J. D. Fortenberry, "Picturing Sexual Spaces in Everyday Life: Exploring the Construction of Sexuality and Sexual Behavior Among Early Adult Women," *Sexuality Research & Social Policy* 8(4) (2011): 267–81; Isaac/Amy flash mob proposal, 2012, http://www.youtube.com/watch?v=5_v7QrIW0zY (accessed 7 May 2014); Hazelton, *Everything Women Always*, 30–32; Kenneth Hey, "Cars and Films in American Culture, 1929–1959," *Michigan Quarterly Review* 19(4) (Fall 1980), 588–89, 594.

57. Bailey, *From Front Porch*, 91, 97; 1930s postcard IAP; Chuck Berry, "No Particular Place to Go" (1964), http://www.azlyrics.com/lyrics/chuckberry/noparticularplacetogo.html (accessed 3 August 2014); Sanger, "Girls and the Getaway," 734–38, 748.

58. Hazelton, *Everything Women Always*, 175–76; Keith Bradsher, "Cars Lose Sex Appeal: New Models Cramp Style," *The Gazette* (Montreal, Quebec), 2 February 1997; Flink, *The Automobile Age*, 160–61; "Study Reveals Women Drivers Fix Their Hair Behind the Wheel," 31 July 2001, http://www.prnewswire.com/news-releases/study-reveals-women-drivers-fix-their-hair-behind-the-wheel-dr-joyce-brothers-shares-insights-about-womens-obsessions-with-hair-71530242.html (accessed 23 February 2016); Derek Thompson and Jordan Weissman, "The Cheapest Generation," *Atlantic*, 22 August 2012, http://

www.theatlantic.com/magazine/archive/2012/09/the-cheapest-generation/309060/; Alex Taylor III, "Say Good-bye to the Honda Element," *Fortune*, 10 December 2010, http://archive.fortune.com/2010/12/10/autos/honda_element_rip.fortune/index.htm (accessed 7 August 2014).

59. Hensel, "Picturing Sexual Spaces," 272; Vanessa Carlton, "White Houses," 2004, http://www.azlyrics.com/lyrics/vanessacarlton/whitehouses.html; Audi commercial, http://www.youtube.com/watch?v=MxkqGaklR68 (both accessed 7 May 2014); 1953 study cited in McShane, *Down the Asphalt*, 168.

60. Berger, "Women Drivers!" 262; Gulf Oil ad, 1984, IAP; Volkswagen ad, 2000, IAP; Clarke, *Driving Women*, 119.

61. Robyn Meredith, "In Detroit, a Sex Change," *NYT*, 16 May 1999; Welsh, "Automobiles"; Gunjan Bagla, "Seeking Customers, Not Bodies," http://www.imediaconnection.com/content/3893.asp (accessed 12 August 2014); Marsh and Collett, *Driving Passion*, 62–64.

Epilogue

1. Anthropologist Grant McCracken has noted, "The observer can tell at a glance from the physical possessions of the status-claimer whether there is foundation for these claims." In this case, it is gender that defines the patina, the marked identity of the car in the twentieth and twenty-first centuries, rather than the more traditional emphasis on class and consumerism studied by scholars exploring the meaning of goods in the eighteenth and nineteenth centuries. Gender identity across class, race, and religious boundaries enabled men "the opportunity of immediate detection. . . . It creates a status of symbolism that is immediately detectable by all." Grant McCracken, *Culture and Consumption* (Bloomington: Indiana University Press, 1988), 31–37, 71; Thorstein Veblen, *The Theory of the Leisure Class*, ed. Martha Banta (1899, (New York: Oxford University Press, 2009); Clay McShane, *Down the Asphalt Path: The Automobile and the American City* (New York: Columbia University Press, 1994), 125–34; Cotton Seiler, *Republic of Drivers: A Cultural History of Automobility in America* (Chicago: University of Chicago Press, 2008), 86–89; Rudy Volti, "A Century of Automobility," *Technology and Culture* 37(4) (October 1996): 667.

As Mary Douglas and Baron Isherwood concluded about the role of goods, they are "needed for making visible and stable the categories of culture." No category has been more significant to culturally delineate in twentieth-century America than gender. Mary Douglas and Baron Isherwood, *The World of Goods* (New York: Basic Books, 1979), 59.

Scholars in several disciplines apply the theory of patina, with social work applying it to gender in Elizabeth G. DePoy and Stephen F. Gilson's *Human Behavior Theory and Applications: A Critical Thinking Approach* (Thousand Oaks, Calif.: SAGE Publications, 2011), 101, 352.

2. McCracken, *Culture and Consumption*; Mihaly Csikszentmihalyi and Eugene Rocheberg-Halton, *The Meaning of Things: Domestic Symbols and the Self* (New York: Cambridge University Press, 1989), 141–42; Jeremy Packer, *Mobility Without Mayhem: Safety, Cars, and Citizenship* (Durham, N.C.: Duke University Press, 2008), 195–209;

Charles L. Sanford, "'Woman's Place' in American Car Culture," in *The Automobile and American Culture*, ed. David L. Lewis and Laurence Goldstein (Ann Arbor: University of Michigan Press, 1983), 138; Seiler, *Republic of Drivers*, 50–51.

3. Letters to the Editor, *PM*, May 2004, 12, and July 2004, 12; Jill Avery, "Defending the Markers of Masculinity: Consumer Resistance to Brand Gender-Bending," *International Journal of Research in Marketing* 23 April 2012; Laura Mulvey, *Visual and Other Pleasures* (Bloomington: Indiana University Press, 1989), 15, 19; Tom Vanderbilt, "Dude, Where's Your Car?" *Slate*, 30 July 2010, http://www.slate.com/articles/life/transport/2010/07/dude_wheres_your_car.html.

4. Allan Johnson, *The Gender Knot: Unraveling Our Patriarchal Legacy* (Delhi, India: Pearson, 1997, 2005), 5; Sylvia Walby, *Theorizing Patriarchy* (Cambridge, Mass.: Blackwell, 1997), 20–24, 178–82, 200–201; Tom McCarthy, *Auto Mania: Cars, Consumers, and the Environment* (New Haven, Conn.: Yale University Press, 2007), 53–54.

INDEX

Page numbers in italics refer to figures.

Index

Index

ACKNOWLEDGMENTS

I MIGHT HAVE FINISHED the book more quickly if I had only taken the express highways between major cities, but this journey took me down many one-lane roads and to many unexpected places in my quest to understand the history of women and cars. I have so many students, colleagues, friends, and family members to thank for enriching my trip, and for giving me wonderful car materials and asking great questions over these many years.

I am grateful for funding from Monmouth University, including a Sabbatical Grant, a Summer Faculty Fellowship, Research and Creativity Grants, and student research assistance. Financial assistance helped offset the cost of editing and preparing the images, as well as traveling to transportation libraries and archives in California, Delaware, Florida, Indiana, Massachusetts, Michigan, North Carolina, Ohio, and Pennsylvania. A Clark Travel Grant enabled me to work at the Benson Ford Research Center in Dearborn, Michigan, and a J. Walter Thompson Research Grant helped me to travel to the Hartman Center at Duke University. Librarians and archivists proved themselves consummate professionals by connecting me with the richness of their collections. In particular, thank you to Tammy Travis at the American Automobile Association; Chris Ritter at the Antique Automobile Club of America Library and Research Center; Judith Endelman, Linda Skolarus, and Suzanne Fischer at the Henry Ford; Martha Sachs and Heidi Abbey Moyer at the Alice Marshall Women's History Archive; Christo Datini at the General Motors Heritage Center; Craig Holbert at Goodyear; Tim Rivers at the Elwood Haynes Museum; and Jacqueline Reid Wachholz at the Hartman Center at Duke University. As always, Monmouth's librarians proved invaluable, bringing the world to me: Thank you especially to Sherri Xie and Linda Silverstein. Thank you to Yvette Lane for her editing assistance. I am grateful to Ferdinand Fasce and Jen Scanlon who generously shared their work and thoughtfully commented on my own. I am also grateful to those whose work and lives informed my research and I thank in particular, Robert Austin, Marti Barletta, Joan E. Biren, Julie Candler, Michal Clements, Daniel Freidan, Kathy Fuller-Seeley, Daniel Horowitz, Michelle Mock, Lou Reiter, Barbara Roos, and Ren Volpe for taking time to help me.

Several people who started out as students and are now dear friends and colleagues have greatly contributed to my work and I would like to thank them for research and organizational assistance, for reading many drafts, and fundamentally for their support and friendship: Annie Gill, Trish Maloney, Felicia Norott, Jenna Tshudy, and Melissa Ziobro. Felicia, in particular, deserves mention for accompanying me to an archive that was located in a parking garage with no electrical outlets, windows, or Internet access. Thank you also to my former students who contributed to the research and continued to reach out with both automotive tidbits and good cheer, I am so grateful for both: Carolyn Cimusz, Cindy Coffey, John Grant, Kyle Lamey, Dominic Longo, Sandra Meola, Kristen Renda, Mark Skesavage, Jessica Solano, Brian Sudol, and the late Kathy Shapiro, who helped me with my earliest forays into this research.

At Monmouth University I am surrounded by amazing colleagues who have always supported me and my work. In my department, I am so grateful to Julius Adekunle, Cindy Bell, Heidi Bludau, Ken Campbell, Veronica Davidov, Hillary DelPrete, Chris DeRosa, Maureen Dorment, Susan Douglas, George Gonzalez, Walter Greason, Brian Greenberg, Adam Heinrich, Fred McKitrick, Bill Mitchell, Brooke Nappi, Matthew O'Brien, Tom Pearson, Karen Schmelzkopf, Rich Veit, and Hettie Williams. Across the university, I have also been so fortunate to have thoughtful friends and colleagues. A special thanks to Stanley Blair, Susan Bucks, Corey Dzenko, Andi Hope, Susan Marshall, Mike and Rachel Phillips-Anderson, Dennis and Rebecca Rhoads, Paul Savoth, and Marie Mele Thomas. Thank you, too, to colleagues at conferences and students in my classes across the years whose feedback helped shape this project and enriched my thinking.

With dinners, vacations, archive trips, marathon phone conversations, and email, my friends have sustained me. Thank you to Brian and Susan Greenberg, Lindsay Currie and Joel Yaccarino, Samantha Yates Francois, Frank and Ditta Hoeber, Robin Levine, Celia Feinstein, Kathy Miller, Jim and Dianne Lemanowicz, Lisa Sonneborn and Andrew Pickering, Alexandra Friedrich and Markus Oebbecke, Lillian Pelios and George Katsikas, Bill and Beth Ashbaugh, Mustafa Aksakal, Dave and Tobey Stern, and John and Patty Connelly. My undergraduate sociology professor and dear friend Arlene Eskilson first introduced me to the scholarly study of feminism that has defined my work; for this and her quirky, wonderful take on the world and loving support of me, I am so grateful. Margaret Marsh has meant so much to me and, along with all she taught me, she continues to model professionalism and kindness—I treasure our friendship. Thirty years ago, Nancy Banks and I started "bombing around"; thank you for all our adventures in San Juan, Maine, New Jersey, and New York City, and for being an incredible friend. From offering a port in the storm that was Sandy to sharing in adventures from D.C. to Amherst, a huge thanks to Trish Maloney for her friendship, for reading countless drafts, and for introducing us to the Blue Swan. Thank you to Julie Berebitsky for all of your support, for wielding an expert purple pen, and for introducing me to Prosecco; you are a wonderful friend.

I am so grateful for the love and support of my family. My mother, Marilyn Parkin, read and commented on the entire manuscript and facilitated all of my Kokomo research; accompanied me on a research trip to Michigan; whisked away grandchildren so that I could work both in archives and at home; and was an incredible support to me. Joe and Esther DeRosa, Jon and Amelia DeRosa, Ben DeRosa and Katelyn Mullen, and Joyce and Peter Forte all loved and supported me. A special thank you to Ben for doing such an amazing job with my images. Thank you all.

Finally, my husband Chris DeRosa and my daughters Vivian Parkin DeRosa and Quinn Parkin DeRosa are everything to me. Always supportive and encouraging, they cheered my "triumphancy" in completing this book on "wams" and cars. From drawing pictures of women and cars to adorn my walls to accompanying me on research trips and to the office, my girls have been a part of this work from its inception and I hope it makes them proud, as they make me proud. Chris, I am so lucky. You are my colleague, my best friend, my editor, my husband. Thank you for believing in me, pushing me to greater heights, and holding me through it all. My love.